D

THE
HACKER
CRACKDOWN

BOOKS BY BRUCE STERLING

THE HACKER

HACKER

CRACKDOWN

LAW AND DISORDER ON THE
ELECTRONIC FRONTIER

BRUCE STERLING

BANTAM BOOKS

NEW YORK   TORONTO   LONDON   SYDNEY   AUCKLAND

THE HACKER CRACKDOWN

A Bantam Book / November 1992

364.168
$5838h$

BOOK DESIGN BY CAROL MALCOLM-RUSSO

COMPUTER-GENERATED ART PROVIDED BY DENNIS BREEN

Library of Congress Cataloging-in-Publication Data

Sterling, Bruce.
 The hacker crackdown : law and disorder on the electronic frontier / Bruce Sterling.
  p. cm.
 Includes index.
 ISBN 0-553-08058-X
 1. Computer crimes—United States. 2. Telephone—United States—Corrupt
practices. 3. Programming (Electronic computers)—United States—Corrupt practices. I.
Title.
HV6773.2.S74 1992
364.1′68—dc20   92-17496
                                                                     CIP

Published simultaneously in the United States and Canada

Bantam Books are published by Bantam Books, a division of Bantam Doubleday Dell
Publishing Group, Inc. Its trademark, consisting of the words "Bantam Books" and the
portrayal of a rooster, is Registered in U.S. Patent and Trademark Office and in other
countries. Marca Registrada. Bantam Books, 666 Fifth Avenue, New York, New York 10103.

PRINTED IN THE UNITED STATES OF AMERICA

BVG   0 9 8 7 6 5 4 3 2 1

CONTENTS

CHRONOLOGY OF THE HACKER CRACKDOWN

1865   U.S. Secret Service (USSS) founded.

1876   Alexander Graham Bell invents telephone.

1878   First teenage males flung off phone system by enraged authorities.

1939   "Futurians" science-fiction group raided by Secret Service.

1971   Yippie phone phreaks start *YIPL/TAP* magazine.

1972   *Ramparts* magazine seized in blue-box rip-off scandal.

1978   Ward Christensen and Randy Seuss create first personal computer bulletin board system.

1982   William Gibson coins term *cyberspace*.
1982   "414 gang" raided.
1982–83   AT&T dismantled in divestiture.

1984   Congress passes Comprehensive Crime Control Act giving USSS jurisdiction over credit card fraud and computer fraud.
1984   "Legion of Doom" formed.
1984   *2600* magazine founded.
1984   *Whole Earth Software Catalog* published.

1985   First police "sting" bulletin board systems established.
1985   Whole Earth 'Lectronic Link computer conference (WELL) goes on-line.

1986   Computer Fraud and Abuse Act passed.
1986   Electronic Communications and Privacy Act passed.

1987   Chicago federal prosecutors form Computer Fraud and Abuse Task Force.

1988

July   Secret Service covertly videotapes "SummerCon" hacker convention.

September   "Prophet" cracks BellSouth AIMSX computer network and downloads E911 Document to his own computer and to Jolnet.

September   AT&T Corporate Information Security informed of Prophet's action.

October   Bellcore Security informed of Prophet's action.

1989

January   "Prophet" uploads E911 Document to Knight Lightning.

February 25   Knight Lightning publishes E911 Document in *Phrack* electronic newsletter.

May   Chicago Task Force raids and arrests "Kyrie."

June   "NuPrometheus League" distributes Apple Computer proprietary software.

June 13   Florida probation office crossed with phone-sex line in switching-station stunt.

July   "Fry Guy" raided by USSS and Chicago Computer Fraud and Abuse Task Force.

July   Secret Service raids "Prophet," "Leftist," and "Urvile" in Georgia.

1990

January 15   Martin Luther King Day Crash strikes AT&T long-distance system nationwide.

January 18–19   Chicago Task Force raids Knight Lightning in St. Louis.

January 24   USSS and New York State Police raid "Phiber Optik," "Acid Phreak," and "Scorpion" in New York City.

February 1   USSS raids "Terminus" in Maryland.

February 3   Chicago Task Force raids Richard Andrews' home.

February 6   Chicago Task Force raids Richard Andrews' business.

February 6   USSS arrests Terminus, Prophet, Leftist, and Urvile.

February 9   Chicago Task Force arrests Knight Lightning.

February 20   AT&T Security shuts down public-access "attctc" computer in Dallas.

February 21   Chicago Task Force raids Robert Izenberg in Austin.

March 1   Chicago Task Force raids Steve Jackson Games, Inc., "Mentor," and "Erik Bloodaxe" in Austin.

May 7, 8, 9   USSS and Arizona Organized Crime and Racketeering Unit conduct "Operation Sundevil" raids in Cincinnati, Detroit, Los Angeles, Miami, Newark, Phoenix, Pittsburgh, Richmond, Tucson, San Diego, San Jose, and San Francisco.

May   FBI interviews John Perry Barlow re NuPrometheus case.

June   Mitch Kapor and Barlow found Electronic Frontier Foundation; Barlow publishes *Crime and Puzzlement* manifesto.

July 24–27   Trial of Knight Lightning.

1991

February   CPSR Roundtable in Washington, D.C.

March 25–28   Computers, Freedom and Privacy conference in San Francisco.

May 1   Electronic Frontier Foundation, Steve Jackson, and others file suit against members of Chicago Task Force.

July 1–2   Switching station phone software crash affects Washington, Los Angeles, Pittsburgh, San Francisco.

September 17   AT&T phone crash affects New York City and three airports.

INTRODUCTION

          This is a book about cops, and wild teenage whiz kids, and lawyers, and hairy-eyed anarchists, and industrial technicians, and hippies, and high-tech millionaires, and game hobbyists, and computer security experts, and Secret Service agents, and grifters, and thieves.

This book is about the electronic frontier of the 1990s. It concerns activities that take place inside computers and over telephone lines.

A science-fiction writer coined the useful term *cyberspace* in 1982. But the territory in question, the electronic frontier, is about 130 years old. Cyberspace is the "place" where a telephone conversation appears to occur. Not inside your actual phone, the plastic device on your desk. Not inside the other person's phone, in some other city. *The place between* the phones. The indefinite place *out there*, where the two of you, two human beings, actually meet and communicate.

Although it is not exactly "real," "cyberspace" is a genuine place. Things happen there that have very genuine consequences. This "place" is not "real," but it is serious, it is earnest. Tens of thousands of people have dedicated their lives to it, to the public service of public communication by wire and electronics.

People have worked on this "frontier" for generations now. Some people became rich and famous from their efforts there. Some just played in it, as hobbyists. Others soberly pondered it, and wrote about it, and regulated it, and negotiated over it in international forums, and sued one another about it, in gigantic, epic court battles that lasted for years. And almost since the beginning, some people have committed crimes in this place.

But in the past twenty years, this electrical "space," which was once thin and dark and one-dimensional—little more than a narrow speaking tube, stretching from phone to phone—has flung itself open like a gigantic jack-in-the-box. Light has flooded upon it, the eerie light of the glowing computer screen. This dark electric netherworld has become a vast flowering electronic landscape. Since the 1960s, the world of the telephone has crossbred itself with computers and television, and though there is still no substance to cyberspace—nothing you can handle—it has a strange kind of physicality now. It makes good sense today to talk of cyberspace as a place all its own.

Because people live in it now. Not just a few people, not just a few technicians and eccentrics, but thousands of people, quite normal people. And not just for a little while, either, but for hours straight, over weeks, and months, and years. Cyberspace today is a "Net," a "Matrix," international in scope and growing swiftly and steadily. It's growing in size, and wealth, and political importance.

People are making entire careers in modern cyberspace. Scientists and technicians, of course; they've been there for twenty years now. But increasingly, cyberspace is filling with journalists and doctors and lawyers and artists and clerks. Civil servants make their careers there now, "on-line" in vast government data banks; and so do spies, industrial, political, and just plain snoops; and so do police, at least a few of them. And there are children living there now.

People have met there and been married there. There are entire living communities in cyberspace today: chattering, gossiping, planning, conferring and scheming, leaving one another voice mail and electronic mail, giving one another big weightless chunks of valuable data, both legitimate and illegitimate. They busily pass one another computer software and the occasional festering computer virus.

We do not really understand how to live in cyberspace yet. We are feeling our way into it, blundering about. That is not surprising. Our lives in the physical world, the "real" world, are also far from perfect, despite a lot more practice. Human lives, real lives, are imperfect by their nature, and there are human beings in cyberspace. The way we live in cyberspace is a funhouse mirror of the way we live in the real world. We take both our advantages and our troubles with us.

This book is about trouble in cyberspace. Specifically, this book is about certain strange events in the year 1990, an unprecedented and startling year for the growing world of computerized communications.

In 1990 there came a nationwide crackdown on illicit computer hackers, with arrests, criminal charges, one dramatic show trial, several guilty pleas, and huge confiscations of data and equipment all over the United States.

The Hacker Crackdown of 1990 was larger, better organized, more deliberate, and more resolute than any previous effort in the brave new world of computer crime. The U.S. Secret Service, private telephone security, and state and local law enforcement groups across the country all joined forces in a determined attempt to break the back of America's electronic underground. It was a fascinating effort, with very mixed results.

The Hacker Crackdown had another unprecedented effect; it spurred the creation, within "the computer community," of the Electronic Frontier Foundation, a new and very odd interest group, fiercely dedicated to the establishment and preservation of electronic civil liberties. The crackdown, remarkable in itself, has created a melee of debate over electronic crime, punishment, freedom of the press, and issues of search and seizure. Politics has entered cyberspace. Where people go, politics follow.

This is the story of the people of cyberspace.

THE
HACKER
CRACKDOWN

1

CRASHING
THE SYSTEM

On January 15, 1990, AT&T's long-distance telephone switching system crashed.

This was a strange, dire, huge event. Sixty thousand people lost their telephone service completely. During the nine long hours of frantic effort that it took to restore service, some 70 million telephone calls went uncompleted.

Losses of service, known as "outages" in the telco trade, are a known and accepted hazard of the telephone business. Hurricanes hit, and phone cables get snapped by the thousands. Earthquakes wrench through buried fiber-optic lines. Switching stations catch fire and burn to the ground. These things do happen. There are contingency plans for them, and decades of experience in dealing with them. But the Crash of January 15 was unprecedented. It was unbelievably huge, and it occurred for no apparent physical reason.

The crash started on a Monday afternoon in a single switching station in Manhattan. But, unlike any mere physical damage, it spread and spread. Station after station across America collapsed in a chain reaction, until fully half of AT&T's network had gone haywire and the remaining half was hard put to handle the overflow.

Within nine hours, AT&T software engineers more or less understood what had caused the crash. Replicating the problem exactly, poring over software line by line, took them a couple of weeks. But because it was hard to understand technically, the full truth of the matter and its implications were not widely and thoroughly aired and explained. The root cause of the crash remained obscure, surrounded by rumor and fear.

The crash was a grave corporate embarrassment. The "culprit" was a bug in AT&T's own software—not the sort of admission the telecommunications giant wanted to make, especially in the face of increasing competition. Still, the truth *was* told, in the baffling technical terms necessary to explain it.

Somehow the explanation failed to persuade American law enforcement officials and even telephone corporate security personnel. These people were not technical experts or software wizards, and they had their own suspicions about the cause of this disaster.

The police and telco security had important sources of information denied to mere software engineers. They had informants in the computer underground and years of experience in dealing with high-tech rascality that seemed to grow ever more sophisticated. For years they had been expecting a direct and savage attack against the American national telephone system. And with the Crash of January 15—in the first month of a new, high-tech decade—their predictions, fears, and suspicions seemed at last to have entered the real world. A world where the telephone system had not merely crashed but, quite likely, *been* crashed—by "hackers."

The crash created a large, dark cloud of suspicion that would color certain people's assumptions and actions for months. The fact that it took place in the realm of software was suspicious on its face. The fact that it occurred on Martin Luther King Day, still the most politically touchy of American holidays, made it more suspicious yet.

The Crash of January 15 gave the Hacker Crackdown its sense of edge and its sweaty urgency. It made people, powerful people in positions of public authority, willing to believe the worst. And, most fatally, it helped to give investigators a willingness to take extreme measures and the determination to preserve almost total secrecy.

> *The Crash of January 15 gave the Hacker Crackdown its sense of sweaty urgency.*

An obscure software fault in an aging switching system in New York was to lead to a chain reaction of legal and constitutional trouble all across the country.

Like the crash in the telephone system, this chain reaction was ready and waiting to happen. During the 1980s, the American legal system was extensively patched to deal with the novel issues of computer crime. There was, for instance, the Electronic Communications Privacy Act of 1986 (eloquently described as "a stinking mess" by a prominent law enforcement official). And there was the draconian Computer Fraud and Abuse Act of 1986, passed unanimously by the U.S. Senate, which later would reveal a large number of flaws. Extensive, well-meant efforts had been made to keep the legal system up-to-date. But in the day-to-day grind of the real world, even the most elegant software tends to crumble and suddenly reveal its hidden bugs.

Like the advancing telephone system, the American legal system was certainly not ruined by its temporary crash; but for those caught under the weight of its collapse, life became a series of blackouts and anomalies.

In order to understand why these weird events occurred, both in the world of technology and in the world of law, it's not enough to understand the merely technical problems. We will get to those; but first and foremost, we must try to understand the telephone, and the business of telephones, and the community of human beings that telephones have created.

Technologies have life cycles, as cities do, as institutions do, as laws and governments do.

The first stage of any technology is the Question Mark, often known as the "Golden Vaporware" stage. At this early point, the technology is only a phantom, a mere gleam in the inventor's eye. One such inventor was a speech teacher and electrical tinkerer named Alexander Graham Bell.

Bell's early inventions, while ingenious, failed to move the world. In 1863, the teenage Bell and his brother Melville made an artificial talking mechanism out of wood, rubber, gutta-percha, and tin. This weird device had a rubber-covered "tongue" made of movable wooden segments, with vibrating rubber "vocal cords," and rubber "lips" and "cheeks." While Melville puffed a bellows into a tin tube, imitating the lungs, young Alec Bell would manipulate the lips, teeth, and tongue, causing the thing to emit high-pitched falsetto gibberish.

Another would-be technical breakthrough was the Bell "phonautograph" of 1874, actually made out of a human cadaver's ear. Clamped into place on a tripod, this grisly gadget drew sound-wave images on smoked glass through a thin straw glued to its vibrating earbones.

By 1875, Bell had learned to produce audible sounds—ugly shrieks and squawks—by using magnets, diaphragms, and electrical current.

Most Golden Vaporware technologies go nowhere.

But the second stage of technology is the Rising Star, or the

"Goofy Prototype," stage. The telephone, Bell's most ambitious gadget yet, reached this stage on March 10, 1876. On that great day, Alexander Graham Bell became the first person to transmit intelligible human speech electrically. As it happened, young Professor Bell, industriously tinkering in his Boston lab, had spattered his trousers with acid. His assistant, Mr. Watson, heard his cry for help—over Bell's experimental audio-telegraph. This was an event without precedent.

Technologies in their Goofy Prototype stage rarely work very well. They're experimental, and therefore half-baked and rather frazzled. The prototype may be attractive and novel, and it does look as if it ought to be good for something-or-other. But nobody, including the inventor, is quite sure what. Inventors, and speculators, and pundits may have very firm ideas about its potential use, but those ideas are often very wrong.

The natural habitat of the Goofy Prototype is in trade shows and in the popular press. Infant technologies need publicity and investment money like a tottering calf needs milk. This was very true of Bell's machine. To raise research and development money, Bell toured with his device as a stage attraction.

Contemporary press reports of the stage debut of the telephone showed pleased astonishment mixed with considerable dread. Bell's stage telephone was a large wooden box with a crude speaker-nozzle, the whole contraption about the size and shape of an overgrown Brownie camera. Its buzzing steel soundplate, pumped up by powerful electromagnets, was loud enough to fill an auditorium. Bell's assistant Mr. Watson, who could manage on the keyboards fairly well, kicked in by playing the organ from distant rooms and, later, distant cities. This feat was considered marvelous, but very eerie indeed.

Bell's original notion for the telephone, an idea promoted for a couple of years, was that it would become a mass medium. We might recognize Bell's idea today as something close to modern "cable radio." Telephones at a central source would transmit music, Sunday sermons, and important public speeches to a paying network of wired-up subscribers.

At the time, most people thought this notion made good sense. In fact, Bell's idea was workable. In Hungary, this philosophy of the telephone was successfully put into everyday practice. In Budapest, for decades, from 1893 until after World War I, there was a government-run information service called "Telefon Hirmondó." Hirmondó was a centralized source of news and entertainment and culture, including stock reports, plays, concerts, and novels read aloud. At certain hours of the day, the phone would ring, you would plug in a loudspeaker for the use of the family, and Telefon Hirmondó would be on the air—or rather, on the phone.

Hirmondó is dead tech today, but it might be considered a spiritual ancestor of the modern telephone-accessed computer data services, such as CompuServe, GEnie, or Prodigy. The principle behind Hirmondó is also not too far from computer "bulletin board systems" or BBS's, which arrived in the late 1970s, spread rapidly across America, and will figure largely in this book.

We are used to using telephones for individual person-to-person speech, because we are used to the Bell system. But this was just one possibility among many. Communication networks are very flexible and protean, especially when their hardware becomes sufficiently advanced. They can be put to all kinds of uses. And they have been—and they will be.

Bell's telephone was bound for glory, but this was due to a combination of political decisions, canny infighting in court, inspired industrial leadership, receptive local conditions, and outright good luck. Much the same is true of communications systems today.

As Bell and his backers struggled to install their newfangled system in the real world of nineteenth-century New England, they had to fight against skepticism and industrial rivalry. There was already a strong electrical communications network present in America: the telegraph. The head of the Western Union telegraph system dismissed Bell's prototype as "an electrical toy" and refused to buy the rights to Bell's patent. The telephone, it seemed, might be all right as a parlor entertainment—but not for serious business.

Telegrams, unlike mere telephones, left a permanent physical record of their messages. Telegrams, unlike telephones, could be answered whenever the recipient had time and convenience. And the telegram had a much longer distance range than Bell's early telephone. These factors made telegraphy seem a much more sound and businesslike technology—at least to some.

The telegraph system was huge, and well entrenched. In 1876, the United States had 214,000 miles of telegraph wire and 8,500 telegraph offices. There were specialized telegraphs for businesses and stock traders, government, police, and fire departments. And Bell's "toy" was best known as a stage-magic musical device.

The third stage of technology is known as the "Cash Cow" stage. In this stage, a technology finds its place in the world, matures, and becomes settled and productive. After a year or so, Alexander Graham Bell and his capitalist backers concluded that eerie music piped from nineteenth-century cyberspace was not the real selling point of his invention. Instead, the telephone was about speech—individual, personal speech, the human voice, human conversation, and human interaction. The telephone was not to be managed from any centralized broadcast center. It was to be a personal, intimate technology.

When you picked up a telephone, you were not absorbing the cold output of a machine—you were speaking to another human being. Once people realized this, their instinctive dread of the telephone as an eerie, unnatural device swiftly vanished. A "telephone call" was not a "call" from a "telephone" itself, but a call from another human being, someone you would generally know and recognize. The real point was not what the machine could do for you (or to you), but what you yourself, a person and citizen, could do *through* the machine. This decision on the part of the young Bell company was absolutely vital.

The first telephone networks went up around Boston—mostly among the technically curious and the well-to-do. (Much the same segment of the American populace that, a hundred years later, would be buying personal computers.) Entrenched backers of the telegraph continued to scoff.

But in January 1878, a disaster made the telephone famous. A train crashed in Tarriffville, Connecticut. Forward-looking doctors in the nearby city of Hartford had had Bell's "speaking telephone" installed. An alert local druggist was able to telephone an entire community of local doctors, who rushed to the site to give aid. The disaster, as disasters do, aroused intense press coverage. The phone had proven its usefulness in the real world.

After Tarriffville, the telephone network spread like crabgrass. By 1890, it was all over New England. By 1893, out to Chicago. By 1897, into Minnesota, Nebraska, and Texas. By 1904, it was all over the continent.

Alexander Graham Bell was a prototype of the high-tech entrepreneur.

The telephone had become a mature technology. Professor Bell (now generally known as "Dr. Bell" despite his lack of a formal degree) became quite wealthy. He lost interest in the tedious day-to-day business muddle of the booming telephone network and gratefully returned his attention to creatively hacking around in his various laboratories, which were now much larger, better ventilated, and gratifyingly better equipped. Bell was never to have another great inventive success, though his speculations and prototypes anticipated fiber-optic transmission, manned flight, sonar, hydrofoil ships, tetrahedral construction, and Montessori education. The "decibel," the standard scientific measure of sound intensity, was named after Bell.

Not all Bell's vaporware notions were inspired. He was fascinated by human eugenics. He also spent many years developing a weird personal system of astrophysics in which gravity did not exist.

Bell was a definite eccentric. He was something of a hypochondriac, and throughout his life he habitually stayed up until four A.M., refusing to rise before noon. But Bell had accomplished a great feat; he was an idol of millions and his influence, wealth, and great personal charm, combined with his eccentricity, made him something of a loose cannon on deck. Bell maintained a thriving scientific salon in his winter mansion in Washington, D.C., which gave him considerable backstage influence in governmental and scientific circles. He was a major financial backer of the magazines *Science* and *National Geographic*, both still flourishing today as important organs of the American scientific establishment.

There would never be another Alexander Graham Bell, but in years to come there would be surprising numbers of people like him. Bell was a prototype of the high-tech entrepreneur. High-tech entrepreneurs will play a very prominent role in this book: not merely as technicians and businessmen, but as pioneers of the technical frontier, who can carry the power and prestige they derive from high technology into the political and social arena.

Like later entrepreneurs, Bell was fierce in defense of his own technological territory. As the telephone began to flourish, Bell was soon involved in violent lawsuits in the defense of his patents. His Boston lawyers were excellent, however, and Bell himself, as an election teacher and gifted public speaker, was a devastatingly effective legal witness. In the eighteen years of Bell's patents, the Bell company was involved in 600 separate lawsuits. The legal records printed filled 149 volumes. The Bell company won every single suit.

After Bell's exclusive patents expired, rival telephone companies sprang up all over America. Bell's company, American Bell Telephone, was soon in deep trouble. In 1907, it fell into the hands of the rather sinister J. P. Morgan financial cartel, robber-baron speculators who dominated Wall Street.

At this point, history might have taken a different turn. America might well have been served forever by a patchwork of locally owned telephone companies. Many state politicians and local businessmen considered this an excellent solution.

But the new Bell holding company, American Telephone and Telegraph, or AT&T, put in a new man at the helm, a visionary industrialist named Theodore Vail. Vail, a former Post Office manager, understood large organizations and had an innate feeling for the nature of large-scale communications. Vail quickly saw to it that AT&T seized the technological edge once again. The Pupin and Campbell "loading coil" and the deForest "audion" are both extinct technology today, but in 1913 they gave Vail's company the best *long-distance* lines ever built. By controlling long distance—the links between, over, and above the smaller local phone companies—AT&T swiftly gained the whip hand over them, and was soon devouring them right and left.

Vail plowed the profits back into research and development, starting the Bell tradition of huge-scale and brilliant industrial research.

Technically and financially, AT&T gradually steamrollered the opposition. Independent telephone companies never became entirely extinct, and hundreds of them flourish today. But Vail's AT&T became the supreme communications company. At one point, Vail's AT&T bought Western Union itself, the very company that had derided Bell's telephone as a "toy." Vail thoroughly reformed Western Union's hidebound business along his modern principles; but when the federal government grew anxious at this centralization of power, Vail politely gave Western Union back.

This centralizing process was not unique. Very similar events had happened in American steel, oil, and railroads. But AT&T, unlike the other companies, was to remain supreme. The monopolistic robber barons of those other industries were humbled and shattered by government trust-busting.

Vail, the former Post Office official, was quite willing to accommodate the U.S. government; in fact, he would forge an active alliance with it. AT&T would become almost a wing of the American government, almost another Post Office—though not quite. AT&T would willingly submit to federal regulation, but in return, it would use the government's regulators as its own police, who would keep out competitors and assure the Bell system's profits and preeminence.

This was the second birth—the political birth—of the American telephone system. Vail's arrangement was to persist, with vast success, for many decades, until 1982. His system was an odd kind of American industrial socialism. It was born at about the same time as Leninist communism, and it lasted almost as long —and, it must be admitted, to considerably better effect.

Vail's system worked. Except perhaps for aerospace, there has been no technology more thoroughly dominated by Americans than the telephone. The telephone was seen from the beginning as a quintessentially American technology. Bell's policy, and the policy of Theodore Vail, was a profoundly democratic one of *universal access.* Vail's famous corporate slogan, "One Policy, One System, Universal Service," was a political slogan, with a very American ring to it.

The American telephone was not to become the specialized tool of government or business, but a general public utility. At first, it was true, only the wealthy could afford private telephones, and Bell's company pursued the business markets primarily. The American phone system was a capitalist effort, meant to make money; it was not a charity. But from the first, almost all communities with telephone service had public telephones. And many stores—especially drugstores—offered public use of their phones. You might not own a telephone—but you could always get into the system, if you really needed to.

There was nothing inevitable about this decision to make telephones "public" and "universal." Vail's system involved a profound act of trust in the public. This decision was a political one, informed by the basic values of the American republic. The situation might have been very different; and in other countries, under other systems, it certainly was.

Joseph Stalin, for instance, vetoed plans for a Soviet phone system soon after the Bolshevik revolution. Stalin was certain that publicly accessible telephones would become instruments of anti-Soviet counterrevolution and conspiracy. (He was probably right.) When telephones did arrive in the Soviet Union, they would be instruments of Party authority, and always heavily tapped. (Alexander Solzhenitsyn's prison-camp novel *The First Circle* describes efforts to develop a phone system more suited to Stalinist purposes.)

France, with its tradition of rational centralized government, had fought bitterly even against the electric telegraph, which seemed to the French entirely too anarchical and frivolous. For decades, nineteenth-century France communicated via the "visual telegraph," a nation-spanning, government-owned semaphore system of huge stone towers that signaled from hilltops, across vast distances, with big windmill-like arms. In 1846, one Dr. Barbay, a semaphore enthusiast, memorably uttered an early version of what might be called "the security expert's argument" against the open media:

> No, the electric telegraph is not a sound invention. It will always be at the mercy of the slightest disruption, wild youths, drunkards, bums, etc. . . . The electric telegraph meets those destructive elements with only a few meters of wire over which supervision is impossible. A single man could, without being seen, cut the telegraph wires leading to Paris, and in twenty-four hours cut in ten different places the wires of the same line, without being arrested. The visual telegraph, on the contrary, has its towers, its high walls, its gates well-guarded from inside by strong armed men. Yes, I declare, substitution of the electric telegraph for the visual one is a dreadful measure, a truly idiotic act.

Dr. Barbay and his high-security stone machines were eventually unsuccessful, but his argument—that communication exists for the safety and convenience of the state, and must be carefully protected from the wild boys and the gutter rabble who might want to crash the system—would be heard again and again.

When the French telephone system finally did arrive, its snarled inadequacy was to be notorious. Devotees of the American Bell System often recommended a trip to France, for skeptics.

In Edwardian Britain, issues of class and privacy were a ball-and-chain for telephonic progress. It was considered outrageous that anyone—any wild fool off the street—could simply barge bellowing into one's office or home, preceded only by the ringing of a telephone bell. In Britain, phones were tolerated for the use of business, but private phones tended to be stuffed away into closets, smoking rooms, or servants' quarters. Telephone operators were resented in Britain because they did not seem to "know their place." And no one of breeding would print a telephone number on a business card; this seemed a crass attempt to make the acquaintance of strangers.

But phone access in America was to become a popular right —something like universal suffrage, only more so. American women could not yet vote when the phone system came through; yet from the begin-

> *No one of breeding would print a telephone number on a business card.*

ning American women doted on the telephone. This "feminization" of the American telephone was often commented on by foreigners. Phones in America were not censored or stiff or formalized; they were social, private, intimate, and domestic. In America, Mother's Day is by far the busiest day of the year for the phone network.

The early telephone companies, and especially AT&T, were among the foremost employers of American women. They employed the daughters of the American middle class in great armies: in 1891, eight thousand women; by 1946, almost a quarter of a million. Women seemed to enjoy telephone work; it was respectable, it was steady, it paid fairly well as women's work went, and—not least—it seemed a genuine contribution to the social good of the community. Women found Vail's ideal of public service attractive. This was especially true in rural areas, where women operators, running extensive rural party lines, enjoyed considerable social power. The operator knew everyone on the party line, and everyone knew her.

Although Bell himself was an ardent suffragist, the telephone company did not employ women for the sake of advancing female liberation. AT&T did this for sound commercial reasons. The first telephone operators of the Bell system were not women, but teenage American boys. They were telegraphic messenger boys (a group about to be rendered technically obsolescent), who swept up around the phone office, dunned customers for bills, and made phone connections on the switchboard, all on the cheap.

Within its first year of operation, Bell's company learned a sharp lesson about combining boys and telephone switchboards.

Within its very first year of operation, 1878, Bell's company learned a sharp lesson about combining teenage boys and telephone switchboards. Putting teenage boys in charge of the phone system brought swift and consistent disaster. Bell's chief engineer described them as "Wild Indians." The boys were openly rude to customers. They talked back to subscribers, saucing off, uttering facetious remarks, and generally giving lip. The rascals took Saint Patrick's Day off without permission. And worst of all, they played clever tricks with the switchboard plugs: disconnecting calls, crossing lines so that customers found themselves talking to strangers, and so forth.

This combination of power, technical mastery, and effective anonymity seemed to act like catnip on teenage boys.

This wild-kid-on-the-wires phenomenon was not confined to the United States; from the beginning, the same was true of the British phone system. An early British commentator kindly remarked: "No doubt boys in their teens found the work not a little irksome, and it is also highly probable that under the early conditions of employment the adventurous and inquisitive spirits of which the average healthy boy of that age is possessed, were not always conducive to the best attention being given to the wants of the telephone subscribers."

So the boys were flung off the system—or, at least, deprived of control of the switchboard. But the "adventurous and inquisitive spirits" of the teenage boys would be heard from in the world of telephony, again and again.

The fourth stage in the technological life cycle is death: "the Dog," dead tech. The telephone has so far avoided this fate. On the contrary, it is thriving, still spreading, still evolving, and at increasing speed.

The telephone has achieved a rare and exalted state for a technological artifact: It has become a *household object.* The telephone, like the clock, like pen and paper, like kitchen utensils and running water, has become a technology that is visible only by its absence. The telephone is technologically transparent. The global telephone system is the largest and most complex machine in the world, yet it is easy to use. More remarkable yet, the telephone is almost entirely physically safe for the user.

For the average citizen in the 1870s, the telephone was weirder, more shocking, more "high tech" and harder to comprehend, than the most outrageous stunts of advanced computing for us Americans in the 1990s. In trying to understand what is happening to us today, with our bulletin board systems, direct overseas dialing, fiber-optic transmissions, computer viruses, hacking stunts, and a vivid tangle of new laws and new crimes, it is important to realize that our society has been through a similar challenge before—and that, all in all, we did rather well by it.

Bell's stage telephone seemed bizarre at first. But the sensations of weirdness vanished quickly, once people began to hear the familiar voices of relatives and friends, in their own homes on their own telephones. The telephone changed from a fearsome high-tech totem to an everyday pillar of human community.

This has also happened, and is still happening, to computer networks. Computer networks such as NSFnet, BITNET, USENET, JANET are technically advanced, intimidating, and much harder to use than telephones. Even the popular, commercial computer networks, such as GEnie, Prodigy, and CompuServe, cause much head-scratching and have been described as "user-hateful." Nevertheless, they too are changing from fancy high-tech items into everyday sources of human community.

The words *community* and *communication* have the same root. Wherever you put a communications network, you put a community as well. And whenever you *take away* that network—confiscate it, outlaw it, crash it, raise its price beyond affordability—then you hurt that community.

Communities will fight to defend themselves. People will fight harder and more bitterly to defend their communities than they will fight to defend their own individual selves. And this is very true of the "electronic community" that arose around computer networks in the 1980s—or rather, the *various* electronic communities, in telephony, law enforcement, computing, and the digital underground that, by the year 1990, were raiding, rallying, arresting, suing, jailing, fining, and issuing angry manifestos.

None of the events of 1990 was entirely new. Nothing happened in 1990 that did not have some kind of earlier and more understandable precedent. What gave the Hacker Crackdown its new sense of gravity and importance was the feeling—the *community* feeling—that the political stakes had been raised; that trouble in cyberspace was no longer mere mischief or inconclusive skirmishing, but a genuine fight over genuine issues, a fight for community survival and the shape of the future.

These electronic communities, having flourished throughout the 1980s, were becoming aware of themselves and, increasingly, becoming aware of other, rival communities. Worries were sprouting up right and left, with complaints, rumors, uneasy speculations. But it would take a catalyst, a shock, to make the new world evident. Like Bell's great publicity break, the Tarriffville Rail Disaster of January 1878, it would take a cause célèbre.

That cause was the AT&T Crash of January 15, 1990. After the crash, the wounded and anxious telephone community would come out fighting hard.

The community of telephone technicians, engineers, operators, and researchers is the oldest community in cyberspace. These are the veterans, the most developed group, the richest, the most respectable, in most ways the most powerful. Whole generations have come and gone since Alexander Graham Bell's day, but the community he founded survives; people work for the phone system today whose great-grandparents worked for the phone system. Its specialty magazines, such as *Telephony, AT&T Technical Journal, Telephone Engineer and Management,* are decades old; they make computer publications such as *Macworld* and *PC Week* look like amateur johnny-come-latelies.

And the phone companies take no back seat in high technology either. Other companies' industrial researchers may have won new markets, but the researchers of Bell Labs have won *seven Nobel Prizes.* One potent device that Bell Labs originated, the transistor, has created entire *groups* of industries. Bell Labs are world-famous for generating "a patent a day," and even have made vital discoveries in astronomy, physics, and cosmology.

Throughout its seventy-year history, "Ma Bell" was not so much a company as a way of life. Until the cataclysmic divestiture of the 1980s, Ma Bell was perhaps the ultimate maternalist mega-employer. The AT&T corporate image was the "gentle giant," "the voice with a smile," a vaguely socialist-realist world of clean-shaven linemen in shiny helmets and blandly pretty phone girls in headsets and nylons. Bell System employees were famous as rock-ribbed Kiwanis and Rotary members, Little League enthusiasts, school board people.

During the long heyday of Ma Bell, the Bell employee corps were nurtured top-to-bottom on a corporate ethos of public service. There was good money in Bell, but Bell was not *about* money; Bell used public relations, but never mere marketeering. People went into the Bell System for a good life, and they had a good life. But it was not mere money that led Bell people out in the midst of storms and earthquakes to fight with toppled phone poles, to wade in flooded manholes, to pull the red-eyed graveyard shift over collapsing switching systems. The Bell ethic was the electrical equivalent of the postman's: Neither rain, nor snow, nor gloom of night would stop these couriers.

It is easy to be cynical about this, as it is easy to be cynical about any political or social system; but cynicism does not change the fact that thousands of people took these ideals very seriously. And some still do.

The Bell ethos was about public service, and that was gratifying; but it was also about private *power*, and that was gratifying too. As a corporation, Bell was very special. Bell was privileged. Bell had snuggled up close to the state. In fact, Bell was as close to government as you could get in America and still make a whole lot of legitimate money.

But unlike other companies, Bell was above and beyond the vulgar commercial fray. Through its regional operating companies, Bell was omnipresent, local, and intimate, all over America; but the central ivory towers at its corporate heart were the tallest and the ivoriest around.

There were other phone companies in America, to be sure; the so-called independents. Rural cooperatives, mostly; small fry, mostly tolerated, sometimes warred upon. For many decades, independent American phone companies lived in fear and loathing of the official Bell monopoly (or the "Bell Octopus," as Ma Bell's nineteenth-century enemies described her in many angry newspaper manifestos). Some few of these independent entrepreneurs, while legally in the wrong, fought so bitterly against the Octopus that their illegal phone networks were cast into the street by Bell agents and publicly burned.

The pure technical sweetness of the Bell System gave its operators, inventors, and engineers a deeply satisfying sense of power and mastery. They had devoted their lives to improving this vast nation-spanning machine; over years, whole human lives, they had watched it improve and grow. It was like a great technological temple. They were an elite, and they knew it—even if others did not; in fact, they felt even more powerful *because* others did not understand.

The deep attraction of this sensation of elite technical power should *never* be underestimated. "Technical power" is not for everybody; for many people, it simply has no charm at all. But for some people, it becomes the core of their lives. For a few, it is overwhelming, obsessive; it becomes something close to an addiction. People—especially clever teenage boys whose lives are otherwise mostly powerless and put-upon—love this sensation of secret power and are willing to do all sorts of amazing things to achieve it. The technical *power* of electronics has motivated many strange acts detailed in this book, which would otherwise be inexplicable.

So Bell had power beyond mere capitalism. The Bell service ethos worked, and it was often propagandized in a rather saccharine fashion. Over the decades, people slowly grew tired of this. And then openly

> *The deep attraction of elite technical power should never be underestimated.*

impatient with it. By the early 1980s, Ma Bell was to find herself with scarcely a real friend in the world. Vail's industrial socialism had become hopelessly out of fashion politically. Bell would be punished for that. And that punishment would fall harshly upon the people of the telephone community.

In 1983, Ma Bell was dismantled by federal court action. The pieces of Bell are now separate corporate entities. The core of the company became AT&T Communications and AT&T Industries (formerly Western Electric, Bell's manufacturing arm). AT&T Bell Labs became Bell Communications Research, Bellcore. Then there are the Regional Bell Operating Companies, or RBOCs, pronounced "arbocks."

Bell was a titan and even these regional chunks are gigantic enterprises: Fortune 50 companies with plenty of wealth and power behind them. But the clean lines of "One Policy, One System, Universal Service" have been shattered, apparently forever.

The "One Policy" of the early Reagan administration was to shatter a system that smacked of noncompetitive socialism. Since that time, there has been no real telephone "policy" on the federal level. Despite the breakup, the remnants of Bell have never been set free to compete in the open marketplace.

The RBOCs are still very heavily regulated, but not from the top. Instead, they struggle politically, economically, and legally, in what seems an endless turmoil, in a patchwork of overlapping federal and state jurisdictions. Increasingly, like other major American corporations, the RBOCs are becoming multinational, acquiring important commercial interests in Europe, Latin America, and the Pacific Rim. But this, too, adds to their legal and political predicament.

The people of what used to be Ma Bell are not happy about their fate. They feel ill used. They might have been grudgingly willing to make a full transition to the free market, to become just companies amid other companies. But this never happened. Instead, AT&T and the RBOCs (the "Baby Bells") feel themselves wrenched from side to side by state regulators, Congress, the Federal Communications Commission (FCC), and especially the federal court of Judge Harold Greene, the magistrate who ordered the Bell breakup and who has been the de facto czar of American telecommunications ever since 1983.

Bell people feel that they exist in a kind of paralegal limbo today. They don't understand what's demanded of them. If it's "service," why aren't they treated like a public service? And if it's money, then why aren't they free to compete for it? No one seems to know, really. Those who claim to know keep changing their minds. Nobody in authority seems willing to grasp the nettle for once and all.

Telephone people from other countries are amazed by the American telephone system today. Not that it works so well; for nowadays even the French telephone system works, more or less. They are amazed that the American telephone system *still* works *at all*, under these strange conditions.

Bell's "One System" of long-distance service is now only about 80 percent of a system, with the remainder held by Sprint, MCI, and the midget long-distance companies. Ugly wars over dubious corporate practices such as "slamming" (an underhanded method of snitching clients from rivals) break out with some regularity in the realm of long-distance service. The battle to break Bell's long-distance monopoly was long and ugly, and since the breakup, the battlefield has not become much prettier. AT&T's famous shame-and-blame advertisements, which emphasized the shoddy work and purported ethical shadiness of its competitors, were much remarked on for their studied psychological cruelty.

There is much bad blood in this industry and much long-treasured resentment. AT&T's postbreakup corporate logo, a striped sphere, is known in the industry as the "Death Star" (a reference from the movie *Star Wars*, in which the Death Star was the spherical high-tech fortress of the harsh-breathing imperial ultra-baddie, Darth Vader). Even AT&T employees are less than thrilled by the Death Star. A popular (though banned) T-shirt among AT&T employees bears the old-fashioned bell logo of the Bell System, plus the newfangled striped sphere, with the before-and-after comments: "This is your brain—This is your brain on drugs!" AT&T made a very well-financed and determined effort to break into the personal computer market; it was disastrous, and telco computer experts are derisively known by their competitors as "the pole-climbers." AT&T and the Baby Bell RBOCs still seem to have few friends.

Under conditions of sharp commercial competition, a crash like that of January 15, 1990, was a major embarrassment to AT&T. It was a direct blow against their much-treasured reputation for reliability. Within days of the crash, AT&T's chief executive officer, Bob Allen, officially apologized, in terms of deeply pained humility:

> AT&T had a major service disruption last Monday. We didn't live up to our own standards of quality, and we didn't live up to yours. It's as simple as that. And that's not acceptable to us. Or to you. . . . We understand how much people have come to depend upon AT&T service, so our AT&T Bell Laboratories scien-

tists and our network engineers are doing everything possible to
guard against a recurrence. . . . We know there's no way to make
up for the inconvenience this problem may have caused you.

Mr. Allen's "open letter to customers" was printed in lavish ads
all over the country: in the *Wall Street Journal, USA Today, The
New York Times, Los Angeles Times, Chicago Tribune, Philadelphia
Inquirer, San Francisco Chronicle Examiner, Boston Globe, Dallas
Morning News, Detroit Free Press, Washington Post, Houston
Chronicle,* Cleveland *Plain Dealer, Atlanta Journal Constitution,
Minneapolis Star Tribune, St. Paul Pioneer Press Dispatch, Seattle
Times/Post Intelligencer, Tacoma News Tribune, Miami Herald,
Pittsburgh Press, St. Louis Post Dispatch, Denver Post, Phoenix
Republic Gazette,* and *Tampa Tribune.*

In another press release, AT&T went to some pains to suggest
that this "software glitch" *might* have happened just as easily to
MCI, although, in fact, it hadn't. (MCI's switching software was
quite different from AT&T's—though not necessarily any safer.)
AT&T also announced plans to offer a rebate of service on Valen-
tine's Day to make up for the loss during the Crash.

"Every technical resource available, including Bell Labs scientists and engineers, has been devoted to assuring it will not occur
again," the public was told. They were further assured that "The
chances of a recurrence are small—a problem of this magnitude
never occurred before."

In the meantime, however, police and corporate security maintained their own suspicions about "the chances of recurrence"
and the real reason why a "problem of this magnitude" had appeared, seemingly out of nowhere. Police and security knew for a
fact that hackers of unprecedented sophistication were illegally
entering, and reprogramming, certain digital switching stations.
Rumors of hidden "viruses" and secret "logic bombs" in the
switches ran rampant in the underground, with much chortling
over AT&T's predicament and idle speculation over what unsung
hacker genius was responsible for it. Some hackers, including po-

lice informants, were trying hard to finger one another as the true culprits of the crash.

Telco people found little comfort in objectivity when they contemplated these possibilities. It was just too close to the bone for them; it was embarrassing; it hurt so much, it was hard even to talk about.

There had always been thieving and misbehavior in the phone system. There had always been trouble with the rival independents and in the local loops. But to have such trouble in the core of the system, the long-distance switching stations, was a horrifying affair. To telco people, this was all the difference between finding roaches in your kitchen and big horrid sewer rats in your bedroom.

From the outside, to the average citizen, the telcos still seem gigantic and impersonal. The American public seems to regard them as something akin to Soviet apparats. Even when the telcos do their best corporate-citizen routine, subsidizing magnet high schools

It was all the difference between finding roaches in your kitchen and big horrid sewer rats in your bedroom.

and sponsoring news shows on public television, they seem to win little except public suspicion.

But from the inside, all this looks very different. There's harsh competition and a legal and political system that seems baffled and bored, when not actively hostile to telco interests. There's a loss of morale, a deep sensation of having somehow lost the upper hand. Technological change has caused a loss of data and revenue to other, newer forms of transmission. There's theft, and new forms of theft, of growing scale and boldness and sophistication. With all these factors, it was no surprise to see the telcos, large and small, break out in a litany of bitter complaint.

In late 1988 and throughout 1989, telco representatives grew shrill in their complaints to those few American law enforcement

officials who make it their business to try to understand what
telephone people are talking about. Telco security officials had
discovered the computer-hacker underground, infiltrated it thoroughly, and become deeply alarmed at its growing expertise. Here
they had found a target that was not only loathsome on its face,
but clearly ripe for counterattack.

Those bitter rivals—AT&T, MCI, and Sprint, and a crowd of
Baby Bells: PacBell, Bell South, Southwestern Bell, NYNEX,
U S West, as well as the Bell
research consortium Bellcore
and the independent long-distance carrier Mid-American—
all were to have their role in the great hacker dragnet of 1990.

Hackers and code thieves were wily prey.

After years of being battered and pushed around, the telcos had,
at least in a small way, seized the initiative again. After years of
turmoil, telcos and government officials were once again to work
smoothly in concert in defense of the System. Optimism blos-
somed; enthusiasm grew on all sides; the taste of prospective
vengeance was sweet.

From the beginning—even before the crackdown had a name
—secrecy was a big problem. There were many good reasons for
secrecy in the hacker crackdown. Hackers and code thieves were
wily prey, slinking back to their bedrooms and basements and
destroying vital incriminating evidence at the first hint of trouble.
Furthermore, the crimes themselves were heavily technical and
difficult to describe, even to police—much less the general public.

When such crimes *had* been described intelligibly to the public, in the past, that very publicity had tended to *increase* the
crimes enormously. Telco officials, while painfully aware of the
vulnerabilities of their systems, were anxious not to publicize
those weaknesses. Experience showed them that those weaknesses, once discovered, would be exploited pitilessly by tens of
thousands of people—not only by professional grifters and by
underground hackers and phone phreaks, but by many otherwise

more-or-less honest everyday folks, who regarded stealing service from the faceless, soulless "Phone Company" as a kind of harmless indoor sport. When it came to protecting their interests, telcos had long since given up on general public sympathy for "the Voice with a Smile." Nowadays the telco's "Voice" was very likely to be a computer's; and the American public showed much less of the proper respect and gratitude due the fine public service bequeathed them by Dr. Bell and Mr. Vail. The more efficient, high tech, computerized, and impersonal the telcos became, it seemed, the more they were met by sullen public resentment and amoral greed.

Telco officials wanted to punish the phone-phreak underground, in as public and exemplary a manner as possible. They wanted to make dire examples of the worst offenders, to seize the ringleaders and intimidate the small fry, to discourage and frighten the wacky hobbyists, and to send the professional grifters to jail. To do all this, publicity was vital.

Yet operational security was even more so. If word got out that a nationwide crackdown was coming, the hackers might simply vanish: destroy the evidence, hide their computers, go to earth, and wait for the campaign to blow over. Even the young hackers were crafty and suspicious; as for the professional grifters, they tended to split for the nearest state line at the first sign of trouble. For the crackdown to work well, they would all have to be caught red-handed, swept upon suddenly, out of the blue, from every corner of the compass.

There was another strong motive for secrecy. In the worst-case scenario, a blown campaign might leave the telcos open to a devastating hacker counterattack. If saboteurs had caused the January 15 crash—if indeed there were gifted hackers loose in the nation's long-distance switching systems—then they might react unpredictably to a crackdown. Even if caught, they might have talented and vengeful friends still running around loose. Conceivably, it could turn ugly. Very ugly. In fact, it was hard to imagine just how ugly things might turn, given that possibility.

Counterattack from hackers was a genuine concern for the

telcos. In point of fact, they would never suffer any such counter-attack. But in months to come, they would be at some pains to publicize this notion and to utter grim warnings about it.

Still, that risk seemed well worth running. Better to run the risk of vengeful attacks than to live at the mercy of potential crashers. Any cop would tell you that a protection racket had no real future.

And publicity was such a useful thing. Corporate security officers, including telco security, generally work under conditions of great discretion. And security officials do not make money for their companies. Their job is to *prevent the loss* of money, which is much less glamorous than actually winning profits.

If you are a corporate security official, and you do your job brilliantly, then nothing bad happens to your company at all. Because of this, you appear completely superfluous. This is one of the many unattractive aspects of security work. It's rare that these folks have the chance to draw some healthy attention to their efforts.

Publicity also served the interest of their friends in law enforcement. Public officials, including those in law enforcement, thrive by attracting favorable public interest. A brilliant prosecution in a matter of vital public interest can make the career of a prosecuting attorney. And for a police officer, good publicity opens the purses of the legislature; it may bring a citation, or a promotion, or at least a rise in status and the respect of one's peers.

But to have both publicity and secrecy is to have one's cake and eat it too. In months to come, as we will show, this impossible act was to cause great pain to the agents of the crackdown. But early on, it seemed possible—maybe even likely—that the crackdown could successfully combine the best of both worlds. The *arrest* of hackers would be heavily publicized. The actual *deeds* of the hackers, which were technically hard to explain and also a security risk, would be left decently obscured. The *threat* hackers posed would be heavily trumpeted; the likelihood of their actually committing such fearsome crimes would be left to the public's imagination. The spread of the computer underground, and its growing technical sophistication, would be heavily promoted; the actual hackers themselves, mostly bespectacled middle-class white suburban teenagers, would be denied any personal publicity.

It does not seem to have occurred to any telco official that the hackers accused would demand a day in court; that journalists would smile upon the hackers as "good copy"; that wealthy high-tech entrepreneurs would offer moral and financial support to crackdown victims; that constitutional lawyers would show up with briefcases, frowning mightily. This possibility does not seem to have ever entered the game plan.

But even if it had, it probably would not have slowed the ferocious pursuit of a stolen phone-company document, mellifluously known as "Control Office Administration of Enhanced 911 Services for Special Services and Major Account Centers."

In the pages to follow, we will explore the worlds of police and the computer underground, and the large shadowy area where they overlap. But first, we must explore the battleground. Before we leave the world of the telcos, we must understand what a switching system actually is and how your telephone actually works.

To the average citizen, the idea of the telephone is represented by, well, a *telephone*: a device that you talk into. To a telco professional, however, the telephone itself is known, in lordly fashion, as a "subset." The subset in your house is a mere adjunct, a distant nerve ending, of the central switching stations, which are ranked in levels of hierarchy, up to the long-distance electronic switching stations, which are some of the largest computers on earth.

Let us imagine that it is, say, 1925, before the introduction of computers, when the phone system was simpler and somewhat easier to grasp. Let's further imagine that you are Miss Leticia Luthor, a fictional operator for Ma Bell in New York City of the 1920s.

Basically, you, Miss Luthor, *are* the "switching system." You are sitting in front of a large vertical switchboard, known as a "cordboard," made of shiny wooden panels, with ten thousand metal-rimmed holes punched in them, known as jacks. The engineers would have put more holes into your switchboard, but ten thousand is as many as you can reach without actually having to get up out of your chair.

Each of these ten thousand holes has its own little electric light bulb, known as a "lamp," and its own neatly printed number code.

With the ease of long habit, you are scanning your board for lit-up bulbs. This is what you do most of the time, so you are used to it.

A lamp lights up. This means that the phone at the end of that line has been taken off the hook. Whenever a handset is taken off the hook, that closes a circuit inside the phone that then signals the local office—you—automatically. There might be somebody calling, or then again the phone might be simply off the hook, but this does not matter to you yet. The first thing you do is record that number in your logbook, in your fine American public-school handwriting. This comes first, naturally, because it is done for billing purposes.

You now take the plug of your answering cord, which goes directly to your headset, and plug it into the lit-up hole. "Operator," you announce.

In operator's classes, before taking this job, you have been issued a large pamphlet full of canned operator's responses for all kinds of contingencies, which you had to memorize. You have also been trained in a proper nonregional, nonethnic pronunciation and tone of voice. You rarely have the occasion to make any spontaneous remark to a customer, and in fact this is frowned upon (except out on the rural lines where people have time on their hands and get up to all kinds of mischief).

A tough-sounding user's voice at the end of the line gives you a number. Immediately, you write that number down in your logbook, next to the caller's number, which you just wrote earlier.

You then look and see if the number this guy wants is in fact on your switchboard, which it generally is, as most calls are local ones. Long distance costs so much that people use it sparingly.

Only then do you pick up a calling cord from a shelf at the base of the switchboard. This is a long elastic cord mounted on a kind of reel so that it will zip back in when you unplug it.

> Some of the girls think there are bugs living in those cable holes.

There are a lot of cords down there, and when a bunch of them are out at once they look like a nest of snakes. Some of the girls think there are bugs living in those cable holes. They're called "cable mites" and are supposed to bite your hands and give you rashes. You don't believe this yourself.

Gripping the head of your calling cord, you slip the tip of it deftly into the sleeve of the jack for the called person. Not all the way in, though. You just touch it. If you hear a clicking sound, that means the line is busy and you can't put the call through. If the line is busy, you have to stick the calling cord into a "busy-tone jack," which will give the guy a busy tone. This way you don't have to talk to him yourself and absorb his natural human frustration.

But the line isn't busy. So you pop the cord all the way in. Relay circuits in your board make the distant phone ring, and if somebody picks it up off the hook, then a phone conversation starts. You can hear this conversation on your answering cord, until you unplug it. In fact you could listen to the whole conversation if you wanted, but this is sternly frowned upon by management, and frankly, when you've overheard one, you've pretty much heard 'em all.

You can tell how long the conversation lasts by the glow of the calling cord's lamp, down on the calling cord's shelf. When it's over, you unplug and the calling cord zips back into place.

Having done this stuff a few hundred thousand times, you become quite good at it. In fact you're plugging, and connecting, and disconnecting ten, twenty, forty cords at a time. It's a manual handicraft, really, quite satisfying in a way, rather like weaving on an upright loom.

Should a long-distance call come up, it would be different, but not all that different. Instead of connecting the call through your own local switchboard, you have to go up the hierarchy, onto the long-distance lines, known as "trunklines." Depending on how far the call goes, it may have to work its way through a whole series of operators, which can take quite a while. The caller doesn't wait on the line while this complex process is negotiated across the country by the gaggle of operators. Instead, the caller hangs up, and you call him back yourself when the call has finally worked its way through.

After four or five years of this work, you get married, and you have to quit your job, this being the natural order of womanhood in the American 1920s. The phone company has to train somebody else—maybe two people, since the phone system has grown somewhat in the meantime. And this costs money.

In fact, using any kind of human being as a switching system is a very expensive proposition. Eight thousand Leticia Luthors would be bad enough, but a quarter of a million of them is a military-scale proposition and makes drastic measures in automation financially worthwhile.

Although the phone system continues to grow today, the number of human beings employed by telcos has been dropping steadily for years. Phone "operators" now deal with nothing but unusual contingencies, all routine operations having been shrugged off onto machines. Consequently, telephone operators are considerably less machinelike nowadays, and have been known to have accents and actual character in their voices. When you reach human operators today, they are rather more "human" than they were in Leticia's day—but on the other hand, human beings in the phone system are much harder to reach in the first place.

Over the first half of the twentieth century, "electromechanical" switching systems of growing complexity were introduced cautiously into the phone system. In certain backwaters, some of these hybrid systems are still in use. But after 1965, the phone system began to go completely electronic, and this is by far the dominant mode today. Electromechanical systems have "cross-bars," and "brushes," and other large moving mechanical parts, which, while faster and cheaper than Leticia, are still slow and tend to wear out fairly quickly.

But fully electronic systems are inscribed on silicon chips, and are lightning-fast and quite durable. They are much cheaper to maintain than even the best electromechanical systems, and they fit into half the space. And with every year, the silicon chip grows smaller, faster, and cheaper yet. Best of all, automated electronics work around the clock and don't have salaries or health insurance.

There are, however, quite serious drawbacks to the use of computer chips. When they do break down, it is a daunting challenge to figure out what the heck has gone wrong with them. A broken cordboard generally had a problem in it big enough to see. A broken chip has invisible, microscopic faults. And the faults in bad software can be so subtle as to be practically theological.

If you want a mechanical system to do something new, then you must travel to where it is, pull pieces out of it, and wire in new pieces. This costs money. However, if you want a chip to do something new, all

The faults in bad software can be so subtle as to be practically theological.

you have to do is change its software, which is easy, fast, and dirt cheap. You don't even have to see the chip to change its program. Even if you did see the chip, it wouldn't look like much. A chip with program X doesn't look one whit different from a chip with program Y.

With the proper codes and sequences, and access to specialized phone lines, you can change electronic switching systems all over America from anywhere you please.

And so can other people. If they know how, and if they want to, they can sneak into a microchip via the special phone lines and diddle with it, leaving no physical trace at all. If they broke into the operator's station and held Leticia at gunpoint, that would be very obvious. If they broke into a telco building and went after an electromechanical switch with a toolbelt, that would at least leave many traces. But people can do all manner of amazing things to computer switches just by typing on a keyboard, and keyboards are everywhere today. The extent of this vulnerability is deep, dark, broad, almost mind-boggling, and yet this is a basic, primal fact of life about any computer on a network.

Security experts over the past twenty years have insisted, with growing urgency, that this basic vulnerability represents an entirely new level of risk, of unknown but obviously dire potential to society. And they are right.

An electronic switching station does pretty much everything Letitia did, except in nanoseconds and on a much larger scale. Compared to Miss Luthor's 10,000 jacks, even a primitive 1ESS switching computer, 1960s vintage, has 128,000 lines. And the current AT&T system of choice is the monstrous fifth-generation 5ESS.

An Electronic Switching Station can scan every line on its "board" in a tenth of a second, and it does this over and over, tirelessly, around the clock. Instead of eyes, it uses "ferrod scanners" to check the condition of local lines and trunks. Instead of hands, it has "signal distributors," "central pulse distributors," "magnetic latching relays," and "reed switches," which complete and break the calls. Instead of a brain, it has a "central processor." Instead of an instruction manual, it has a program. Instead of a handwritten logbook for recording and billing calls, it has magnetic tapes. And it never has to talk to anybody. Everything a customer might say to it is done by punching the direct-dial tone buttons on your subset.

Although an Electronic Switching Station can't talk, it does need an interface, some way to relate to its, er, employers. This interface is known as the "master control center." (This interface might be better known simply as "the interface," as it doesn't actually "control" phone calls directly. However, a term such as "master control center" is just the kind of rhetoric that telco maintenance engineers—and hackers—find particularly satisfying.)

Using the master control center, a phone engineer can test local and trunk lines for malfunctions. He (rarely she) can check various alarm displays, measure traffic on the lines, examine the records of telephone usage and the charges for those calls, and change the programming.

So, of course, can anybody else who gets into the master control center by remote control, if he (rarely she) has managed to figure out how—or, more likely, has swiped the knowledge from people who already know.

In 1989 and 1990, one particular RBOC, BellSouth, which felt particularly troubled, spent a purported $1.2 million on computer security. Some think it spent as much as $2 million, if you count all the associated costs. Two million dollars is still very little compared to the great cost-saving utility of telephonic computer systems.

Unfortunately, computers are also stupid. Unlike human beings, computers possess the truly profound stupidity of the inanimate.

In the 1960s, in the first shocks of spreading computerization, there was much easy talk about the stupidity of computers—how they could "only follow the program" and were rigidly required to do "only what they were told." There has been rather less talk about the stupidity of computers since they began to achieve grandmaster status in chess tournaments and to manifest many other impressive forms of apparent cleverness.

Nevertheless, computers *still* are profoundly brittle and stupid; they are simply vastly more subtle in their stupidity and brittleness. The computers of the 1990s are much more reliable in their components than earlier computer systems, but they are also called upon to do far more complex things, under far more challenging conditions.

On a basic mathematical level, every single line of a software program offers a chance for some possible screwup. Software does not sit still when it works; it "runs," it interacts with itself and with its own inputs and outputs. By analogy, it stretches like putty into millions of possible shapes and conditions, so many shapes that they can never all be successfully tested, not even in the life span of the universe. Sometimes the putty snaps.

The stuff we call "software" is not like anything that human society is used to thinking about. Software is something like a machine, and something like mathematics, and something like language, and something like thought, and art, and information . . . but software is not in fact any of those other things. The protean quality of software is one of the great sources of its fascination. It also makes software very powerful, very subtle, very unpredictable, and very risky.

Some software is bad and buggy. Some is "robust," even "bulletproof." The best software is that which has been tested by thousands of users under thousands of different conditions, over years. It is then known as "stable." This does *not* mean that the software is now flawless, free of bugs. It generally means that there are plenty of bugs in it, but the bugs are well identified and fairly well understood.

There is simply no way to assure that software is free of flaws. Though software is mathematical in nature, it cannot be "proven" like a mathematical theorem; software is more like language, with inherent ambiguities, with different definitions, different assumptions, different levels of meaning that can conflict.

Human beings can manage, more or less, with human language because we can catch the gist of it.

Computers, despite years of effort in "artificial intelligence," have proven spectacularly bad in "catching the gist" of anything at all. The tiniest bit of semantic grit still may bring the mightiest computer tumbling down. One of the most hazardous things you can do to a computer program is try to improve it—to try to make it safer. Software "patches" represent new, untried un-"stable" software, which is by definition riskier.

The modern telephone system has come to depend, utterly

and irretrievably, upon software. And the System Crash of January 15, 1990, was caused by an *improvement* in software. Or rather, an *attempted* improvement.

As it happened, the problem itself—the problem per se—took this form. A piece of telco software had been written in C language, a standard language of the telco field. Within the C software was a long "do . . . while" construct. The "do . . . while" construct contained a "switch" statement. The "switch" statement contained an "if" clause. The "if" clause contained a "break." The "break" was *supposed* to break the "if" clause. Instead, the "break" broke the "switch" statement.

That was the problem, the actual reason why people picking up phones on January 15, 1990, could not talk to one another.

Or at least, that was the subtle, abstract, cyberspatial seed of the problem. This is how the problem manifested itself from the realm of programming into the realm of real life.

The System 7 software for AT&T's 4ESS switching station, the "Generic 44E14 Central Office Switch Software," had been extensively tested, and was considered very stable. By the end of 1989, eighty of AT&T's switching systems nationwide had been programmed with the new software. Cautiously, thirty-four stations were left to run the slower, less-capable System 6, because AT&T suspected there might be shakedown problems with the new and unprecedentedly sophisticated System 7 network.

The stations with System 7 were programmed to switch over to a backup net in case of any problems. In mid-December 1989, however, a new high-velocity, high-security software patch was distributed to each of the 4ESS switches that would enable them to switch over even more quickly, making the System 7 network that much more secure.

Unfortunately, every one of these 4ESS switches was now in possession of a small but deadly flaw.

In order to maintain the network, switches must monitor the condition of other switches—whether they are up and running, whether they have temporarily shut down, whether they are overloaded and in need of assistance, and so forth. The new software helped control this bookkeeping function by monitoring the status calls from other switches.

It only takes four to six seconds for a troubled 4ESS switch to rid itself of all its calls, drop everything temporarily, and reboot its software from scratch. Starting over from scratch generally will rid the switch of any software problems that may have developed in the course of running the system. Bugs that arise will be simply wiped out by this process. It is a clever idea. This process of automatically rebooting from scratch is known as the "normal fault recovery routine." Because AT&T's software is in fact excep-

Unfortunately, every one of these 4ESS switches was now in possession of a small but deadly flaw.

tionally stable, systems rarely have to go into "fault recovery" in the first place; but AT&T has long boasted of its "real-world" reliability, and this tactic is a belt-and-suspenders routine.

The 4ESS switch used its new software to monitor its fellow switches as they recovered from faults. As other switches came back on line after recovery, they would send their "OK" signals to the switch. The switch would make a little note to that effect in its "status map," recognizing that the fellow switch was back and ready to go, and should be sent some calls and put back to regular work.

Unfortunately, while it was busy bookkeeping with the status map, the tiny flaw in the brand-new software came into play. The flaw caused the 4ESS switch to interact, subtly but drastically, with incoming telephone calls from human users. If—and only if —two incoming phone calls happened to hit the switch within a hundredth of a second, then a small patch of data would be garbled by the flaw.

But the switch had been programmed to monitor itself constantly for any possible damage to its data. When the switch perceived that its data had been garbled somehow, then it too would go down, for swift repairs to its software. It would signal its fellow switches not to send any more work. It would go into the fault-recovery mode for four to six seconds. And then the switch would be fine again, and would send out its "OK, ready for work" signal.

However, the "OK, ready for work" signal was the *very thing that had caused the switch to go down in the first place.* And *all* the System 7 switches had the same flaw in their status-map software. As soon as they stopped to make the bookkeeping note that their fellow switch was "OK," then they too would become vulnerable to the slight chance that two phone calls would hit them within a hundredth of a second.

At approximately 2:25 P.M. EST on Monday, January 15, 1990, one of AT&T's 4ESS toll switching systems in New York City had an actual, legitimate, minor problem. It went into fault recovery routines, announced, "I'm going down," then announced, "I'm back, I'm OK." And this cheery message then blasted throughout the network to many of its fellow 4ESS switches.

Many of the switches, at first, escaped trouble. These lucky switches were not hit by the coincidence of two phone calls within a hundredth of a second. Their software did not fail—at first. But three switches—in Atlanta, St. Louis, and Detroit— were unlucky and were caught with their hands full. They went down. And came back up, almost immediately. And they too began to broadcast the lethal message that they were "OK" again, activating the lurking software bug in yet other switches.

As more and more switches did have that bit of bad luck and collapsed, the call traffic became more and more densely packed in the remaining switches, which were groaning to keep up with the load. And of course, as the calls became more densely packed, the switches were *much more likely* to be hit twice within a hundredth of a second.

It only took four seconds for a switch to get well. There was no *physical* damage of any kind to the switches, after all. Physically, they were working perfectly. This situation was "only" a software problem.

But the 4ESS switches were leaping up and down every four to six seconds, in a virulent spreading wave all over America, in utter, manic, mechanical stupidity. They kept *knocking* one another down with their contagious "OK" messages.

It took about ten minutes for the chain reaction to cripple the network. Even then, switches would periodically luck out and manage to resume their normal work. Many calls—millions of them—were managing to get through. But millions weren't.

The switching stations that used System 6 were not directly affected. Thanks to these old-fashioned switches, AT&T's national system avoided complete collapse. This fact also made it clear to engineers that System 7 was at fault.

Bell Labs engineers, working feverishly in New Jersey, Illinois, and Ohio, tried their entire repertoire of standard network remedies on the malfunctioning System 7. None of the remedies worked, of course, because nothing like this had ever happened to any phone system before.

By cutting out the backup safety network entirely, they were able to reduce the frenzy of "OK" messages by about half. The system then began to recover, as the chain reaction slowed. By 11:30 P.M. on Monday, January 15, sweating engineers on the midnight shift breathed a sigh of relief as the last switch cleared up.

By Tuesday they were pulling all the brand-new 4ESS software and replacing it with an earlier version of System 7.

If these had been human operators, rather than computers at work, someone would simply have eventually stopped screaming. It would have been *obvious* that the situation was not "OK," and common sense would have kicked in. Humans possess common sense—at least to some extent. Computers simply don't.

On the other hand, computers can handle hundreds of calls per second. Humans simply can't. If every human being in America worked for the phone company, we couldn't match the performance of digital switches: direct dialing, three-way calling, speed-calling, call waiting, Caller ID, all the rest of the cornucopia of digital bounty. Replacing computers with operators is simply not an option anymore.

And yet we still, anachronistically, expect humans to be running our phone system. It is hard for us to understand that we have sacrificed huge amounts of initiative and control to senseless yet powerful machines. When the phones fail, we want somebody to be responsible. We want somebody to blame.

When the Crash of January 15 happened, the American populace simply was not prepared to understand that enormous landslides in cyberspace, like the crash itself, can happen and can be nobody's fault in particular. It was easier to believe, maybe even in some odd way more *reassuring* to believe, that some evil person, or evil group, had done this to us. "Hackers" had done it. With a virus. A Trojan horse. A software bomb. A dirty plot of some kind. People believed this, responsible people. In 1990, they were looking hard for evidence to confirm their heartfelt suspicions.

And they would look in a lot of places.

Come 1991, however, the outlines of an apparent new reality would begin to emerge from the fog.

On July 1 and 2, 1991, computer-software collapses in telephone switching stations disrupted service in Washington, D.C., Pittsburgh, Los Angeles, and San Francisco. Once again, seemingly minor maintenance problems had crippled the digital System 7. About 12 million people were affected in the Crash of July 1, 1991.

Said *The New York Times* service: "Telephone company executives and federal regulators said they were not ruling out the possibility of sabotage by computer hackers, but most seemed to think the problems stemmed from some unknown defect in the software running the networks."

And sure enough, within the week, a red-faced software company, DSC Communications Corporation of Plano, Texas, owned up to "glitches" in the "signal transfer point" software that DSC had designed for Bell Atlantic and Pacific Bell. The immediate cause of the July 1 crash was a single mistyped character: one tiny typographical flaw in one single line of the software. One mistyped letter, in one single line, had deprived the nation's capital of phone service. It was not particularly surprising that this tiny flaw had escaped attention; a typical System 7 station requires *10 million* lines of code.

On Tuesday, September 17, 1991, came the most spectacular outage yet. This case had nothing to do with software failures—at least, not directly. Instead, a group of AT&T's switching stations in New York City had simply run out of electrical power and shut down cold. Their backup batteries had failed. Automatic warning systems were supposed to warn of the loss of battery power, but those automatic systems had failed as well.

This time, Kennedy, La Guardia, and Newark airports all had their voice and data communications cut. This horrifying event was particularly ironic, as hacker attacks on airport computers had long been a standard nightmare scenario, much trumpeted by computer-security experts who feared the computer underground. There had even been a Hollywood thriller about sinister hackers ruining airport computers—*Die Hard II*.

Now AT&T itself had crippled airports with computer malfunctions—not just one airport, but three at once, some of the busiest in the world.

Air traffic came to a standstill throughout the Greater New York area, causing more than 500 flights to be canceled, in a spreading wave all over America and even into Europe. Another 500 or so flights were delayed, affecting, all in all, about 85,000 passengers. (One of these passengers was the chairman of the Federal Communications Commission.)

Stranded passengers in New York and New Jersey were further infuriated to discover that they could not even manage to make a long-distance phone call to explain their delay to loved ones or business associates. Thanks to the crash, about four and a half million domestic calls and half a million international calls failed to get through.

The September 17 New York City crash, unlike the previous ones, involved not a whisper of "hacker" misdeeds. On the contrary, by 1991, AT&T itself was suffering much of the vilification that had formerly been directed at hackers. Congresspeople were grumbling. So were state and federal regulators. And so was the press.

For its part, ancient rival MCI took out snide full-page newspaper ads in New York, offering its own long-distance services for the "next time that AT&T goes down."

"You wouldn't find a classy company like AT&T using such advertising," protested AT&T Chairman Robert Allen, unconvincingly. Once again, out came the full-page AT&T apologies in newspapers, apologies for "an inexcusable culmination of both human and mechanical failure." (This time, however, AT&T offered no discount on later calls. Unkind critics suggested that AT&T was worried about setting any precedent for refunding the financial losses caused by telephone crashes.)

Industry journals asked publicly if AT&T was "asleep at the switch." The telephone network, America's purported marvel of high-tech reliability, had gone down three times in eighteen months. *Fortune* magazine listed the Crash of September 17 among the "Biggest Business Goofs of 1991," cruelly parodying AT&T's ad campaign in an article entitled "AT&T Wants You Back (Safely On the Ground, God Willing)."

Why had those New York switching systems simply run out of power? Because no human being had attended to the alarm system. Why did the alarm systems blare automatically, without any human being noticing? Because the three telco technicians who *should* have been listening were absent from their stations in the power room, on another floor of the building—attending a training class. A training class about the alarm systems for the power room!

"Crashing the System" was no longer "unprecedented" by late 1991. On the contrary, it no longer even seemed an oddity. By 1991, it was clear that all the police in the world could no longer "protect" the phone system from crashes. By far the worst crashes the system had ever had, had been inflicted, by the system, upon *itself*. And this time nobody was making cocksure statements that this was an anomaly, something that would never happen again. By 1991 the System's defenders had met their nebulous Enemy, and the Enemy was—the System.

PART

2

THE DIGITAL
UNDERGROUND

The date was May 9, 1990. The Pope was touring Mexico City. Hustlers from the Medellín Cartel were trying to buy black-market Stinger missiles in Florida. On the comics page, Doonesbury character Andy was dying of AIDS. And then . . . a highly unusual item whose novelty and calculated rhetoric won it headscratching attention in newspapers all over America.

The U.S. Attorney's office in Phoenix, Arizona, had issued a press release announcing a nationwide law enforcement crackdown against "illegal computer hacking activities." The sweep was officially known as "Operation Sundevil."

Eight paragraphs in the press release gave the bare facts: twenty-seven search warrants carried out on May 8, with three arrests, and 150 agents on the prowl in twelve cities across America. (Different counts in local press reports yielded "thirteen," "fourteen," and "sixteen" cities.) Officials estimated that criminal losses of revenue to telephone companies "may run into millions of dollars." Credit for the Sundevil investigations was taken by the U.S. Secret Service, Assistant U.S. Attorney Tim Holtzen of Phoenix, and the assistant attorney general of Arizona, Gail Thackeray.

The prepared remarks of Garry M. Jenkins, appearing in a U.S. Department of Justice press release, were of particular interest. Mr. Jenkins was the assistant director of the U.S. Secret Service and the highest-ranking federal official to take any direct public role in the hacker crackdown of 1990.

> Today, the Secret Service is sending a clear message to those computer hackers who have decided to violate the laws of this nation in the mistaken belief that they can successfully avoid detection by hiding behind the relative anonymity of their computer terminals. . . .
>
> Underground groups have been formed for the purpose of exchanging information relevant to their criminal activities. These groups often communicate with each other through message systems between computers called "bulletin boards."
>
> Our experience shows that many computer hacker suspects are no longer misguided teenagers, mischievously playing games with their computers in their bedrooms. Some are now high tech computer operators using computers to engage in unlawful conduct.

Who *were* these "underground groups" and "high tech computer operators"? Where had they come from? What did they want? Were they "mischievous"? Were they dangerous? How had "misguided teenagers" managed to alarm the U.S. Secret Service? And just how widespread was this sort of thing?

Of all the major players in the Hacker Crackdown—the phone

companies, law enforcement, the civil libertarians, and the hackers themselves—the hackers are by far the most mysterious, by far the hardest to understand, by far the *weirdest*.

Legitimate "hackers," those computer enthusiasts who are independent-minded but law-abiding, generally trace their spiritual ancestry to elite technical universities, especially MIT and Stanford, in the 1960s.

How had "misguided teenagers" managed to alarm the U.S. Secret Service?

But the genuine roots of the modern hacker *underground* probably can be traced most successfully to a now much-obscured hippie anarchist movement known as the Yippies. The Yippies, who took their name from the largely fictional "Youth International Party," carried out a loud and lively policy of surrealistic subversion and outrageous political mischief. Their basic tenets were flagrant sexual promiscuity, open and copious drug use, the political overthrow of any powermonger over thirty years of age, and an immediate end to the war in Vietnam, by any means necessary, including the psychic levitation of the Pentagon.

The two most visible Yippies were Abbie Hoffman and Jerry Rubin. Rubin eventually became a Wall Street broker. Hoffman, ardently sought by federal authorities, went into hiding for seven years in Mexico, France, and the United States. While on the lam, Hoffman continued to write and publish, with help from sympathizers in the American anarcho-leftist underground. Mostly, Hoffman survived through false ID and odd jobs. Eventually he underwent facial plastic surgery and adopted an entirely new identity as one "Barry Freed." After surrendering himself to authorities in 1980, Hoffman spent a year in prison on a cocaine conviction.

Hoffman's worldview grew much darker as the glory days of the 1960s faded. In 1989, he purportedly committed suicide, under odd and, to some, rather suspicious circumstances.

Abbie Hoffman is said to have caused the Federal Bureau of

Investigation to amass the single largest investigation file ever opened on an individual American citizen. (If this is true, it is still questionable whether the FBI regarded Hoffman as a serious public threat—quite possibly, his file was enormous simply because Hoffman left colorful legendry wherever he went.) He was a gifted publicist, who regarded electronic media as both playground and weapon. He actively enjoyed manipulating network television and other gullible, image-hungry media, with various weird lies, mindboggling rumors, impersonation scams, and other sinister distortions, all absolutely guaranteed to upset cops, presidential candidates, and federal judges. Hoffman's most famous work was a book self-reflexively titled *Steal This Book*, which publicized a number of methods by which young, penniless hippie agitators might live off the fat of a system supported by humorless drones. *Steal This Book*, whose title urged readers to damage the very means of distribution that had put it into their hands, might be described as a spiritual ancestor of a computer virus.

Hoffman, like many a later conspirator, made extensive use of pay phones for his agitation work—in his case, generally through the use of cheap brass washers as coin slugs.

During the Vietnam War, a federal surtax was imposed on telephone service; Hoffman and his cohorts could, and did, argue that in systematically stealing phone service they were engaging in civil disobedience: virtuously denying tax funds to an illegal and immoral war.

But this thin veil of decency was soon dropped entirely. Ripping off the System found its justification in deep alienation and a basic outlaw contempt for conventional bourgeois values. Ingenious, vaguely politicized varieties of rip-off, which might be described as "anarchy by convenience," became very popular in Yippie circles, and because rip-off was so useful, it was to outlast the Yippie movement itself.

In the early 1970s, it required fairly limited expertise and ingenuity to cheat pay phones, to divert "free" electricity and gas service, or to rob vending machines and parking meters for handy

pocket change. It also required a conspiracy to spread this knowledge, and the gall and nerve actually to commit petty theft, but
the Yippies had these qualifications in plenty. In June 1971, Abbie Hoffman and a telephone enthusiast sarcastically known as
"Al Bell" began publishing a newsletter called *Youth International
Party Line.* This newsletter was dedicated to collating and spreading Yippie rip-off techniques, especially of phones, to the joy of
the freewheeling underground and the insensate rage of all
straight people.

As a political tactic, phone-service theft ensured that Yippie
advocates would always have ready access to the long-distance
telephone as a medium, despite the Yippies' chronic lack of organization, discipline, money, or even a steady home address.

Party Line was run out of Greenwich Village for a couple of
years, then Al Bell more or less defected from the faltering ranks
of Yippiedom, changing the newsletter's name to *TAP*, or *Technical Assistance Program.* After the Vietnam War ended, the steam
began leaking out of American radical dissent. But by this time,
Bell and his dozen or so core contributors had the bit between
their teeth and had begun to derive tremendous gut-level satisfaction from the sensation of pure *technical power.*

TAP articles, once highly politicized, became pitilessly jargon-
ized and technical, in homage or parody to the Bell System's own
technical documents, which *TAP* studied closely, gutted, and reproduced without permission. The *TAP* elite reveled in gloating
possession of the specialized knowledge necessary to beat the
System.

Al Bell dropped out of the game by the late 1970s, and "Tom
Edison" took over; *TAP* readers (some 1,400 of them, all told)
now began to show more interest in telex switches and the growing phenomenon of computer systems.

In 1983, Tom Edison had his computer stolen and his house
set on fire by an arsonist. This was an eventually mortal blow to
TAP (though the legendary name was to be resurrected in 1990 by
a young Kentuckian computer outlaw named "Predat0r").

* * *

Ever since telephones began to make money, there have been people willing to rob and defraud phone companies. The legions of petty phone thieves vastly outnumber those "phone phreaks" who "explore the system" for the sake of the intellectual challenge. The New York metropolitan area (long in the vanguard of American crime) claims over 150,000 physical attacks on pay telephones every year! Studied carefully, a modern pay phone reveals itself as a little fortress, carefully designed and redesigned over generations, to resist coin slugs, zaps of electricity, chunks of coin-shaped ice, prybars, magnets, lockpicks, blasting caps. Public pay phones must survive in a world of unfriendly, greedy people, and a modern pay phone is as exquisitely evolved as a cactus.

> *A modern pay phone is as exquisitely evolved as a cactus.*

Because the phone network predates the computer network, the scofflaws known as "phone phreaks" predate the scofflaws known as "computer hackers." In practice, today, the line between "phreaking" and "hacking" is very blurred, just as the distinction between telephones and computers has blurred. The phone system has been digitized, and computers have learned to "talk" over phone lines. What's worse—and this was the point of Mr. Jenkins of the Secret Service—some hackers have learned to steal, and some thieves have learned to hack.

Despite the blurring, one can still draw a few useful behavioral distinctions between phreaks and hackers. Hackers are intensely interested in the "System" per se and enjoy relating to machines. Phreaks are more social, manipulating the System in a rough-and-ready fashion in order to get through to other human beings, fast, cheap, and under the table.

Phone phreaks love nothing so much as "bridges," illegal conference calls of ten or twelve chatting conspirators, seaboard to seaboard, lasting for many hours—and running, of course, on somebody else's tab, preferably a large corporation's.

As phone-phreak conferences wear on, people drop out (or

simply leave the phone off the hook, while they sashay off to work or school or baby-sitting), and new people are phoned up and invited to join in, from some other continent, if possible. Technical trivia, boasts, brags, lies, head-trip deceptions, weird rumors, and cruel gossip are all freely exchanged.

The lowest rung of phone-phreaking is the theft of telephone access codes. Charging a phone call to somebody else's stolen number is, of course, a pig-easy way of stealing phone service, requiring practically no technical expertise. This practice has been very widespread, especially among lonely people without much money who are far from home. Code theft has flourished especially in college dorms, military bases, and, notoriously, among roadies for rock bands. Of late, code theft has spread very rapidly among Third Worlders in the United States, who pile up enormous unpaid long-distance bills to the Caribbean, South America, and Pakistan.

The simplest way to steal phone codes is to look over a victim's shoulder as he punches in his own code number on a public pay phone. This technique is known as "shoulder-surfing" and is especially common in airports, bus terminals, and train stations. The code is then sold by the thief for a few dollars. The buyer abusing the code has no computer expertise, but calls his mom in New York, Kingston, or Caracas and runs up a huge bill with impunity. The losses from this primitive phreaking activity are far, far greater than the monetary losses caused by computer-intruding hackers.

In the mid-to-late 1980s, until the introduction of sterner telco security measures, *computerized* code theft worked like a charm and was virtually omnipresent throughout the digital underground, among phreaks and hackers alike. This was accomplished through programming one's computer to try random code numbers over the telephone until one of them worked. Simple programs to do this were widely available in the underground; a computer running all night was likely to come up with a dozen or so useful hits. This could be repeated week after week until one had a large library of stolen codes.

Nowadays, the computerized dialing of hundreds of numbers can be detected within hours and swiftly traced. If a stolen code is abused repeatedly, this too can be detected within a few hours. But for years in the 1980s, the publication of stolen codes was a kind of elementary etiquette for fledgling hackers. The simplest way to establish your bona-fides as a raider was to steal a code through repeated random dialing and offer it to the "community" for use. Codes could be both stolen and used, simply and easily, from the safety of one's own bedroom, with very little fear of detection or punishment.

Before computers and their phone-line modems entered American homes in gigantic numbers, phone phreaks had their own special telecommunications hardware gadget, the famous "blue box." This fraud device (now rendered increasingly useless by the digital evolution of the phone system) could trick switching systems into granting free access to long-distance lines. It did this by mimicking the system's own signal, a tone of 2600 hertz.

Steven Jobs and Steve Wozniak, the founders of Apple Computer, Inc., once dabbled in selling blue boxes in college dorms in California. For many, in the early days of phreaking, blue-boxing was scarcely perceived as "theft," but rather as a fun (if sneaky) way to use excess phone capacity harmlessly. After all, the long-distance lines were *just sitting there.* . . . Whom did it hurt, really? If you're not *damaging* the system, and you're not *using up any tangible resource,* and if nobody *finds out* what you did, then what real harm have you done? What exactly *have* you "stolen," anyway? If a tree falls in the forest and nobody hears it, how much is the noise worth? Even now this remains a rather dicey question.

Blue-boxing was no joke to the phone companies, however. Indeed, when *Ramparts* magazine, a radical publication in California, printed the wiring schematics necessary to create a mute box in June 1972, the magazine was seized by police and Pacific Bell phone company officials. The mute box, a blue-box variant, allowed its user to receive long-distance calls free of charge to the caller. This device was closely described in a *Ramparts* article wryly titled, "Regulating the Phone Company in Your Home." Publication of this article was held to be in violation of California State Penal Code section 502.7, which outlaws ownership of wire-fraud devices and the selling of "plans or instructions for any instrument, apparatus, or device intended to avoid telephone toll charges."

Issues of *Ramparts* were recalled or seized on the newsstands, and the resultant loss of income helped put the magazine out of business. This was an ominous precedent for free-expression issues, but the telco's crushing of a radical-fringe magazine passed without serious challenge at the time. Even in the freewheeling California 1970s, it was widely felt that there was something sacrosanct about what the phone company knew; that the telco had a legal and moral right to protect itself by shutting off the flow of such illicit information. Most telco information was so "specialized" that it would scarcely be understood by any honest member of the public. If not published, it would not be missed. To print such material did not seem part of the legitimate role of a free press.

In 1990, there would be a similar telco-inspired attack on the electronic phreak/hacking "magazine" *Phrack*. The *Phrack* legal case became a central issue in the Hacker Crackdown and gave rise to great controversy. *Phrack* would also be shut down, for a time, at least, but this time both the telcos and their law enforcement allies would pay a much larger price for their actions. The *Phrack* case will be examined in detail later.

Phone-phreaking as a social practice is still very much alive at this moment. Today, phone-phreaking is thriving much more vigorously than the better-known and worse-feared practice of "computer hacking." New forms of phreaking are spreading rapidly, following new vulnerabilities in sophisticated phone services.

Cellular phones are especially vulnerable; their chips can be reprogrammed to present a false caller ID and avoid billing. Doing so also avoids police tapping, making cellular-phone abuse a favorite among drug dealers. "Call-sell operations" using pirate cellular phones can, and have, been run right out of the backs of cars, which move from "cell" to "cell" in the local phone system, retailing stolen long-distance service, like some kind of demented electronic version of the neighborhood ice-cream truck.

Private branch-exchange (PBX) phone systems in large corporations can be penetrated; phreaks dial up a local company, enter its internal phone system, hack it, then use the company's own PBX system to dial back out over the public network, causing the company to be stuck with the resulting long-distance bill. This technique is known as "diverting." Diverting can be very costly, especially because phreaks tend to travel in packs and never stop talking. Perhaps the worst by-product of this PBX fraud is that victim companies and telcos have sued one another over the financial responsibility for the stolen calls, thus enriching not only shabby phreaks but well-paid lawyers.

"Voice-mail systems" can also be abused; phreaks can seize their own sections of these sophisticated electronic answering machines and use them for trading codes or knowledge of illegal techniques. Voice-mail abuse does not hurt the company directly, but finding supposedly empty slots in your company's answering machine all crammed with phreaks eagerly chattering and hey-duding one another in impenetrable jargon can cause sensations of almost mystical repulsion and dread.

Worse yet, phreaks sometimes have been known to react trucu-lently to attempts to "clean up" the voice-mail system. Rather than humbly acquiescing to being thrown out of their play-ground, they may very well call up the company officials at work (or at home) and loudly demand free voice-mail addresses of their very own. Such bullying is taken very seriously by spooked victims.

Acts of phreak revenge against straight people are rare, but voice-mail systems are especially tempting and vulnerable, and an infestation of angry phreaks in one's voice-mail system is no joke. They can erase legitimate messages, or spy on private messages, or harass users with recorded taunts and obscenities. They've even been known to seize control of voice-mail security and lock out legitimate users, or even shut down the system entirely.

Cellular phone calls, cordless phones, and ship-to-shore tele-phony all can be monitored by various forms of radio; this kind of "passive monitoring" is spreading explosively today. Eavesdrop-ping on other people's cordless and cellular phone calls is the fastest-growing area in phreaking today. This practice strongly appeals to the lust for power and conveys gratifying sensations of technical superiority over the eavesdropping victim. Monitoring is rife with all manner of tempting evil mischief. Simple prurient snooping is by far the most common activity. But credit card numbers unwarily spoken over the phone can be recorded, stolen, and used. And tapping people's phone calls (whether through active telephone taps or passive radio monitors) does lend itself conveniently to activities such as blackmail, industrial espio-nage, and political dirty tricks.

An infestation of angry phone phreaks in one's voice-mail system is no joke.

It should be repeated that telecommunications fraud, the theft of phone service, causes vastly greater monetary losses than the practice of entering into computers by stealth. As mentioned, hackers are mostly young suburban American white males, and exist in the hundreds—but phreaks come from both sexes and from many nationalities, ages, and ethnic backgrounds, and are flourishing in the thousands.

✡The term *hacker* has had an unfortunate history. This book, *The Hacker Crackdown*, has little to say about "hacking" in its finer, original sense. The term can signify the free-wheeling intel-lectual exploration of the highest and deepest potential of com-puter systems. Hacking can describe the determination to make access to computers and information as free and open as possible. Hacking can involve the heartfelt conviction that beauty can be found in computers, that the fine aesthetic in a perfect program can liberate the mind and spirit. This is hacking as it was defined in Steven Levy's much-praised history of the pioneer computer milieu, *Hackers*, published in 1984.

Hackers of all kinds are absolutely soaked through with heroic antibureaucratic sentiment. Hackers long for recognition as a praiseworthy cultural archetype, the postmodern electronic equivalent of the cowboy and mountain man. Whether they deserve such a reputation is something for history to decide. But many hackers—including those outlaw hackers who are computer intruders and whose activities are defined as criminal—actually attempt to *live up to* this techno-cowboy reputation. And given that electronics and telecommunications are still largely unexplored territories, there is simply *no telling* what hackers might uncover.

For some people, this freedom is the very breath of oxygen, the inventive spontaneity that makes life worth living and that flings open doors to marvelous possibility and individual empowerment. But for many people—and increasingly so—the hacker is an ominous figure, a smart-aleck sociopath ready to burst out of his basement wilderness and savage other people's lives for his own anarchical convenience.

Any form of power without responsibility, without direct and formal checks and balances, is frightening to people—and reasonably so. It should be frankly admitted that some hackers *are* frightening and that the basis of this fear is not irrational.

Fear of hackers goes well beyond the fear of merely criminal activity.

Subversion and manipulation of the phone system is an act with disturbing political overtones. In America, computers and telephones are potent symbols of organized authority and the technocratic business elite.

But there is an element in American culture that has always strongly rebelled against these symbols, rebelled against all large industrial computers and all phone companies. A certain anarchical tinge deep in the American soul delights in causing confusion and pain to all bureaucracies, including technological ones.

There is sometimes malice and vandalism in this attitude, but it is a deep and cherished part of the American national character. The outlaw, the rebel, the rugged individual, the pioneer, the sturdy Jeffersonian yeoman, the private citizen resisting interference in his pursuit of happiness—these are figures that all Americans recognize and that many will strongly applaud and defend.

Many scrupulously law-abiding citizens today do cutting-edge work with electronics—work that has already had tremendous social influence and will have much more in years to come. In all truth, these talented, hardworking, law-abiding, mature, adult people are far more disturbing to the peace and order of the current status quo than any scofflaw group of romantic teenage punk kids. These law-abiding hackers have the power, ability, and willingness to influence other people's lives quite unpredictably. They have means, motive, and opportunity to meddle drastically with the American social order. When corraled into governments, universities, or large multinational companies, and forced to follow rulebooks and wear suits and ties, they at least have some conventional halters on their freedom of action. But when loosed alone, or in small groups, and fired by imagination and the entrepreneurial spirit, they can move mountains—causing landslides that will likely crash directly into your office and living room.

These people, as a class, instinctively recognize that a public, politicized attack on hackers will eventually spread to them—that the term "hacker," once demonized, might be used to knock their hands off the levers of power and choke them out of existence. There are hackers today who fiercely and publicly resist any besmirching of the noble title of hacker. Naturally and understandably, they deeply resent the attack on their values implicit in using the word "hacker" as a synonym for computer criminal.

This book, sadly but in my opinion unavoidably, rather adds to the degradation of the term. It concerns itself mostly with hacking in its commonest latter-day definition, that is, intruding into computer systems by stealth and without permission.

The term "hacking" is used routinely today by almost all law enforcement officials with any professional interest in computer fraud and abuse. American police describe almost any crime committed with, by, through, or against a computer as hacking.

Most important, "hacker" is what computer intruders choose to call *themselves*. Nobody who hacks into systems willingly describes himself (rarely, herself) as a "computer intruder," "computer trespasser," "cracker," "wormer," "darkside hacker," or "high-tech street gangster." Several other demeaning terms have been invented in the hope that the press and public will leave the original sense of the word alone. But few people actually use these terms. (I exempt the term "cyberpunk," which a few hackers and law enforcement people actually do use. The term is drawn from literary criticism and has some odd and unlikely resonances, but, like hacker, cyberpunk too has become a criminal pejorative today.)

In any case, breaking into computer systems was hardly alien to the original hacker tradition. The first tottering systems of the 1960s required fairly extensive internal surgery merely to function day by day. Their users "invaded" the deepest, most arcane recesses of their operating software almost as a matter of routine. "Computer security" in these early, primitive systems was at best an afterthought. What security existed was entirely physical, for it was assumed that anyone allowed near this expensive, arcane hardware would be a fully qualified professional expert.

In a campus environment, though, this meant that grad students, teaching assistants, undergraduates, and, eventually, all manner of dropouts and hangers-on ended up accessing and often running the works.

Universities, even modern universities, are not in the business of maintaining security over information. On the contrary, universities, as institutions, predate the "information economy" by many centuries and are not-for-profit cultural entities, whose reason for existence (purportedly) is to discover truth, codify it through techniques of scholarship, and then teach it. Universities are meant to *pass the torch of civilization*, not just download data into student skulls, and the values of the academic community are strongly at odds with those of all would-be information empires. Teachers at all levels, from kindergarten up, have proven to be shameless and persistent software and data pirates. Universities do not merely "leak information" but vigorously broadcast free thought.

This clash of values has been fraught with controversy. Many hackers of the 1960s remember their professional apprenticeship as a long guerilla war against the uptight mainframe-computer "information priesthood." These computer-hungry youngsters had to struggle hard for access to computing power, and many of them were not above certain, er, shortcuts. But, over the years, this practice freed computing from the sterile reserve of lab-coated technocrats and was largely responsible for the explosive growth of computing in general society—especially *personal* computing.

Access to technical power acted like catnip on certain of these youngsters. Most of the basic techniques of computer intrusion—password cracking, trapdoors, backdoors, Trojan horses—were invented in college environments in the 1960s, in the early days of network computing. Some off-the-cuff experience at computer intrusion was to be in the informal résumé of most hackers and many future industry giants. Outside of the tiny cult of computer enthusiasts, few people thought much about the implications of "breaking into" computers. This sort of activity had not yet been publicized, much less criminalized.

In the 1960s, definitions of "property" and "privacy" had not yet been extended to cyberspace. Computers were not yet indispensable to society. There were no vast data banks of vulnerable, proprietary information stored in computers, which might be accessed, copied without permission, erased, altered, or sabotaged. The stakes were low in the early days—but they grew every year, exponentially, as computers themselves grew.

By the 1990s, commercial and political pressures had become overwhelming, and they broke the social boundaries of the hacking subculture. Hacking had become too important to be left to the hackers. Society was now forced to tackle the intangible nature of cyberspace-as-property, cyberspace as privately owned unreal estate. In the new, severe, responsible, high-stakes context of the "Information Society" of the 1990s, hacking was called into question.

What did it mean to break into a computer without permission and use its computational power, or look around inside its files without hurting anything? What were computer-intruding hackers anyway—how should society, and the law, best define their actions? Were they just *browsers*, harmless intellectual explorers? Were they *voyeurs*, snoops, invaders of privacy? Should they be sternly treated as potential *agents of espionage*, or perhaps as *industrial spies*? Or were they best defined as *trespassers*, a very common teenage misdemeanor? Was hacking *theft of service*? (After all, intruders were getting someone else's computer to carry out their orders, without permission and without paying.) Was hacking *fraud*? Maybe it was best described as *impersonation*. The commonest mode of computer intrusion was (and is) to swipe or snoop somebody else's password and then enter the computer in the guise of another person—who is commonly stuck with the blame and the bills.

Perhaps a medical metaphor was better—hackers should be defined as "sick," as *computer addicts* unable to control their irresponsible, compulsive behavior.

But these weighty assessments meant little to the people who were actually being judged. From inside the underground world of hacking itself, all these perceptions seem quaint, wrongheaded, stupid, or meaningless. The most important self-perception of underground hackers—from the 1960s, right through to the present day—is that they are an *elite*. The day-to-day struggle in the underground is not over sociological definitions—who cares?—but for power, knowledge, and status among one's peers.

When you are a hacker, it is your own inner conviction of your elite status that enables you to break, or let us say "transcend," the rules. It is not that *all* rules go by the board. The rules habitually broken by hackers are *unimportant* rules—the rules of dopey greedhead telco bureaucrats and pig-ignorant government pests.

Hackers have their *own* rules, which separate behavior that is cool and elite from behavior that is rodentlike, stupid, and losing. These "rules," however, are mostly unwritten and enforced by peer pressure and tribal feeling. Like all rules that depend on the unspoken conviction that everybody else is a good old boy, these rules are ripe for abuse. The mechanisms of hacker peer pressure, "teletrials" and ostracism, are rarely used and rarely work. Backstabbing slander, threats, and electronic harassment are freely employed in down-and-dirty intrahacker feuds, but this rarely forces a rival out of the scene entirely. The only real solution to the problem of an utterly losing, treacherous, and rodentlike hacker is to *turn him in to the police.* Unlike the Mafia or Medellín Cartel, the hacker elite cannot simply execute the bigmouths, creeps, and troublemakers among their ranks, so they turn one another in with astonishing frequency.

There is no tradition of silence or *omerta* in the hacker underworld. Hackers can be shy, even reclusive, but when they do talk, they tend to brag, boast, and strut. Almost everything hackers do is *invisible;* if they don't brag, boast, and strut about it, then *nobody will ever know.* If you don't have something to brag, boast, and strut about, then nobody in the underground will recognize you and favor you with vital cooperation and respect.

The way to win a solid reputation in the underground is by telling other hackers things that could have been learned only by exceptional cunning and stealth. Forbidden knowledge, therefore, is the basic currency of the digital underground, like seashells among Trobriand Islanders. Hackers hoard this knowledge, and dwell upon it obsessively, and refine it, and bargain with it, and talk and talk about it.

> *Forbidden knowledge is the basic currency of the digital underground.*

Many hackers even suffer from a strange obsession to *teach*— to spread the ethos and the knowledge of the digital underground. They'll do this even when it gains them no particular advantage and presents a grave personal risk.

And when that risk catches up with them, they will go right on teaching and preaching—to a new audience this time, their inter-rogators from law enforcement. Almost every hacker arrested tells everything he knows—all about his friends, his mentors, his disciples—legends, threats, horror stories, dire rumors, gossip, hallucinations. This is, of course, convenient for law enforcement —except when law enforcement begins to believe hacker leg-endry.

Phone phreaks are unique among criminals in their willingness to call up law enforcement officials—in the office, at their homes —and give them an extended piece of their mind. It is hard not to interpret this as *begging for arrest,* and in fact it is an act of incredible foolhardiness. Police are naturally nettled by these acts of chutzpah and will go well out of their way to bust these flaunt-ing idiots. But it can also be interpreted as a product of a worldview so elitist, so closed and hermetic, that electronic police simply are not perceived as "police" but rather as *enemy phone phreaks* who should be scolded into behaving "decently."

Hackers at their most grandiloquent perceive themselves as the elite pioneers of a new electronic world. Attempts to make them obey the democratically established laws of contemporary Ameri-can society are seen as repression and persecution. After all, they argue, if Alexander Graham Bell had gone along with the rules of the Western Union telegraph company, there would have been no telephones. If Jobs and Wozniak had believed that IBM was the be-all and end-all, there would have been no personal com-puters. If Benjamin Franklin and Thomas Jefferson had tried to "work within the system," there would have been no United States.

Not only do hackers privately believe this as an article of faith, but they have been known to write ardent manifestos about it. Here are some revealing excerpts from an especially vivid hacker manifesto: "The Techno-Revolution" by "Dr. Crash," which ap-peared in electronic form in *Phrack,* Volume 1, Issue 6, Phile 3.

To fully explain the true motives behind hacking, we must first take a quick look into the past. In the 1960s, a group of MIT students built the first modern computer system. This wild, rebellious group of young men were the first to bear the name "hackers." The systems that they developed were intended to be used to solve world problems and to benefit all of mankind.

As we can see, this has not been the case. The computer system has been solely in the hands of big businesses and the government. The wonderful device meant to enrich life has become a weapon which dehumanizes people. To the government and large businesses, people are no more than disk space, and the government doesn't use computers to arrange aid for the poor, but to control nuclear death weapons. The average American can only have access to a small microcomputer which is worth only a fraction of what they pay for it. The businesses keep the true state-of-the-art equipment away from the people behind a steel wall of incredibly high prices and bureaucracy. It is because of this state of affairs that hacking was born. . . .

Of course, the government doesn't want the monopoly of technology broken, so they have outlawed hacking and arrest anyone who is caught. . . . The phone company is another example of technology abused and kept from people with high prices. . . .

Hackers often find that their existing equipment, due to the monopoly tactics of computer companies, is inefficient for their purposes. Due to the exorbitantly high prices, it is impossible to legally purchase the necessary equipment. This need has given still another segment of the fight: Credit Carding. Carding is a way of obtaining the necessary goods without paying for them. It is again due to the companies' stupidity that Carding is so easy, and shows that the world's businesses are in the hands of those with considerably less technical know-how than we, the hackers. . . .

Hacking must continue. We must train newcomers to the art of hacking. . . . And whatever you do, continue the fight. Whether you know it or not, if you are a hacker, you are a revolutionary. Don't worry, you're on the right side.

The defense of "carding" is rare. Most hackers regard credit card theft as "poison" to the underground, a sleazy and immoral effort that, worse yet, is hard to get away with. Nevertheless, manifestos advocating credit card theft, the deliberate crashing of computer systems, and even acts of violent physical destruction such as vandalism and arson do exist in the underground. These boasts and threats are taken quite seriously by the police. And not every hacker is an abstract, platonic computer nerd. Some few are quite experienced at picking locks, robbing phone trucks, and breaking and entering buildings.

Hackers vary in their degree of hatred for authority and the violence of their rhetoric. But, at the bottom line, they are scofflaws. They don't regard the current rules of electronic behavior as respectable efforts to preserve law and order and protect public safety. They regard these laws as immoral efforts by soulless corporations to protect their profit margins and to crush dissidents. "Stupid" people, including police, businessmen, politicians, and journalists, simply have no right to judge the actions of those possessed of genius, techno-revolutionary intentions, and technical expertise.

Hackers are generally teenagers and college kids not engaged in earning a living. They often come from fairly well-to-do middle-class backgrounds, and are markedly antimaterialistic (except, that is, when it comes to computer equipment). Anyone motivated by greed for mere money (as opposed to the greed for power, knowledge, and status) is swiftly written off as a narrow-minded breadhead whose interests can only be corrupt and contemptible. Having grown up in the 1970s and 1980s, the young Bohemians of the digital underground regard straight society as awash in plutocratic corruption, where everyone from the President down is for sale and whoever has the gold makes the rules.

Interestingly, there's a funhouse mirror image of this attitude on the other side of the conflict. The police are also one of the most markedly antimaterialistic groups in American society, motivated not by mere money but by ideals of service, justice, esprit-de-corps, and, of course, their own brand of specialized knowledge and power. Remarkably, the propaganda war between cops and hackers has always involved angry allegations that the other side is trying to make a sleazy buck. Hackers consistently sneer that antiphreak prosecutors are angling for cushy jobs as telco lawyers and that computer-crime police are aiming to cash in later as well-paid computer-security consultants in the private sector.

For their part, police publicly conflate all hacking crimes with robbing pay phones with crowbars. Allegations of "monetary losses" from computer intrusion are notoriously inflated. The act of illicitly copying a document from a computer is equated with that of directly robbing a company of, say, half a million dollars. The teenage computer intruder in possession of this "proprietary" document certainly has not sold it for such a sum, would likely have little idea how to sell it at all, and quite probably doesn't even understand what he has. He has not made a cent in profit from his felony but is still morally equated with a thief who has robbed the church poorbox and lit out for Brazil.

Police want to believe that all hackers are thieves. It is a tortuous and almost unbearable act for the American justice system to put people in jail because they want to learn things which are forbidden for them to know. In an American context, almost any pretext for punishment is better than jailing people to protect certain restricted kinds of information. Nevertheless, *policing information* is part and parcel of the struggle against hackers.

> *Police want to believe that all hackers are thieves.*

This dilemma is well exemplified by the remarkable activities of "Emmanuel Goldstein," editor and publisher of a print magazine known as *2600: The Hacker Quarterly.* Goldstein was an English major at Long Island's State University of New York in the 1970s, when he became involved with the local college radio station. His growing interest in electronics caused him to drift into Yippie TAP circles and thus into the digital underground, where he became a self-described techno-rat. His magazine publishes techniques of computer intrusion and telephone "exploration" as well as gloating exposés of telco misdeeds and governmental failings.

Goldstein lives quietly and very privately in a large, crumbling Victorian mansion in Setauket, New York. The seaside house is decorated with telco decals, chunks of driftwood, and the basic bric-a-brac of a hippie crash pad. He is unmarried, mildly unkempt, and survives mostly on TV dinners and turkey stuffing eaten straight out of the bag. Goldstein is a man of considerable charm and fluency, with a brief, disarming smile and the kind of pitiless, stubborn, thoroughly recidivist integrity that America's electronic police find genuinely alarming.

Goldstein took his nom-de-plume, or "handle," from a character in Orwell's *1984*, which may be taken, correctly, as a symptom of the gravity of his sociopolitical worldview. He himself is not a practicing computer intruder, though he vigorously abets these actions, especially when they are pursued against large corporations or governmental agencies. Nor is he a thief, for he loudly scorns mere theft of phone service in favor of "exploring and manipulating the system." He is probably best described and understood as a *dissident.*

Weirdly, Goldstein is living in modern America under conditions very similar to those of former East European intellectual dissidents. In other words, he flagrantly espouses a value system that is deeply and irrevocably opposed to the system of those in power and the police. The values in *2600* are generally expressed in terms that are ironic, sarcastic, paradoxical, or just downright confused. But there's no mistaking their radically anti-authoritarian tenor. *2600* holds that technical power and specialized knowledge, of any kind obtainable, belong by right in the hands of those individuals brave and bold enough to discover them—by whatever means necessary. Devices, laws, or systems that forbid access, and the free spread of knowledge, are provocations that any free and self-respecting hacker should relentlessly attack. The "privacy" of governments, corporations, and other soulless technocratic organizations should never be protected at the expense of the liberty and free initiative of the individual techno-rat.

However, in our contemporary workaday world, both governments and corporations are very anxious indeed to police information that is secret, proprietary, restricted, confidential, copyrighted, patented, hazardous, illegal, unethical, embarrassing, or otherwise sensitive. This makes Goldstein persona non grata and his philosophy a threat.

Very little about the conditions of Goldstein's daily life would astonish, say, Vàclav Havel. (We may note in passing that President Havel once had his word processor confiscated by the Czechoslovak police.) Goldstein lives by *samizdat*, acting semi-openly as a data center for the underground, while challenging the powers-that-be to abide by their own stated rules: freedom of speech and the First Amendment.

Goldstein thoroughly looks and acts the part of techno-rat, with shoulder-length ringlets and a piratical black fisherman's cap set at a rakish angle. He often shows up like Banquo's ghost at meetings of computer professionals, where he listens quietly, half smiling and taking thorough notes.

Computer professionals generally meet publicly, and find it very difficult to rid themselves of Goldstein and his ilk without extralegal and unconstitutional actions. Sympathizers, many of them quite respectable people with responsible jobs, admire Goldstein's attitude and surreptitiously pass him information. An unknown but presumably large proportion of Goldstein's 2,000-plus readership are telco security personnel and police, who are forced to subscribe to 2600 to stay abreast of new developments in hacking. They thus find themselves *paying this guy's rent* while grinding their teeth in anguish, a situation that would have delighted Abbie Hoffman (one of Goldstein's few idols).

Goldstein is probably the best-known public representative of the hacker underground today, and certainly the best hated. Police regard him as a Fagin, a corrupter of youth, and speak of him with untempered loathing. He is quite an accomplished gadfly.

After the Martin Luther King Day Crash of 1990, for instance,

Goldstein adeptly rubbed salt into the wound in the pages of 2600. "Yeah, it was fun for the phone phreaks as we watched the network crumble," he admitted cheerfully. "But it was also an ominous sign of what's to come. . . . Some AT&T people, aided by well-meaning but ignorant media, were spreading the notion that many companies had the same software and therefore could face the same problem someday. Wrong. This was entirely an AT&T software deficiency. Of course, other companies could face entirely *different* software problems. But then, so too could AT&T."

After a technical discussion of the system's failings, the Long Island techno-rat went on to offer thoughtful criticism to the gigantic multinational's hundreds of professionally qualified engineers. "What we don't know is how a major force in communications like AT&T could be so sloppy. What happened to backups? Sure, computer systems go down all the time, but people making phone calls are not the same as people logging on to computers. We must make that distinction. It's not acceptable for the phone system or any other essential service to 'go down.' If we continue to trust technology without understanding it, we can look forward to many variations on this theme.

"AT&T owes it to its customers to be prepared to *instantly* switch to another network if something strange and unpredictable starts occurring. The news here isn't so much the failure of a computer program, but the failure of AT&T's entire structure."

The very idea of this . . . this *person* . . . offering "advice" about "AT&T's entire structure" is more than some people can easily bear. How dare this near criminal dictate what is or isn't "acceptable" behavior from AT&T? Especially when he's publishing, in the very same issue, detailed schematic diagrams for creating various switching-network signaling tones unavailable to the public.

"See what happens when you drop a 'silver box' tone or two down your local exchange or through different long distance service carriers," advises 2600 contributor "Mr. Upsetter" in "How to Build a Signal Box." "If you experiment systematically and keep good records, you will surely discover something interesting."

This is, of course, the scientific method, generally regarded as a praiseworthy activity and one of the flowers of modern civilization. One can indeed learn a great deal with this sort of structured intellectual activity. Telco employees regard this mode of "exploration" as akin to flinging sticks of dynamite into their pond to see what lives on the bottom.

> *Telco employees regard this "exploration" as akin to flinging sticks of dynamite into their pond to see what lives on the bottom.*

2600 has been published consistently since 1984. It has also run a bulletin board computer system, printed 2600 T-shirts, taken fax calls. . . . The Spring 1991 issue has an interesting announcement on page 45: "We just discovered an extra set of wires attached to our fax line and heading up the pole. (They've since been clipped.) Your faxes to us and to anyone else could be monitored."

In the worldview of 2600, the tiny band of techno-rat brothers (rarely, sisters) are a besieged vanguard of the truly free and honest. The rest of the world is a maelstrom of corporate crime and high-level governmental corruption, occasionally tempered with well-meaning ignorance. To read a few issues in a row is to enter a nightmare akin to Solzhenitsyn's, somewhat tempered by the fact that 2600 is often extremely funny.

Goldstein did not become a target of the Hacker Crackdown, though he protested loudly, eloquently, and publicly about it, and it added considerably to his fame. It was not that he is not regarded as dangerous, because he is so regarded. Goldstein has had brushes with the law in the past: In 1985, a 2600 bulletin board computer was seized by the FBI, and some software on it was formally declared "a burglary tool in the form of a computer program." But Goldstein escaped direct repression in 1990, because his magazine is printed on paper and recognized as subject to constitutional freedom of the press protection. As was seen in the *Ramparts* case, this is far from an absolute guarantee. Still, as a practical matter, shutting down *2600* by court order would create so much legal hassle that it is simply unfeasible, at least for the present. Throughout 1990, both Goldstein and his magazine were peevishly thriving.

Instead, the Crackdown of 1990 would concern itself with the computerized version of forbidden data. The crackdown itself, first and foremost, was about *bulletin board systems*. Bulletin board systems, most often known by the ugly and unpluralizable acronym "BBS," are the life-blood of the digital underground. Boards were also central to law enforcement's tactics and strategy in the Hacker Crackdown.

A "bulletin board system" can be formally defined as a computer that serves as an information and message-passing center for users dialing up over the phone lines through the use of modems. A "modem," or modulator-demodulator, is a device that translates the digital impulses of computers into audible analog telephone signals, and vice versa. Modems connect computers to phones and thus to each other.

Large-scale mainframe computers have been connected since the 1960s, but *personal* computers, run by individuals out of their homes, were first networked in the late 1970s. The "board" created by Ward Christensen and Randy Seuss in February 1978, in Chicago, Illinois, is generally regarded as the first personal-computer bulletin board system worthy of the name.

Boards run on many different machines, employing many different kinds of software. Early boards were crude and buggy, and their managers, known as "system operators" or "sysops," were hardworking technical experts who wrote their own software. But like most everything else in the world of electronics, boards became faster, cheaper, better designed, and generally far more sophisticated throughout the 1980s. They also moved swiftly out of the hands of pioneers and into those of the general public. By 1985 there were something in the neighborhood of 4,000 boards in America. By 1990 it was calculated, vaguely, that there were about 30,000 boards in the United States, with uncounted thousands overseas.

Computer bulletin boards are unregulated enterprises. Running a board is a rough-and-ready, catch-as-catch-can proposition. Basically, anybody with a computer, modem, software, and a phone line can start a board. With secondhand equipment and public-domain free software, the price of a board might be quite small—less than it would take to publish a magazine or even a decent pamphlet. Entrepreneurs eagerly sell bulletin board software and will coach nontechnical amateur sysops in its use.

Boards are not "presses." They are not magazines, or libraries, or phones, or CB radios, or traditional cork bulletin boards down at the local laundry, though they have some passing resemblance to those earlier media. Boards are a new medium—they may even be a *large number* of new media.

Consider these unique characteristics: Boards are cheap, yet they can have a national, even global reach. Boards can be contacted from anywhere in the global telephone network, at *no cost* to the person running the board—the caller pays the phone bill, and if the caller is local, the call is free. Boards do not involve an editorial elite addressing a mass audience. The sysop of a board is not an exclusive publisher or writer—he is managing an electronic salon, where individuals can address the general public, play the part of the general public, and also exchange private mail with other individuals. And the "conversation" on boards, though fluid, rapid, and highly interactive, is not spoken but written. It is also relatively anonymous, sometimes completely so.

And because boards are cheap and ubiquitous, regulations and licensing requirements likely would be practically unenforceable. It would almost be easier to "regulate," "inspect," and "license" the content of private mail—probably more so, because the mail system is operated by the federal government. Boards are run by individuals, independently, entirely at their own whim.

For the sysop, the cost of operation is not the primary limiting factor. Once the investment in a computer and modem has been made, the only steady cost is the charge for maintaining a phone line (or several phone lines). The primary limits for sysops are time and energy. Boards require upkeep. New users are generally "validated"—they must be issued individual passwords and called at home by voice-phone, so that their identity can be verified. Obnoxious users, who exist in plenty, must be chided or purged. Proliferating messages must be deleted when they grow old, so that the capacity of the system is not overwhelmed. And software programs (if such things are kept on the board) must be examined for possible computer viruses. If there is a financial charge to use the board (increasingly common, especially in larger and fancier systems), then accounts must be kept and users must be billed. And if the board crashes—a very common occurrence—then repairs must be made.

Boards can be distinguished by the amount of effort spent in regulating them. First, we have the completely open board, whose sysop is off chugging brews and watching reruns while his users generally degenerate over time into peevish anarchy and eventual silence. Second comes the supervised board, where the sysop breaks in every once in a while to tidy up, calm brawls, issue announcements, and rid the community of dolts and troublemakers. Third is the heavily supervised board, which sternly urges adult and responsible behavior and swiftly edits any message considered offensive, impertinent, illegal, or irrelevant. And last comes the completely edited "electronic publication," which is presented to a silent audience that is not allowed to respond directly in any way.

Boards can also be grouped by their degree of anonymity. There is the completely anonymous board, where everyone uses pseudonyms—"handles"—and even the sysop is unaware of a user's true identity. The sysop himself is likely pseudonymous on a board of this type. Second, and rather more common, is the board where the sysop knows (or thinks he knows) the true names and addresses of all users, but the users don't know one another's names and may not know his. Third is the board where everyone

has to use real names and role-playing and pseudonymous postur-
ing are forbidden.

Boards can be grouped by their immediacy. "Chat lines" are
boards linking several users together over several different phone
lines simultaneously, so that people exchange messages at the
very moment that they type. (Many large boards feature chat
capabilities along with other services.) Less immediate boards,
perhaps with a single phone line, store messages serially, one at a
time. And some boards are open for business only in daylight
hours or on weekends, which greatly slows response. A *network* of
boards, such as "FidoNet," can carry electronic mail from board
to board, continent to continent, across huge distances—but at a
relative snail's pace, so that a message can take several days to
reach its target audience and elicit a reply.

Boards can be grouped by their degree of community. Some
boards emphasize the exchange of private, person-to-person electronic mail. Others emphasize public postings and may even
purge people who "lurk," merely reading posts but refusing to
participate openly. Some boards are intimate and neighborly.
Others are frosty and highly technical. Some are little more than
storage dumps for software, where users "download" and
"upload" programs but interact among themselves little if at all.

Boards can be grouped by their ease of access. Some boards are
entirely public. Others are private and restricted only to personal
friends of the sysop. Some boards divide users by status. On these
boards, some users, especially beginners, strangers, or children,
will be restricted to general topics and perhaps forbidden to post.
Favored users, though, are granted the ability to post as they
please and to stay on-line as long as they like, even to the disad-
vantage of other people trying to call in. High-status users can be
given access to hidden areas in the board, such as off-color topics,
private discussions, and/or valuable software. Favored users may
even become "remote sysops" with the power to take remote
control of the board through their own home computers. Quite
often remote sysops end up doing all the work and taking formal

control of the enterprise, despite the fact that it's physically located in someone else's house. Sometimes several "co-sysops" share power.

And boards can also be grouped by size. Massive, nationwide commercial networks, such as CompuServe, Delphi, GEnie, and Prodigy, are run on mainframe computers and are generally not considered boards, though they share many of their characteristics, such as electronic mail, discussion topics, libraries of software, and persistent and growing problems with civil-liberties issues. Some private boards have as many as thirty phone lines and quite sophisticated hardware. And then there are tiny boards.

Boards vary in popularity. Some are huge and crowded, where users must claw their way in against a constant busy signal. Others are huge and empty—there are few things sadder than a formerly flourishing board where no one posts any longer and the dead conversations of vanished users lie about gathering digital dust. Some boards are tiny and intimate, their telephone numbers intentionally kept confidential so that only a small number can log on.

And some boards are *underground.*

Boards can be mysterious entities. The activities of their users can be hard to differentiate from conspiracy. Sometimes they *are* conspiracies. Boards have harbored, or have been accused of harboring, all manner of fringe groups, and have abetted, or been accused of abetting, every manner of frowned-upon, sleazy, radical, and criminal activity. There are Satanist boards. Nazi boards. Pornographic boards. Pedophile boards. Drug-dealing boards. Anarchist boards. Communist boards. Gay and lesbian boards (these exist in great profusion, many of them quite lively with well-established histories). Religious cult boards. Evangelical boards. Witchcraft boards, hippie boards, punk boards, skateboarder boards. Boards for UFO believers. There may well be boards for serial killers, airline terrorists, and professional assassins. There is simply no way to tell. Boards spring up, flourish, and disappear in large numbers, in most every corner of the developed world. Even apparently innocuous public boards can, and sometimes do, harbor secret areas known only to a few. And even on the vast, public, commercial services, private mail is very private—and quite possibly criminal.

Boards cover most every topic imaginable, and some that are hard to imagine. They cover a vast spectrum of social activity. However, all board users do have something in common: their possession of computers and phones. Naturally, computers and phones are primary topics of conversation on almost every board.

And hackers and phone phreaks, those utter devotees of computers and phones, live by boards. They swarm by boards. They are bred by boards. By the late 1980s, phone-phreak groups and hacker groups, united by boards, had proliferated fantastically.

As evidence, here is a list of hacker groups compiled by the editors of *Phrack* on August 8, 1988.

The Administration. Advanced Telecommunications, Inc. ALIAS. American Tone Travelers. Anarchy Inc. Apple Mafia. The Association. Atlantic Pirates Guild.

Bad Ass Mother Fuckers. Bellcore. Bell Shock Force. Black Bag.

Camorra. C&M Productions. Catholics Anonymous. Chaos Computer Club. Chief Executive Officers. Circle of Death. Circle of Deneb. Club X. Coalition of Hi-Tech Pirates. Coast-to-Coast. Corrupt Computing. Cult of the Dead Cow. Custom Retaliations.

Damage Inc. D&B Communications. The Dange Gang. Dec Hunters. Digital Gang. DPAK.

Eastern Alliance. The Elite Hackers Guild. Elite Phreakers and Hackers Club. The Elite Society of America. EPG. Executives of Crime. Extasyy Elite.

Fargo 4A. Farmers of Doom. The Federation. Feds R Us. First Class. Five 0. Five Star. Force Hackers. The 414s.

Hack-A-Trip. Hackers of America. High Mountain Hackers. High Society. The Hitchhikers.

IBM Syndicate. The Ice Pirates. Imperial Warlords. Inner Circle. Inner Circle II. Insanity Inc. International Computer Underground Bandits.

Justice League of America.

Kaos Inc. Knights of Shadow. Knights of the Round Table.

League of Adepts. Legion of Doom. Legion of Hackers. Lords of Chaos. Lunatic Labs, Unlimited.

Master Hackers. MAD! The Marauders. MD/PhD. Metal Communications, Inc. MetalliBashers, Inc. MBI. Metro Communications. Midwest Pirates Guild.

NASA Elite. The NATO Association. Neon Knights. Nihilist Order.

Order of the Rose. OSS.

Pacific Pirates Guild. Phantom Access Associates. PHido PHreaks. The Phirm. Phlash. PhoneLine Phantoms. Phone Phreakers of America. Phortune 500. Phreak Hack Delinquents. Phreak Hack Destroyers. Phreakers, Hackers, and Laundromat Employees Gang (PHALSE Gang). Phreaks Against Geeks. Phreaks Against Phreaks Against Geeks. Phreaks and Hackers of America. Phreaks Anonymous World Wide. Project Genesis. The Punk Mafia.

The Racketeers. Red Dawn Text Files. Roscoe Gang.

SABRE. Secret Circle of Pirates. Secret Service. 707 Club. Shadow Brotherhood. Sharp Inc. 65C02 Elite. Spectral Force. Star League. Stowaways. Strata-Crackers.

Team Hackers '86. Team Hackers '87. TeleComputist Newsletter Staff. Tribunal of Knowledge. Triple Entente. Turn Over and Die Syndrome (TOADS). 300 Club. 1200 Club. 2300 Club. 2600 Club. 2601 Club. 2AF.

The United SoftWareZ Force. United Technical Underground.
Ware Brigade. The Warelords. WASP.

Contemplating this list is an impressive, almost humbling business. As a cultural artifact, the thing approaches poetry.

Underground groups—subcultures—can be distinguished from independent cultures by their habit of referring constantly to the parent society. Undergrounds by their nature constantly must maintain a membrane of differentiation. Funny/distinctive clothes and hair, specialized jargon, specialized ghettoized areas in cities, different hours of rising, working, sleeping. . . . The digital underground, which specializes in information, relies very heavily on language to distinguish itself. As can be seen from this list, they make heavy use of parody and mockery. It's revealing to see who they choose to mock.

First, large corporations. We have the Phortune 500, Chief Executive Officers, Bellcore, IBM Syndicate, SABRE (a computerized reservation service maintained by airlines). The common use of "Inc." is telling—none of these groups is an actual corporation, but all take clear delight in mimicking them.

Second, governments and police. NASA Elite, The NATO Association. Feds R Us and Secret Service are fine bits of fleering boldness. OSS—the Office of Strategic Services was the forerunner of the CIA.

Third, criminals. Using stigmatizing pejoratives as a perverse badge of honor is a time-honored tactic for subcultures: punks, gangs, delinquents, mafias, pirates, bandits, racketeers.

Specialized orthography, especially the use of "ph" for "f" and "z" for the plural "s," are instant recognition symbols. So is the use of the numeral "0" for the letter "O"—computer-software orthography generally features a slash through the zero, making the distinction obvious.

Some terms are poetically descriptive of computer intrusion: Stowaways, The Hitchhikers, PhoneLine Phantoms, Coast-To-

Coast. Others are simple bravado and vainglorious puffery. (Note the insistent use of the terms "elite" and "master.") Some terms are blasphemous, some obscene, others merely cryptic—anything to puzzle, offend, confuse, and keep the straights at bay.

Many hacker groups further encrypt their names by the use of acronyms: United Technical Underground becomes UTU, Farmers of Doom become FoD, the United SoftWareZ Force becomes, at its own insistence, TuSwF, and woe to the ignorant rodent who capitalizes the wrong letters.

It should be further recognized that the members of these groups are themselves pseudonymous. If you did, in fact, run across the PhoneLine Phantoms, you would find them to consist of "Carrier Culprit," "The Executioner," "Black Majik," "Egyptian Lover," "Solid State," and "Mr Icom." Carrier Culprit will likely be referred to by his friends as "CC," as in "I got these dialups from CC of PLP."

It's quite possible that this entire list refers to as few as a thousand people. It is not a complete list of underground groups—there has never been such a list, and there never will be. Groups rise, flourish, decline, share membership, maintain a cloud of wannabes and casual hangers-on. People pass in and out, are ostracized, get bored, are busted by police, or are cornered by telco security and presented with huge bills. Many "underground groups" are software pirates, "warez d00dz," who might break copy protection and pirate programs but likely wouldn't dare to intrude on a computer system.

The true population of the digital underground is hard to estimate. There is constant turnover. Most hackers start young, come and go, then drop out at age twenty-two—the age of college graduation. And a large majority access pirate boards, adopt a handle, swipe software and perhaps abuse a phone code or two, while never actually joining the elite.

Some professional informants, who make it their business to retail knowledge of the underground to paymasters in private corporate security, have estimated the hacker population at as high as fifty thousand. This is likely highly inflated, unless one counts every single teenage software pirate and petty phone-booth thief. My best guess is about five thousand people. Of these, I would guess that as few as a hundred are truly "elite"—active computer intruders, skilled enough to penetrate sophisticated systems and truly to worry corporate security and law enforcement.

Another interesting speculation is whether this group is growing or not. Young teenage hackers are often convinced that hackers exist in vast swarms and will soon dominate the cybernetic universe. Older and wiser veterans, perhaps as wizened as twenty-four or twenty-five years old, are convinced that the glory days are long gone, that the cops have the underground's number now, and that kids these days are dirt-stupid and just want to play Nintendo.

My own assessment is that computer intrusion, as a nonprofit act of intellectual exploration and mastery, is in slow decline, at least in the United States; but that electronic fraud, especially telecommunication crime, is growing by leaps and bounds.

One might find a useful parallel to the digital underground in the drug underground. There was a time, now much obscured by historical revisionism, when Bohemians freely shared joints at concerts, and hip, small-scale marijuana dealers might turn people on just for the sake of enjoying a long, stoned conversation about the Doors and Allen Ginsberg. Now drugs are increasingly verboten, except in a high-stakes, highly criminal world of highly addictive drugs. Over years of disenchantment and police harassment, a vaguely ideological, free-wheeling drug underground has relinquished the business of drug-dealing to a far more savage criminal hard core. This is not a pleasant prospect to contemplate, but the analogy is fairly compelling.

What does an underground board look like? What distinguishes it from a standard board? It isn't necessarily the conversation—hackers often talk about common board topics, such as hardware, software, sex, science fiction, current events, politics, movies, personal gossip. Underground boards can best be distinguished by their files, or "philes," precomposed texts that teach the techniques and ethos of the underground. These are prized reservoirs of forbidden knowledge. Some are anonymous, but most proudly bear the handle of the hacker who has created them and his group affiliation, if he has one.

Here is a partial table of contents of philes from an underground board, somewhere in the heart of middle America, circa 1991. The descriptions are mostly self-explanatory.

BANKAMER.ZIP	5406 06-11-91	Hacking Bank America
CHHACK.ZIP	4481 06-11-91	Chilton Hacking
CITIBANK.ZIP	4118 06-11-91	Hacking Citibank
CREDIMTC.ZIP	3241 06-11-91	Hacking Mtc Credit Company
DIGEST.ZIP	5159 06-11-91	Hackers Digest
HACK.ZIP	14031 06-11-91	How To Hack
HACKBAS.ZIP	5073 06-11-91	Basics Of Hacking
HACKDICT.ZIP	42774 06-11-91	Hackers Dictionary
HACKER.ZIP	57938 06-11-91	Hacker Info
HACKERME.ZIP	3148 06-11-91	Hackers Manual
HACKHAND.ZIP	4814 06-11-91	Hackers Handbook
HACKTHES.ZIP	48290 06-11-91	Hackers Thesis
HACKVMS.ZIP	4696 06-11-91	Hacking Vms Systems
MCDON.ZIP	3830 06-11-91	Hacking Macdonalds (Home Of The Archs)
P500UNIX.ZIP	15525 06-11-91	Phortune 500 Guide To Unix
RADHACK.ZIP	8411 06-11-91	Radio Hacking
TAOTRASH.DOC	4096 12-25-89	Suggestions For Trashing
TECHHACK.ZIP	5063 06-11-91	Technical Hacking

The preceding files are do-it-yourself manuals about computer intrusion. The list is only a small section of a much larger library of hacking and phreaking techniques and history. We now move into a different and perhaps surprising area.

```
+-----------+
|           |
| Anarchy   |
|           |
+-----------+
```

ANARC.ZIP	3641 06-11-91	Anarchy Files
ANARCHST.ZIP	63703 06-11-91	Anarchist Book
ANARCHY.ZIP	2076 06-11-91	Anarchy At Home
ANARCHY3.ZIP	6982 06-11-91	Anarchy No 3
ANARCTOY.ZIP	2361 06-11-91	Anarchy Toys
ANTIMODM.ZIP	2877 06-11-91	Anti-modem Weapons
ATOM.ZIP	4494 06-11-91	How To Make An Atom Bomb
BARBITUA.ZIP	3982 06-11-91	Barbiturate Formula
BLCKPWDR.ZIP	2810 06-11-91	Black Powder Formulas
BOMB.ZIP	3765 06-11-91	How To Make Bombs
BOOM.ZIP	2036 06-11-91	Things That Go Boom
CHLORINE.ZIP	1926 06-11-91	Chlorine Bomb
COOKBOOK.ZIP	1500 06-11-91	Anarchy Cook Book
DESTROY.ZIP	3947 06-11-91	Destroy Stuff
DUSTBOMB.ZIP	2576 06-11-91	Dust Bomb
ELECTERR.ZIP	3230 06-11-91	Electronic Terror
EXPLOS1.ZIP	2598 06-11-91	Explosives 1
EXPLOSIV.ZIP	18051 06-11-91	More Explosives
EZSTEAL.ZIP	4521 06-11-91	Ez-stealing

FLAME.ZIP	2240 06-11-91	Flame Thrower
FLASHLT.ZIP	2533 06-11-91	Flashlight Bomb
FMBUG.ZIP	2906 06-11-91	How To Make An Fm Bug
OMEEXPL.ZIP	2139 06-11-91	Home Explosives
HOW2BRK.ZIP	3332 06-11-91	How To Break In
LETTER.ZIP	2990 06-11-91	Letter Bomb
LOCK.ZIP	2199 06-11-91	How To Pick Locks
MRSHIN.ZIP	3991 06-11-91	Briefcase Locks
NAPALM.ZIP	3563 06-11-91	Napalm At Home
NITRO.ZIP	3158 06-11-91	Fun With Nitro
PARAMIL.ZIP	2962 06-11-91	Paramilitary Info
PICKING.ZIP	3398 06-11-91	Picking Locks
PIPEBOMB.ZIP	2137 06-11-91	Pipe Bomb
POTASS.ZIP	3987 06-11-91	Formulas With Potassium
PRANK.TXT	11074 08-03-90	More Pranks To Pull On Idiots!
REVENGE.ZIP	4447 06-11-91	Revenge Tactics
ROCKET.ZIP	2590 06-11-91	Rockets For Fun
SMUGGLE.ZIP	3385 06-11-91	How To Smuggle

Holy cow! The damned thing is full of stuff about bombs! What are we to make of this?

First, it should be acknowledged that spreading knowledge about demolitions to teenagers is a highly and deliberately antisocial act. It is not, however, illegal.

Second, it should be recognized that most of these philes were in fact *written* by teenagers. Most adult American males who can remember their teenage years will recognize that the notion of building a flamethrower in your garage is an incredibly neat-o idea. *Actually* building a flamethrower in your garage, however, is fraught with discouraging difficulty. Stuffing gunpowder into a booby-trapped flashlight, so as to blow the arm off your high school vice-principal, can be a thing of dark beauty to contemplate. Actually committing assault by explosives will earn you the sustained attention of the federal Bureau of Alcohol, Tobacco and Firearms.

Some people, however, actually will try these plans. A determinedly murderous American teenager can probably buy or steal a handgun far more easily than he can brew fake "napalm" in the kitchen sink.

> *Blowing the arm off your high school vice-principal can be a thing of dark beauty to contemplate.*

Nevertheless, if temptation is spread before people a certain number will succumb, and a small minority actually will attempt these stunts. A large minority of that small minority will either fail or, quite likely, maim themselves, since these philes have not been checked for accuracy, are not the product of professional experience, and are often highly fanciful. But the gloating menace of these philes is not to be entirely dismissed.

Hackers may not be "serious" about bombing; if they were, we would hear far more about exploding flashlights, homemade bazookas, and gym teachers poisoned by chlorine and potassium. However, hackers are *very* serious about forbidden knowledge. They are possessed not merely by curiosity but by a positive *lust to know*. The desire to know what others don't is scarcely new. But the *intensity* of this desire, as manifested by these young technophilic denizens of the Information Age, may in fact *be* new and may represent some basic shift in social values—a harbinger of what the world may come to, as society lays more and more value on the possession, assimilation, and retailing of *information* as a basic commodity of daily life.

There have always been young men with obsessive interests in these topics. Never before, however, have they been able to network so extensively and easily, and to propagandize their interests with impunity to random passersby. High school teachers will recognize that there's always one in a crowd, but when the one in a crowd escapes control by jumping into the phone lines and becomes a hundred such kids all together on a board, then trouble is brewing visibly. The urge of authority to *do something*, even something drastic, is hard to resist. And in 1990, authority did something. In fact, authority did a great deal.

The process by which boards create hackers goes something like this. A youngster becomes interested in computers—usually, computer games. He hears from friends that "bulletin boards" exist where games can be obtained for free. (Many computer games are "freeware," not copyrighted—invented simply for the love of it and given away to the public; some of these games are quite good.) He bugs his parents for a modem or, quite often, uses his parents' modem.

The world of boards suddenly opens up. Computer games can be quite expensive, real budget-breakers for a kid, but pirated games, stripped of copy protection, are cheap or free. They are also illegal, but it is very rare, almost unheard of, for a small-scale software pirate to be prosecuted. Once "cracked" of its copy protection, the program, being digital data, becomes infinitely reproducible. Even the instructions to the game, any manuals that accompany it, can be reproduced as text files or photocopied from legitimate sets. Other users on boards can give many useful hints in game-playing tactics. And a youngster with an infinite supply of free computer games can certainly cut quite a swath among his modemless friends.

And boards are pseudonymous. No one need know that you're fourteen years old—with a little practice at subterfuge, you can talk to adults about adult things, and be accepted and taken seriously! You can even pretend to be a girl, or an old man, or anybody you can imagine. If you find this kind of deception gratifying, there is ample opportunity to hone your ability on boards.

But local boards can grow stale. And almost every board maintains a list of phone numbers to other boards, some in distant, tempting, exotic locales. Who knows what they're up to, in Ore-

gon or Alaska or Florida or California? It's very easy to find out—
just order the modem to call through its software; nothing to this,
just typing on a keyboard, the same thing you would do for most
any computer game. The machine reacts swiftly and in a few
seconds you are talking to a bunch of interesting people on another seaboard.

And yet the *bills* for this trivial action can be staggering! Just
by going tippety-tap with your fingers, you may have saddled your
parents with four hundred bucks in long-distance charges and
gotten chewed out but good. That hardly seems fair.

How horrifying to have made friends in another state and to be
deprived of their company—and their software—just because
telephone companies demand absurd amounts of money! How
painful, to be restricted to boards in one's own *area code*—what
the heck is an "area code" anyway, and what makes it so special?
A few grumbles, complaints, and innocent questions of this sort
will often elicit a sympathetic reply from another board user—
someone with some stolen codes to hand. You dither awhile,
knowing this isn't quite right, then you make up your mind to try
them anyhow—*and they work!* Suddenly you're doing something
even your parents can't do. Six months ago you were just some
kid—now you're the Crimson Flash of Area Code 512! You're
bad—you're nationwide!

Maybe you'll stop at a few abused codes. Maybe you'll decide
that boards aren't all that interesting after all, that it's wrong, not
worth the risk—but maybe you won't. The next step is to pick up
your own repeat-dialing program—to learn to generate your own
stolen codes. (This was dead easy five years ago, much harder to
get away with nowadays, but not yet impossible.) And these dialing programs are not complex or intimidating—some are as small
as twenty lines of software.

Now you too can share codes. You can trade codes to learn
other techniques. If you're smart enough to catch on, and obsessive enough to want to bother, and ruthless enough to start seriously bending rules, then you'll get better fast. You start to
develop a rep. You move up to a heavier class of board—one with

a bad attitude, the kind of board that naive dopes like your classmates and your former self have never even heard of! You pick up the jargon of phreaking and hacking from the board. You read a few of those anarchy philes—and man, you never realized you could be a real *outlaw* without ever leaving your bedroom.

You still play other computer games, but now you have a new and bigger game. This one will bring you a different kind of status than destroying even 8 zillion lousy space invaders.

Hackers perceive hacking as a "game." This is not an entirely unreasonable or sociopathic perception. You can win or lose at hacking, succeed or fail, but it never feels "real." It's not simply that imaginative youngsters sometimes have a hard time telling "make-believe" from "real life." Cyberspace is *not real!* "Real" things are physical objects, such as trees and shoes and cars. Hacking takes place on a screen. Words aren't physical, numbers (even telephone numbers and credit card numbers) aren't physical. Sticks and stones may break my bones, but data will never hurt me. Computers *simulate* reality, such as computer games that simulate tank battles or dogfights or spaceships. Simulations are just make-believe, and the stuff in computers is *not real.*

Consider this: If "hacking" is supposed to be so serious and real-life and dangerous, then how come *nine-year-old kids* have computers and modems? You wouldn't give a nine-year-old his own car, or his own rifle, or his own chainsaw—those things are "real."

People underground are perfectly aware that the "game" is frowned upon by the powers that be. Word gets around about busts in the underground. Publicizing busts is one of the primary functions of pirate boards, but they also promulgate an attitude about them, and their own idiosyncratic ideas of justice. The users of underground boards won't complain if some guy is busted for crashing systems, spreading viruses, or stealing money by wire fraud. They may shake their heads with a sneaky grin, but they won't openly defend these practices. But when a kid is charged with some theoretical amount of theft: $233,846.14, for instance, because he sneaked into a computer and copied something, and kept it in his house on a floppy disk—this is regarded as a sign of near insanity on the part of prosecutors, a sign that they've drastically mistaken the immaterial game of computing for their real and boring everyday world of fatcat corporate money.

It's as if big companies and their suck-up lawyers think that computing belongs to them, and they can retail it with price stickers, as if it were boxes of laundry soap! But pricing "information" is like trying to price air or price dreams. Well, anybody on a pirate board knows that computing can be, and ought to be, *free*. Pirate boards are little independent worlds in cyberspace, and they don't belong to anybody but the underground. Underground boards aren't "brought to you by Procter & Gamble."

To log on to an underground board can mean to experience liberation, to enter a world where, for once, money isn't everything and adults don't have all the answers.

Let's sample another vivid hacker manifesto. Here are some excerpts from "The Conscience of a Hacker," by "The Mentor," from *Phrack*, Volume One, Issue 7, Phile 3.

    I made a discovery today. I found a computer.
Wait a second, this is cool. It does what I want
it to. If it makes a mistake, it's because I
screwed it up. Not because it doesn't like
me. . . .
    And then it happened . . . a door opened to a
world . . . rushing through the phone line
like heroin through an addict's veins, an
electronic pulse is sent out, a refuge from
day-to-day incompetencies is sought . . . a
board is found. ''This is it . . . this is
where I belong . . .''
    I know everyone here . . . even if I've never
met them, never talked to them, may never hear
from them again . . . I know you all. . . .
    This is our world now . . . the world of the
electron and the switch, the beauty of the
baud. We make use of a service already

```
existing without paying for what could be
dirt-cheap if it wasn't run by profiteering
gluttons┐ and you call us criminals. We ex-
plore . . . and you call us criminals. We seek
after knowledge . . . and you call us crimi-
nals. We exist without skin color┐ without na-
tionality┐ without religious bias . . . and
you call us criminals. You build atomic bombs┐
you wage wars┐ you murder┐ cheat and lie to us
and try to make us believe that it's for our own
good┐ yet we're the criminals.
     Yes┐ I am a criminal. My crime is that of cu-
riosity. My crime is that of judging people
by what they say and think┐ not what they
look like. My crime is that of outsmarting
you┐ something that you will never forgive me
for.
```

There have been underground boards almost as long as there have been boards. One of the first was 8BBS, which became a stronghold of the West Coast phone-phreak elite. After going on-line in March 1980, 8BBS sponsored "Susan Thunder" and "Tuc" and, most notoriously, "the Condor." The Condor bore the singular distinction of becoming the most vilified American phreak and hacker ever. Angry underground associates, fed up with Condor's peevish behavior, turned him in to police, along with a heaping double-helping of outrageous hacker legendry. As a result, Condor was kept in solitary confinement for seven months, for fear that he might start World War III by triggering missile silos from the prison pay phone. (Having served his time, Condor is now walking around loose; WWIII has thus far conspicuously failed to occur.)

The sysop of 8BBS was an ardent free-speech enthusiast who simply felt that *any* attempt to restrict the expression of his users was unconstitutional and immoral. Swarms of the technically curious entered 8BBS and emerged as phreaks and hackers, until, in 1982, a friendly 8BBS alumnus passed the sysop a new modem that had been purchased by credit card fraud. Police took this opportunity to seize the entire board and remove what they considered an attractive nuisance.

Plovernet was a powerful East Coast pirate board that operated in both New York and Florida. Owned and operated by teenage hacker "Quasi Moto," Plovernet attracted five hundred eager users in 1983. "Emmanuel Goldstein" was one-time co-sysop of Plovernet, along with "Lex Luthor," founder of the "Legion of Doom" group. Plovernet bore the signal honor of being the original home of the Legion of Doom, about which the reader will be hearing a great deal, soon.

Pirate-80, or P-80, run by a sysop known as "Scan Man," got into the game very early in Charleston and continued steadily for years. P-80 flourished so flagrantly that even its most hardened users became nervous, and some slanderously speculated that Scan Man must have ties to corporate security, a charge he vigorously denied.

"414 Private" was the home board for the first *group* to attract conspicuous trouble, the teenage "414 gang," whose intrusions into Sloan-Kettering Cancer Center and Los Alamos military computers were to be a nine-day wonder in 1982.

At about this time, the first software piracy boards began to open up, trading cracked games for the Atari 800 and the Commodore C64. Naturally these boards were heavily frequented by teenagers. And with the 1983 release of the hacker-thriller movie *War Games*, the scene exploded. It seemed that every kid in America had demanded and gotten a modem for Christmas. Most of these dabbler wannabes put their modems in the attic after a few weeks, and most of the remainder minded their Ps and Qs and stayed well out of hot water. But some stubborn and talented diehards had this hacker kid in *War Games* figured for a happening dude. They simply could not rest until they had contacted the underground—or, failing that, created their own.

In the mid-1980s, underground boards sprang up like digital fungi. ShadowSpawn Elite. Sherwood Forest I, II, and III. Digital Logic Data Service in Florida, sysoped by no less a man than

"Digital Logic" himself; Lex Luthor of the Legion of Doom was prominent on this board, because it was in his area code. Lex's own board, Legion of Doom, started in 1984. The Neon Knights ran a network of Apple-hacker boards: Neon Knights North, South, East, and West. Free World II was run by "Major Havoc." Lunatic Labs is still in operation as of this writing. Dr. Ripco in Chicago, an anything-goes anarchist board with an extensive and raucous history, was seized by Secret Service agents in 1990 on Sundevil day but came up again almost immediately, with new machines and scarcely diminished vigor.

The St. Louis scene was not to rank with major centers of American hacking such as New York and L.A. But St. Louis did rejoice in possession of "Knight Lightning" and "Taran King," two of the foremost *journalists* native to the underground. Missouri boards such as Metal Shop AE, Metal Shop Private, and Metal Shop Brewery may not have been the heaviest boards around in terms of illicit expertise. But they became boards where hackers could exchange social gossip and try to figure out what the heck was going on nationally—and internationally. Gossip from Metal Shop was put into the form of news files, then assembled into a general electronic publication, *Phrack*, a portmanteau title coined from "phreak" and "hack." The *Phrack* editors were as obsessively curious about other hackers as hackers were about machines.

Phrack, being free of charge and lively reading, began to circulate throughout the underground. As Taran King and Knight Lightning left high school for college, *Phrack* began to appear on mainframe machines linked to BITNET, and, through BITNET to the Internet, that loose but extremely potent not-for-profit network where academic, governmental, and corporate machines trade data through the UNIX TCP/IP protocol. (The Internet Worm of November 2–3, 1988, created by Cornell grad student Robert Morris, was to be the largest and best-publicized computer-intrusion scandal to date. Morris said that his ingenious "worm" program was meant to explore the Internet harmlessly, but due to bad programming, the worm replicated out of control and crashed some six thousand Internet computers. Smaller-scale and less ambitious Internet hacking was a standard for the underground elite.)

Most any underground board not hopelessly lame and out-of-it would feature a complete run of *Phrack*—and, possibly, the lesser-known standards of the underground: the *Legion of Doom Technical Journal*, the obscene and raucous *Cult of the Dead Cow* files, *P/HUN* magazine, *Pirate*, the *Syndicate Reports*, and perhaps the highly anarcho-political *Activist Times Incorporated*.

Possession of *Phrack* on one's board was prima facie evidence of a bad attitude. *Phrack* was seemingly everywhere, aiding, abetting, and spreading the underground ethos. And this did not escape the attention of corporate security or the police.

We now come to the touchy subject of police and boards. Police do, in fact, own boards. In 1989, there were police-sponsored boards in California, Colorado, Florida, Georgia, Idaho, Michigan, Missouri, Texas, and Virginia: boards such as Crime Bytes, Crimestoppers, All Points, and Bullet-N-Board. Police officers, as private computer enthusiasts, ran their own boards in Arizona, California, Colorado, Connecticut, Florida, Missouri, Maryland, New Mexico, North Carolina, Ohio, Tennessee, and Texas. Police boards have often proved helpful in community relations. Sometimes crimes are reported on police boards.

Sometimes crimes are *committed* on police boards. This has sometimes happened by accident, as naive hackers blunder onto police boards and blithely begin offering telephone codes. Far more often, however, it occurs through the now almost-traditional use of "sting boards." The first police sting boards were established in 1985: Underground Tunnel in Austin, Texas, whose sysop Sergeant Robert Ansley called himself "Pluto"—The Phone Company in Phoenix, Arizona, run by Ken MacLeod of the Maricopa County Sheriff's office—and Sergeant Dan Pasquale's board in Fremont, California. Sysops posed as hackers, and swiftly garnered coteries of ardent users, who posted codes and loaded pirate software with abandon, and came to a sticky end.

Sting boards are cheap to operate; very cheap, by the standards of undercover police operations.

Sting boards, like other boards, are cheap to operate; very cheap, by the standards of undercover police operations. Once accepted by the local underground, sysops will likely be invited into other pirate boards, where they can compile more dossiers. And when the sting is announced and the worst offenders arrested, the publicity is generally gratifying. The resultant paranoia in the underground —perhaps more justly described as a "deterrence effect"—tends to quell local lawbreaking for quite a while.

Obviously police do not have to beat the underbrush for hackers. On the contrary, they can go trolling for them. Those caught can be grilled. Some become useful informants. They can lead the way to pirate boards all across the country.

And boards all across the country showed the sticky fingerprints of *Phrack*, and of that loudest and most flagrant of all underground groups, the Legion of Doom.

The term "Legion of Doom" came from comic books. The Legion of Doom, a conspiracy of costumed supervillains headed by the chrome-domed criminal ultra-mastermind Lex Luthor, gave Superman a lot of four-color graphic trouble for a number of decades. Of course, Superman, that exemplar of Truth, Justice, and the American Way, always won in the long run. This didn't matter to the hacker Doomsters—Legion of Doom was not some thunderous and evil Satanic reference, it was not meant to be taken seriously. Legion of Doom came from funny books and was supposed to be *funny*.

Legion of Doom did have a good, mouth-filling ring to it, though. It sounded really cool. Other groups, such as the Farmers of Doom, closely allied to LoD, recognized this grandiloquent quality and made fun of it. There was even a hacker group called

"Justice League of America," named after Superman's club of true-blue crime-fighting superheros.

But they didn't last; the Legion did.

The original Legion of Doom, hanging out on Quasi Moto's Plovernet board, were phone phreaks. They weren't much into computers. Lex Luthor himself (who was under eighteen when he formed the Legion) was a COSMOS expert, COSMOS being the "Central System for Mainframe Operations," a telco internal computer network. Lex would eventually become quite a dab hand at breaking into IBM mainframes, but although everyone liked Lex and admired his attitude, he was not considered a truly accomplished computer intruder. Nor was he the "mastermind" of the Legion of Doom—LoD was never big on formal leadership. As a regular on Plovernet and sysop of his Legion of Doom BBS, Lex was the Legion's cheerleader and recruiting officer.

Legion of Doom was built on the ruins of an earlier phreak group, The Knights of Shadow. Later, LoD was to subsume the personnel of the hacker group Tribunal of Knowledge. People came and went constantly in LoD; groups split up or formed offshoots.

Early on, the LoD phreaks befriended a few computer-intrusion enthusiasts, who became the associated Legion of Hackers. Then the two groups conflated into the Legion of Doom/Hackers, or LoD/H. When the original "hacker" wing, Messrs. "Compu-Phreak" and "Phucked Agent 04," found other matters to occupy their time, the extra "/H" slowly atrophied out of the name; but by this time the phreak wing, Messrs. Lex Luthor, "Blue Archer," "Gary Seven," "Kerrang Khan," "Master of Impact," "Silver Spy," "The Marauder," and "The Video-smith," had picked up a plethora of intrusion expertise and had become a force to be reckoned with.

LoD members seemed to have an instinctive understanding that the way to real power in the underground lay through covert publicity. LoD was flagrant. Not only was it one of the earliest groups, but members took pains to distribute their illicit knowledge widely. Some LoD members, such as "The Mentor," were close to evangelical about it. *Legion of Doom Technical Journal* began to show up on boards throughout the underground.

LoD Technical Journal was named in cruel parody of the ancient and honored *AT&T Technical Journal.* The material in these two publications was quite similar—much of it adopted from public journals and discussions in the telco community. And yet, the predatory attitude of LoD made even its most innocuous data seem deeply sinister, an outrage, a clear and present danger.

To see why this should be, let's consider the following (invented) paragraphs, as a kind of thought experiment.

(A) W. Fred Brown, AT&T Vice President for Advanced Technical Development, testified May 8 at a Washington hearing of the National Telecommunications and Information Administration (NTIA), regarding Bellcore's GARDEN project. GARDEN (Generalized Automatic Remote Distributed Electronic Network) is a telephone-switch programming tool that makes it possible to develop new telecom services, including hold-on-hold and customized message transfers, from any keypad terminal, within seconds. The GARDEN prototype combines centrex lines with a minicomputer using UNIX operating system software.

(B) Crimson Flash 512 of the Centrex Mobsters reports: DOOdz, you wouldn't believe this GARDEN bullshit Bellcore's just come up with! Now you don't even need a lousy Commodore to reprogram a switch-just log on to GARDEN as a technician, and you can reprogram switches right off the keypad in any public phone booth! You can give yourself hold-on-hold and customized message transfers, and best of all, the thing is run off (notoriously insecure) centrex lines using-get this-standard UNIX software! Ha ha ha ha!

Message (A), couched in typical techno-bureaucratese, appears tedious and almost unreadable, scarcely threatening or menacing.

Message (B), on the other hand, is a dreadful thing, prima facie evidence of a dire conspiracy, definitely not the kind of thing you want your teenager reading.

The *data*, however, are identical. They are *public* data, presented before the federal government in an open hearing. They are not "secret." They are not "proprietary." They are not even "confidential." On the contrary, the development of advanced software systems is a matter of great public pride to Bellcore.

However, when Bellcore publicly announces a project of this kind, it expects a certain attitude from the public—something along the lines of *gosh wow, you guys are great, keep that up, whatever it is*—certainly not cruel mimicry, one-upmanship, and outrageous speculations about possible security holes.

Now put yourself in the place of a policeman confronted by an outraged parent, or telco official, with a copy of version (B). This well-meaning citizen, to his horror, has discovered a local bulletin board carrying outrageous stuff like (B), which his son is examining with a deep and unhealthy interest. If (B) were printed in a book or magazine, you, as an American law enforcement officer, would know that it would take a hell of a lot of trouble to do anything about it; but it doesn't take technical genius to recognize that if there's a computer in your area harboring stuff like (B), there's going to be trouble.

In fact, if you ask around, any computer-literate cop will tell you straight out that boards with stuff like (B) are the *source* of trouble. And the *worst* source of trouble on boards are the ringleaders inventing and spreading stuff like (B). If it weren't for these jokers, there wouldn't *be* any trouble.

And Legion of Doom was on boards like nobody else. Plovernet. The Legion of Doom Board. The Farmers of Doom Board. Metal Shop. OSUNY. Blottoland. Private Sector. Atlantis. Digital Logic. Hell Phrozen Over.

LoD members also ran their own boards. "Silver Spy" started his own board, Catch-22, considered one of the heaviest around. So did Mentor, with his Phoenix Project. When they didn't run boards themselves, they showed up on other people's boards, to brag, boast, and strut. And where they themselves didn't go, their philes went, carrying evil knowledge and an even more evil attitude.

As early as 1986, the police were under the vague impression that *everyone* in the underground was Legion of Doom. LoD was never that large—considerably smaller than either Metal Communications or The Administration, for instance—but LoD got tremendous press. Especially in *Phrack*, which at times read like an LoD fan magazine; and *Phrack* was everywhere, especially in the offices of telco security. You couldn't *get* busted as a phone phreak, a hacker, or even a lousy codes kid or warez dood, without the cops asking if you were LoD.

Somewhere at the center of this conspiracy there had to be some adult masterminds.

This was a difficult charge to deny, as LoD never distributed membership badges or laminated ID cards. If it had, it likely would have died out quickly, for turnover in membership was considerable. LoD was less a high-tech street gang than an ongoing state of mind. LoD was the Gang That Refused to Die. By 1990 LoD had *ruled* for years, and it seemed *weird* to police that they continually were busting people who were only sixteen years old. All these teenage small-timers were pleading the tiresome hacker litany of "just curious, no criminal intent." Somewhere at the center of this conspiracy there had to be some serious adult masterminds, not this seemingly endless supply of myopic suburban white kids with high SATs and funny haircuts.

There was no question that most any American hacker arrested would "know" LoD. They all knew the handles of contributors to *LoD Tech Journal*, and were likely to have learned their craft through LoD boards and LoD activism. But they'd never met anyone from LoD. Even some of the rotating cadre who were actually and formally "in LoD" knew one another only by board mail and pseudonyms. This was a highly unconventional profile for a criminal conspiracy. Computer networking, and the rapid evolution of the digital underground, made the situation very diffuse and confusing.

Furthermore, a big reputation in the digital underground did not coincide with one's willingness to commit "crimes." Instead, reputation was based on cleverness and technical mastery. As a result, it often seemed that the *heavier* the hackers were, the *less* likely they were to have committed any kind of common, easily prosecutable crime. There were some hackers who could really steal. And there were hackers who could really hack. But the two groups didn't seem to overlap much, if at all. For instance, most people in the underground looked up to Emmanuel Goldstein of *2600* as a hacker demigod. But Goldstein's publishing activities were entirely legal—he just printed dodgy stuff and talked about politics, he didn't even hack. When you came right down to it, Goldstein spent half his time complaining that computer security *wasn't strong enough* and ought to be improved drastically across the board!

Truly heavy-duty hackers, those with serious technical skills who had earned the respect of the underground, never stole money or abused credit cards. Sometimes they might abuse phone codes—but often they seemed to get all the free phone time they wanted without leaving a trace of any kind.

The best hackers, the most powerful and technically accomplished, were not professional fraudsters. They raided computers habitually but wouldn't alter anything, or damage anything. They didn't even steal computer equipment—most had day jobs messing with hardware and could get all the cheap secondhand equipment they wanted. The hottest hackers, unlike the teenage wannabes, weren't snobs about fancy or expensive hardware. Their machines tended to be raw secondhand digital hot rods full of custom add-ons that they'd cobbled together out of chicken wire, memory chips, and spit. Some were adults, computer software writers and consultants by trade, and making quite good livings at it. Some of them *actually worked for the phone company* —and for those, the "hackers" actually found under the skirts of Ma Bell, there would be little mercy in 1990.

It has long been an article of faith in the underground that the "best" hackers never get caught. They're far too smart, supposedly. They never get caught because they never boast, brag, or strut. These demigods may read underground boards (with a condescending smile), but they never say anything there. The "best" hackers, according to legend, are adult computer professionals, such as mainframe system administrators, who already know the ins and outs of their particular brand of security. Even the "best" hacker can't break in to just any computer at random: the knowledge of security holes is too specialized, varying widely with different software and hardware. But if people are employed to run, say, a UNIX mainframe or a VAX/VMS machine, then they tend to learn security from the inside out. Armed with this knowledge, they can look into most anybody else's UNIX or VMS without much trouble or risk, if they want to. And, according to hacker legend, of course they want to, so of course they do. They just don't make a big deal of what they've done. So nobody ever finds out.

It is also an article of faith in the underground that professional telco people "phreak" like crazed weasels. *Of course* they spy on Madonna's phone calls—I mean, *wouldn't you?* Of course they give themselves free long distance—why the hell should *they* pay, they're running the whole shebang!

It has, as a third matter, long been an article of faith that any hacker caught can escape serious punishment if he confesses *how he did it*. Hackers seem to believe that governmental agencies and large corporations are blundering about in cyberspace like eyeless jellyfish or cave salamanders. They feel that these large but pathetically stupid organizations will proffer up genuine gratitude, and perhaps even a security post and a big salary, to the hot-shot intruder who will deign to reveal to them the supreme genius of his modus operandi.

In the case of longtime LoD member "Control-C," this actually happened, more or less. Control-C had led Michigan Bell on a merry chase, and when captured in 1987, he turned out to be a bright and apparently physically harmless young fanatic, fascinated by phones. There was no chance in hell that Control-C would actually repay the enormous and largely theoretical sums in long-distance service that he had accumulated from Michigan Bell. He could always be indicted for fraud or computer intrusion, but there seemed little real point in this—he hadn't physically damaged any computer. He'd just plead guilty, and he'd likely get the usual slap on the wrist, and in the meantime it would be a big hassle for Michigan Bell just to bring up the case. But if kept on the payroll, he might at least keep his fellow hackers at bay.

There were uses for him. For instance, a contrite Control-C was featured on Michigan Bell internal posters, sternly warning employees to shred their trash. He'd always gotten most of his best inside info from "trashing"—raiding telco dumpsters, for useful data indiscreetly thrown away. He signed these posters too. Control-C had become something like a Michigan Bell mascot. And in fact, Control-C *did* keep other hackers at bay. Little hackers were quite scared of Control-C and his heavy-duty Legion of Doom friends. And big hackers *were* his friends and didn't want to screw up his cushy situation.

No matter what one might say of LoD, the members did stick together. When "Wasp," an apparently genuinely malicious New York hacker, began crashing Bellcore machines, Control-C received swift volunteer help from The Mentor and the Georgia LoD wing made up of "The Prophet," "Urvile," and "Leftist." Using Mentor's Phoenix Project board to coordinate, the Doomsters helped telco security to trap Wasp, by luring him into a machine with a tap and line trace installed. Wasp lost. LoD won! And my, did they brag.

Urvile, Prophet, and Leftist were well qualified for this activity, probably more so even than the quite accomplished Control-C. The Georgia boys knew all about phone switching stations. Though relative johnny-come-latelies in the Legion of Doom, they were considered some of LoD's heaviest guys, into the hairiest systems around. They had the good fortune to live in or near Atlanta, home of the sleepy and apparently tolerant BellSouth RBOC.

As RBOC security went, BellSouth was "cake." U S West (of Arizona, the Rockies, and the Pacific Northwest) was tough and aggressive, probably the heaviest RBOC around. Pacific Bell, California's PacBell, was sleek, high tech, and a longtime veteran of the L.A. phone-phreak wars. NYNEX had the misfortune to run the New York City area and was warily prepared for most anything. Even Michigan Bell, a division of the Ameritech RBOC, at least had the elementary sense to hire its own hacker as a useful scarecrow. But BellSouth, even though its corporate public relations proclaimed it to have "Everything You Expect From a Leader," was pathetic.

When rumor about LoD's mastery of Georgia's switching network got around to BellSouth through Bellcore and telco security scuttlebutt, at first it refused to believe it. If you paid serious attention to every rumor out and about these hacker kids, you would hear all kinds of wacko saucer-nut nonsense: that the National Security Agency monitored all American phone calls, that the CIA and DEA tracked traffic on bulletin boards with word-analysis programs, that the Condor could start World War III from a pay phone.

If there were hackers into BellSouth switching stations, then how come nothing had happened? Nothing had been hurt. BellSouth's machines weren't crashing. BellSouth wasn't suffering especially badly from fraud. BellSouth's customers weren't complaining. BellSouth was headquartered in Atlanta, ambitious metropolis of the new high-tech Sunbelt; and BellSouth was upgrading its network by leaps and bounds, digitizing the works left, right, and center. It could hardly be considered sluggish or naive. BellSouth's technical expertise was second to none, thank you kindly.

But then came the Florida business.

On June 13, 1989, callers to the Palm Beach County Probation Department, in Delray Beach, Florida, found themselves involved in a remarkable discussion with a phone-sex worker named "Tina" in New York State. Somehow, *any* call to this probation office near Miami was instantly and magically transported across state lines, at no extra charge to the user, to a pornographic phone-sex hotline hundreds of miles away!

This practical joke may seem utterly hilarious at first hearing, and indeed there was a good deal of chuckling about it in phone-phreak circles, including the autumn 1989 issue of *2600.* But for Southern Bell (the division of the BellSouth RBOC supplying local service for Florida, Georgia, North Carolina, and South Carolina), this was a smoking gun. For the first time ever, a computer intruder had broken into a BellSouth central office switching station and reprogrammed it!

Or so BellSouth thought in June 1989. Actually, LoD members had been frolicking harmlessly in BellSouth switches since September 1987. The stunt of June 13—call-forwarding a number through manipulation of a switching station—was child's play for hackers as accomplished as the Georgia wing of LoD. Switching calls interstate sounded like a big deal, but it took only four lines of code to accomplish this. An easy, yet more discreet, stunt would be to call-forward another number to your own house. If you were careful and considerate, and changed the software back later, then not a soul would know. Except you. And whoever you had bragged to about it.

As for BellSouth, what it didn't know wouldn't hurt it.

Except now somebody had blown the whole thing wide open, and BellSouth knew.

A now alerted and considerably paranoid BellSouth began searching switches right and left for signs of impropriety, in that hot summer of 1989. No fewer than forty-two BellSouth employees were put on twelve-hour shifts, twenty-four hours a day, for two solid months, poring over records and monitoring computers for any sign of phony access. These forty-two overworked experts were known as BellSouth's "Intrusion Task Force."

What the investigators found astounded them. Proprietary telco databases had been manipulated: phone numbers had been created out of thin air, with no users' names and no addresses and, perhaps worst of all, no charges and no records of use. The new digital ReMOB (Remote Observation) diagnostic feature had been tampered with extensively—hackers had learned to reprogram ReMOB software, so that they could listen in on any switch-routed call at their leisure! They were using telco property to *spy!*

The electrifying news went out throughout law enforcement in 1989. It had never really occurred to anyone at BellSouth that its prized and brand-new digital switching stations could be *reprogrammed.* People seemed utterly amazed that anyone could have the nerve. Of course these switching stations were "computers," and everybody knew hackers liked to "break into computers." But telephone people's computers were *different* from normal people's computers.

The exact reason *why* these computers were "different" was rather ill defined. It certainly wasn't the extent of their security. The security on these BellSouth computers was lousy; the AIMSX computers, for instance, didn't even have passwords. But there was no question that BellSouth strongly *felt* that its computers were very different indeed. And if there were some criminals out there who had not gotten that message, BellSouth was determined to see that message taught.

After all, a 5ESS switching station was no mere bookkeeping system for some local chain of florists. Public service depended on these stations. Public *safety* depended on these stations.

Hackers could spy on anybody in the local area! And hackers, lurking in there call-forwarding or ReMobbing, could spy on anybody in the local area! They could spy on telco officials! They could spy on police stations! They could spy on local offices of the Secret Service. . . .

In 1989, electronic cops and hacker-trackers began using scrambler phones and secured lines. It only made sense. There was no telling who was into those systems. Whoever they were, they sounded scary. This was some new level of antisocial daring. Could be West German hackers, in the pay of the KGB. That too had seemed a weird and farfetched notion, until Clifford Stoll had poked and prodded a sluggish Washington law-enforcement bureaucracy into investigating a computer intrusion that turned out to be exactly that—*hackers, in the pay of the KGB!* Stoll, the systems manager for an Internet lab in Berkeley, California, had ended up on the front page of *The New York Times*, proclaimed a national hero in the first true story of international computer espionage. Stoll's counterspy efforts, which he related in a best-selling book, *The Cuckoo's Egg*, in 1989, had established the credibility of "hacking" as a possible threat to national security. The U.S. Secret Service doesn't mess around when it suspects a possible action by a foreign intelligence apparat.

The Secret Service scrambler phones and secured lines put a tremendous kink in law enforcement's ability to operate freely; to get the word out, cooperate, prevent misunderstandings. Nevertheless, 1989 scarcely seemed the time for half-measures. If the police and Secret Service themselves were not operationally secure, then how could they reasonably demand measures of security from private enterprise? At least, the inconvenience made people aware of the *seriousness* of the threat.

If there was a final spur needed to get the police off the dime, it came in the realization that the emergency 911 system was vulnerable. The 911 system has its own specialized software, but it is run on the same digital switching systems as the rest of the telephone network. The system is not physically different from normal telephony. But it is certainly *culturally* different, because this is the area of telephonic cyberspace reserved for the police and emergency services.

Your average policeman may not know much about hackers or phone phreaks. Computer people are weird; even computer *cops* are rather weird; the stuff they do is hard to figure out. But a threat to the 911 system is anything but abstract. If the 911 system goes, people can die.

Imagine being in a car wreck, staggering to a phone booth, punching 911, and hearing "Tina" pick up the phone-sex line somewhere in New York! The situation's no longer comical, somehow.

And was it possible? No question. Hackers had attacked 911 systems before. Phreaks can max-out 911 systems just by siccing a bunch of computer modems on them in tandem, dialing them over and over until they clog. That's very crude and low tech, but it's still a serious business.

The time had come for action. It was time to take stern measures with the underground. It was time to start picking up the dropped threads, the loose edges, the bits of braggadocio here and there; it was time to get on the stick and start putting serious casework together. Hackers weren't "invisible." They *thought* they were invisible; but the truth was, they had just been tolerated too long.

Under sustained police attention in the summer of 1989, the digital underground began to unravel as never before.

The first big break in the case came very early on: July 1989, the following month. The perpetrator of the "Tina" switch was caught and confessed. His name was "Fry Guy," a sixteen-year-old in Indiana. Fry Guy had been a very wicked young man.

Fry Guy had earned his handle from a stunt involving French fries. Fry Guy had filched the log-in of a local MacDonald's manager and had logged on to the MacDonald's mainframe on the Sprint Telenet system. Posing as the manager, Fry Guy had altered MacDonald's records and given generous raises to some teenage hamburger-flipping friends. He had not been caught.

Emboldened by success, Fry Guy moved on to credit card abuse. Fry Guy was quite an accomplished talker, with a gift for "social engineering." If you can do social engineering—fast talk, fake-outs, impersonation, conning, scamming—then card abuse comes easy. (Getting away with it in the long run is another question.)

Fry Guy had run across Urvile of the Legion of Doom on the ALTOS Chat board in Bonn, Germany. ALTOS Chat was a sophisticated board, accessible through such globe-spanning computer networks as BITNET, Tymnet, and Telenet. ALTOS was much frequented by members of Germany's Chaos Computer Club. Two Chaos hackers who hung out on ALTOS, "Jaeger" and "Pengo," had been the central villains of Clifford Stoll's *Cuckoo's Egg* case: consorting in East Berlin with a spymaster from the

KGB and breaking into American computers for hire, through the Internet.

When LoD members learned the story of Jaeger's depredations from Stoll's book, they were rather less than impressed, technically speaking. On LoD's own favorite board of the moment, Black Ice, LoD members bragged that they themselves could have done all the Chaos break-ins in a week flat! Nevertheless, LoD was grudgingly impressed by the Chaos rep, the sheer hairy-eyed daring of hash-smoking anarchist hackers who had rubbed shoulders with the fearsome big boys of international Communist espionage. LoD members sometimes traded bits of knowledge with friendly German hackers on ALTOS—phone numbers for vulnerable VAX/VMS computers in Georgia, for instance. Dutch and British phone phreaks, and the Australian clique of "Phoenix," "Nom," and "Electron," were ALTOS regulars too. In underground circles, to hang out on ALTOS was considered the sign of an elite dude, a sophisticated hacker of the international digital jet set.

Fry Guy quickly learned how to raid information from credit card consumer-reporting agencies. He had over a hundred stolen credit card numbers in his notebooks and upward of a thousand swiped long-distance access codes. He knew how to get onto ALTOS and how to talk the talk of the underground convincingly. He now wheedled knowledge of switching-station tricks from Urvile on the ALTOS system.

Combining these two forms of knowledge enabled Fry Guy to bootstrap his way up to a new form of wire fraud. First, he'd snitched credit card numbers from credit-company computers. The data he copied included names, addresses, and phone numbers of the random cardholders.

Then Fry Guy, impersonating a cardholder, called up Western Union and asked for a cash advance on "his" credit card. Western Union, as a security guarantee, would call the customer back, at home, to verify the transaction.

But, just as he had switched the Florida probation office to Tina in New York, Fry Guy switched the cardholder's number to a local pay phone. There he would lurk in wait, muddying his trail by routing and rerouting the call through switches as far away as Canada. When the call came through, he would boldly "social engineer," or con, the Western Union people, pretending to be the legitimate cardholder. Because he'd answered the proper phone number, the deception was not very hard. Western Union's money was then shipped to a confederate of Fry Guy's in his hometown in Indiana.

Fry Guy and his cohort, using LoD techniques, stole $6,000 from Western Union between December 1988 and July 1989. They also dabbled in ordering delivery of stolen goods through card fraud. Fry Guy was intoxicated with success. The sixteen-year-old fantasized wildly to hacker rivals, boasting that he'd used ripped-off money to hire himself a big limousine and had driven out-of-state with a groupie from his favorite heavy-metal band, Motley Crue.

Armed with knowledge, power, and a gratifying stream of free money, Fry Guy now took it upon himself to call local representatives of Indiana Bell security, to brag, boast, strut, and utter tormenting warnings that his powerful friends in the notorious Legion of Doom could crash the national telephone network. Fry Guy even named a date for the scheme: the Fourth of July, a national holiday.

This egregious example of the begging-for-arrest syndrome was followed shortly by Fry Guy's arrest. After the Indiana telephone company figured out who he was, the Secret Service had DNRs— Dialed Number Recorders—installed on his home phone lines. These devices are not taps and can't record the substance of phone calls, but they do record the phone numbers of all calls going in and out. Tracing these numbers showed Fry Guy's long-distance code fraud, his extensive ties to pirate bulletin boards, and numerous personal calls to his LoD friends in Atlanta. By July 11, 1989, Prophet, Urvile, and Leftist also had Secret Service DNR "pen registers" installed on their own lines.

The Secret Service showed up in force at Fry Guy's house on July 22, 1989, to the horror of his unsuspecting parents. The raiders were led by a special agent from the service's Indianapolis office. However, the raiders were accompanied and advised by Timothy M. Foley of the Chicago office (a gentleman about whom we will soon be hearing a great deal).

Following federal computer-crime techniques that had been standard since the early 1980s, the Secret Service searched the house thoroughly and seized all of Fry Guy's electronic equipment and note-

The Secret Service showed up in force, to the horror of Fry Guy's unsuspecting parents.

books. All his equipment went out the door in the custody of the Secret Service, which put a swift end to his depredations.

The Secret Service interrogated Fry Guy at length. His case was put in the charge of Deborah Daniels, the federal U.S. Attorney for the Southern District of Indiana. Fry Guy was charged with eleven counts of computer fraud, unauthorized computer access, and wire fraud. The evidence was thorough and irrefutable. For his part, Fry Guy blamed his corruption on the Legion of Doom and offered to testify against it.

Fry Guy insisted that the Legion intended to crash the phone system on a national holiday. And when AT&T crashed on Martin Luther King Day, 1990, this lent a credence to his claim that genuinely alarmed telco security and the Secret Service.

Fry Guy eventually pled guilty on May 31, 1990. On September 14 he was sentenced to forty-four months' probation and four hundred hours' community service. He could have had it much worse; but it made sense to prosecutors to take it easy on this teenage minor, while zeroing in on the notorious kingpins of the Legion of Doom.

But the case against LoD had nagging flaws. Despite the best effort of investigators, it was impossible to prove that the Legion had crashed the phone system on January 15, because it, in fact, hadn't done so. The investigations of 1989 did show that certain members of the Legion of Doom had achieved unprecedented power over the telco switching stations and that they were in active conspiracy to obtain more power yet. Investigators were privately convinced that the Legion of Doom intended to do awful things with this knowledge, but mere evil intent was not enough to put them in jail.

And although the Atlanta Three—Prophet, Leftist, and especially Urvile—had taught Fry Guy plenty, they were not themselves credit card fraudsters. The only thing they'd "stolen" was long-distance service—and because they'd done much of that through phone-switch manipulation, there was no easy way to judge how much they'd "stolen," or whether this practice was even "theft" of any easily recognizable kind.

Fry Guy's theft of long-distance codes had cost the phone companies plenty. The theft of long-distance service may be a fairly theoretical "loss," but it costs genuine money and genuine time to delete all those stolen codes and to reissue new codes to the innocent owners of the corrupted ones. The owners of the codes themselves are victimized, and lose time and money and peace of mind in the hassle. And then there were the credit card victims to deal with too, and Western Union. When it came to rip-off, Fry Guy was far more of a thief than LoD. It was only when it came to actual computer expertise that Fry Guy was small potatoes.

The Atlanta Three thought most "rules" of cyberspace were for rodents and losers, but they *did* have rules. *They never crashed anything, and they never took money.* These were rough rules of thumb, and rather dubious principles when it comes to the ethical subtleties of cyberspace, but they enabled the Atlanta Three to operate with a relatively clear conscience (though never with peace of mind).

If you didn't hack for money, if you weren't robbing people of actual funds—money in the bank, that is—then nobody *really* got hurt, in LoD's opinion. "Theft of service" was a bogus issue, and "intellectual property" was a bad joke. But LoD had only elitist contempt for rip-off artists, "leechers," thieves. The members considered themselves clean. In their opinion, if you didn't smash up or crash any systems (well, not on purpose, anyhow—accidents can happen, just ask Robert Morris), then it was very unfair to call you a "vandal" or a "cracker." When you were hanging out on-line with your "pals" in telco security, you could face them down from the higher plane of hacker morality. And you could mock the police from the supercilious heights of your hacker's quest for pure knowledge.

But from the point of view of law enforcement and telco security, however, Fry Guy was not really dangerous. The Atlanta Three *were* dangerous. It wasn't the crimes they were committing, but the *danger*, the potential hazard, the sheer *technical power* LoD had accumulated, that had made the situation untenable.

Fry Guy was not LoD. He'd never laid eyes on anyone in LoD; his only contacts with them had been electronic. Core members of the Legion of Doom tended to meet physically for conventions every year or so, to get drunk, give each other the hacker high sign, send out for pizza, and ravage hotel suites. Fry Guy had never done any of this. Deborah Daniels assessed Fry Guy accurately as "an LoD wannabe."

Nevertheless Fry Guy's crimes would be directly attributed to LoD in much future police propaganda. LoD would be described as "a closely knit group" involved in "numerous illegal activities" including "stealing and modifying individual credit histories" and "fraudulently obtaining money and property." Fry Guy did this, but the Atlanta Three didn't; they simply weren't into theft, but rather intrusion. This caused a strange kink in the prosecution's strategy. LoD was accused of "disseminating information about attacking computers to other computer hackers in an effort to shift the focus of law enforcement to those other hackers and away from the Legion of Doom."

This last accusation (taken directly from a press release by the Chicago Computer Fraud and Abuse Task Force) sounds particularly farfetched. One might conclude at this point that investigators would have been well advised to go ahead and "shift their focus" from the Legion of Doom. Maybe they *should* concentrate on "those other hackers"—the ones who were actually stealing money and physical objects.

But the Hacker Crackdown of 1990 was not a simple policing action. It wasn't meant just to walk the beat in cyberspace—it was a *crackdown*, a deliberate attempt to nail the core of the operation, to send a dire and potent message that would settle the hash of the digital underground for good.

By this reasoning, Fry Guy wasn't much more than the electronic equivalent of a cheap streetcorner dope dealer. As long as the masterminds of LoD were still flagrantly operating, pushing their mountains of illicit knowledge right and left and whipping up enthusiasm for blatant lawbreaking, then there would be an *infinite supply* of Fry Guys.

Because LoD was flagrant, it had left trails everywhere, to be picked up by law enforcement in New York, Indiana, Florida, Texas, Arizona, Missouri, even Australia. But 1990's war on the Legion of Doom was led out of Illinois, by the Chicago Computer Fraud and Abuse Task Force.

The Computer Fraud and Abuse Task Force, led by federal prosecutor William J. Cook, had started in 1987 and had swiftly become one of the most aggressive local "dedicated computer-crime units." Chicago was a natural home for such a group. The world's first computer bulletin board system had been invented in Illinois. The state had some of the nation's first and sternest computer crime laws. Illinois State Police were markedly alert to the possibilities of white-collar crime and electronic fraud.

And William J. Cook in particular was a rising star in electronic crime-busting. He and his fellow federal prosecutors at the U.S. Attorney's office in Chicago had a tight relation with the Secret Service, especially go-getting Chicago-based agent Timothy Foley. While Cook and his Department of Justice colleagues plotted strategy, Foley was their man on the street.

Throughout the 1980s, the federal government had given prosecutors an armory of new, untried legal tools against computer crime. Cook and his colleagues were pioneers in the use of these new statutes in the real-life cut-and-thrust of the federal courtroom.

On October 2, 1986, the U.S. Senate had passed the Computer Fraud and Abuse Act unanimously, but there had been pitifully few convictions under this statute. Cook's group took its name from this statute, because it was determined to transform this powerful but rather theoretical act of Congress into a real-life engine of legal destruction against computer fraudsters and scofflaws.

It was not a question of merely discovering crimes, investigating them, and then trying and punishing their perpetrators. The Chicago unit, like most everyone else in the business, already *knew* who the bad guys were: the Legion of Doom and the writers and editors of *Phrack*. The task at hand was to find some legal means of putting these characters away.

This approach might seem a bit dubious to someone not acquainted with the gritty realities of prosecutorial work. But prosecutors don't put people in jail for crimes they have committed; they put people in jail for crimes they have committed *that can be proved in court.* Chicago federal police put Al Capone in prison for income-tax fraud. Chicago is a big town, with a rough-and-ready bare-knuckle tradition on both sides of the law.

Fry Guy had broken the case wide open and alerted telco security to the scope of the problem. But Fry Guy's crimes would not put the Atlanta Three behind bars—much less the wacko underground journalists of *Phrack*. So on July 22, 1989, the same day that Fry Guy was raided in Indiana, the Secret Service descended upon the Atlanta Three.

Likely this was inevitable. By the summer of 1989, law enforcement was closing in on the Atlanta Three from at least six directions at once. First, there were the leads from Fry Guy, which had led to the DNR registers being installed on the lines of the Three. The DNR evidence alone would have finished them off, sooner or later.

But second, the Atlanta lads were already well known to Control-C and his telco security sponsors. LoD's contacts with telco security had made its members overconfident and even more boastful than usual; they felt that they had powerful friends in high places and that they were being tolerated openly by telco security. But BellSouth's Intrusion Task Force was hot on the trail of LoD and sparing no effort or expense.

The Atlanta Three had also been identified by name and listed on the extensive antihacker files maintained, and retailed for pay, by private security operative John Maxfield of Detroit. Maxfield, who had extensive ties to telco security and many informants in the underground, was a bête noire of the *Phrack* crowd, and the dislike was mutual.

The Atlanta Three themselves had written articles for *Phrack*. This boastful act could not possibly escape telco and law enforcement attention.

"Knightmare," a high school–age hacker from Arizona, was a close friend and disciple of Atlanta LoD, but he had been nabbed by the formidable Arizona Organized Crime and Racketeering Unit. Knightmare was on some of LoD's favorite boards—Black Ice in particular—and was privy to their secrets. And to have Gail Thackeray, the assistant attorney general of Arizona, on one's trail was a dreadful peril for any hacker.

And perhaps worst of all, Prophet had committed a major blunder by passing an illicitly copied BellSouth computer file to Knight Lightning, who had published it in *Phrack*. This, as we will see, was an act of dire consequence for almost everyone concerned.

On July 22, 1989, the Secret Service showed up at Leftist's house, where he lived with his parents. A massive squad of some twenty officers surrounded the building: Secret Service, federal marshals, local police, possibly BellSouth telco security; it was hard to tell in the crush. Leftist's dad, at work in his basement office, first noticed a muscular stranger in plain clothes crashing through the backyard with a drawn pistol. As more strangers poured into the house, Leftist's dad naturally assumed there was an armed robbery in progress.

Like most hacker parents, Leftist's mom and dad had only the vaguest notions of what their son had been up to all this time. Leftist had a day job repairing computer hardware. His obsession with computers seemed a bit odd, but harmless enough, and likely to produce a well-paying career. The sudden, overwhelming raid left Leftist's parents traumatized.

Leftist himself had been out after work with his co-workers, surrounding a couple of pitchers of margaritas. As he came trucking on tequila-numbed feet up the pavement, toting a bag full of floppy disks, he noticed a large number of unmarked cars parked in his driveway. All the cars sported tiny microwave antennas.

Like most hacker parents, Leftist's mom and dad had only the vaguest notions of what their son had been up to.

The Secret Service had knocked the front door off its hinges, almost flattening his mom.

Inside, Leftist was greeted by Special Agent James Cool of the U.S. Secret Service, Atlanta office. Leftist was flabbergasted. He'd never met a Secret Service agent before. He could not imagine that he'd ever done anything worthy of federal attention. He'd always figured that if his activities became intolerable, one of his contacts in telco security would give him a private phone call and tell him to knock it off.

But now Leftist was pat-searched for weapons by grim professionals, and his bag of floppies was quickly seized. He and his parents were all shepherded into separate rooms and grilled at length as a score of officers scoured their home for anything electronic.

Leftist was horrified as his treasured IBM AT personal computer with its forty-meg hard disk and his recently purchased 80386 IBM clone with a whopping hundred-meg hard disk both went swiftly out the door in Secret Service custody. They also seized all his disks, all his notebooks, and a tremendous booty in dog-eared telco documents that Leftist had snitched from trash dumpsters.

Leftist figured the whole thing for a big misunderstanding. He'd never been into *military* computers. He wasn't a *spy* or a

Communist. He was just a good ol' Georgia hacker, and now he just wanted all these people out of the house. But it seemed they wouldn't go until he made some kind of statement.

And so, he leveled with them.

And that, Leftist said later from his federal prison camp in Talladega, Alabama, was a big mistake.

The Atlanta area was unique, in that it had three members of the Legion of Doom who actually occupied more or less the same physical locality. Unlike the rest of LoD, who tended to associate by phone and computer, Atlanta LoD actually *were* "tightly knit." It was no real surprise that the Secret Service agents apprehending Urvile at the computer labs at Georgia Tech would discover Prophet with him as well.

Urvile, a twenty-one-year-old Georgia Tech student in polymer chemistry, posed quite a puzzling case for law enforcement. Urvile—also known as "Necron 99," as well as other handles, for he tended to change his cover alias about once a month—was both an accomplished hacker and a fanatic simulation-gamer.

Simulation games are an unusual hobby; but then hackers are unusual people, and their favorite pastimes tend to be somewhat out of the ordinary. The best-known American simulation game is probably Dungeons & Dragons, a multiplayer parlor entertainment played with paper, maps, pencils, statistical tables, and a variety of oddly shaped dice. Players pretend to be heroic characters exploring a wholly invented fantasy world. The fantasy worlds of simulation gaming are commonly pseudomedieval, involving swords and sorcery—spell-casting wizards, knights in armor, unicorns and dragons, demons and goblins.

Urvile and his fellow gamers preferred their fantasies highly technological. They made use of a game known as "GURPS," the "Generic Universal Role Playing System," published by a company called Steve Jackson Games (SJG).

GURPS served as a framework for creating a wide variety of artificial fantasy worlds. Steve Jackson Games published a smorgasboard of books, full of detailed information and gaming hints, which were used to flesh-out many different fantastic back-grounds for the basic GURPS framework. Urvile made extensive use of two SJG books called *GURPS High-Tech* and *GURPS Special Ops.*

In the artificial fantasy world of *GURPS Special Ops,* players entered a modern fantasy of intrigue and international espionage. On beginning the game, players started small and powerless, per-haps as minor-league CIA agents or penny-ante arms dealers. But as players persisted through a series of game sessions (which gen-erally lasted for hours, over long, elaborate campaigns that might be pursued for months on end), they would achieve new skills, new knowledge, new power. They would acquire and hone new abilities, such as marksmanship, karate, wiretapping, or Water-gate burglary. They could also win various kinds of imaginary booty, such as Berettas, or martini shakers, or fast cars with ejec-tion seats and machine guns under the headlights.

As might be imagined from the complexity of these games, Urvile's gaming notes were very detailed and extensive. Urvile was a "dungeonmaster," inventing scenarios for his fellow gamers, giant simulated adventure-puzzles for his friends to unravel. Urvile's game notes covered dozens of pages with all sorts of exotic lunacy, all about ninja raids on Libya and break-ins on encrypted Red Chinese supercomputers. His notes were written on scrap paper and kept in loose-leaf binders.

The handiest scrap paper around Urvile's college digs were the many pounds of BellSouth printouts and documents that he had snitched out of telco dumpsters. His notes were written on the back of misappropriated telco property. Worse yet, the gaming notes were interspersed chaotically with Urvile's hand-scrawled records involving *actual computer intrusions* that he had commit-ted.

Not only was it next to impossible to tell Urvile's fantasy game notes from cyberspace "reality," but Urvile himself barely made this distinction. It's no exaggeration to say that to Urvile it was *all* a game. Urvile was very bright, highly imaginative, and quite careless of other people's notions of propriety. His connection to "reality" was not something to which he paid a great deal of attention.

Hacking was a game for Urvile. It was an amusement he was carrying out, it was something he was doing for fun. And Urvile was an obsessive young man. He could no more stop hacking than he could stop in the middle of a jigsaw puzzle, or stop in the middle of reading a Stephen Donaldson fantasy trilogy. (The name "Urvile" came from a best-selling Donaldson novel.)

Urvile's airy, bulletproof attitude seriously annoyed his interrogators. First of all, he didn't consider that he'd done anything wrong. There was scarcely a shred of honest remorse in him. On the contrary, he seemed privately convinced that his police interrogators were operating in a demented fantasy world all their own. Urvile was too polite and well behaved to say this straight out, but his reactions were askew and disquieting.

For instance, there was the business about LoD's ability to monitor phone calls to the police and Secret Service. Urvile agreed that this was quite possible and posed no big problem for LoD. In fact, he and his friends had kicked the idea around on the Black Ice board, much as they had discussed many other nifty notions, such as building personal flamethrowers and jury-rigging fistsful of blasting caps. They had hundreds of dial-up numbers for government agencies that they'd gotten through scanning Atlanta phones or had pulled from raided VAX/VMS mainframe computers.

Basically, they'd never gotten around to listening in on the cops because the idea wasn't interesting enough to bother with. Besides, if they'd been monitoring Secret Service phone calls, obviously they'd never have been caught in the first place. Right?

The Secret Service was less than satisfied with this rapierlike hacker logic.

Then there was the issue of crashing the phone system. No problem, Urvile admitted sunnily. Atlanta LoD could have shut down phone service all over Atlanta any time it liked. *Even the*

911 service? Nothing special about that, Urvile explained patiently. Bring the switch to its knees, with say the UNIX "makedir" bug, and 911 goes down too as a matter of course. The 911 system wasn't very interesting, frankly. It might be tremendously interesting to cops (for odd reasons of their own), but as technical challenges went, the 911 service was yawnsville.

So of course the Atlanta Three could crash service. They probably could have crashed service all over BellSouth territory, if they'd worked at it for a while. But Atlanta LoD weren't crashers. Only losers and rodents were crashers. LoD were *elite*.

Urvile privately was convinced that sheer technical expertise could win him free of any kind of problem. As far as he was concerned, elite status in the digital underground had placed him permanently beyond the intellectual grasp of cops and straights. Urvile had a lot to learn.

Of the three LoD stalwarts, Prophet was in the most direct trouble. Prophet was a UNIX programming expert who burrowed in and out of the Internet as a matter of course. He'd started his hacking career at around age fourteen, meddling with a UNIX mainframe system at the University of North Carolina.

Prophet himself had written the handy Legion of Doom file "UNIX Use and Security From the Ground Up." UNIX (pronounced "you-nicks") is a powerful, flexible computer operating system for multiuser, multitasking computers. In 1969, when UNIX was created in Bell Labs, such computers were exclusive to large corporations and universities, but today UNIX is run on thousands of powerful home machines. UNIX was particularly well suited to telecommunications programming and had become a standard in the field. Naturally, UNIX also became a standard for the elite hacker and phone phreak.

Lately Prophet had not been so active as Leftist and Urvile, but Prophet was a recidivist. In 1986, when he was eighteen, Prophet had been convicted of "unauthorized access to a computer network" in North Carolina. He'd been discovered breaking into the Southern Bell Data Network, a UNIX-based internal telco network supposedly closed to the public. He'd gotten a typical hacker sentence: six months suspended, 120 hours community service, and three years' probation.

After that humiliating bust, Prophet had gotten rid of most of his tonnage of illicit phreak and hacker data and had tried to go straight. He was, after all, still on probation. But by the autumn of 1988, the temptations of cyberspace had proved too much for young Prophet, and he was shoulder to shoulder with Urvile and Leftist into some of the hairiest systems around.

In early September 1988, he'd broken into BellSouth's centralized automation system, AIMSX, or "Advanced Information Management System." AIMSX was an internal business network for BellSouth, where telco employees stored electronic mail, databases, memos, and calendars, and did text processing. Because AIMSX did not have public dial-ups, it was considered utterly invisible to the public and was not well secured—it didn't even require passwords. Prophet abused an account known as "waa1," the personal account of an unsuspecting telco employee. Disguised as the owner of waa1, Prophet made about ten visits to AIMSX.

Prophet did not damage or delete anything in the system. His presence in AIMSX was harmless and almost invisible. But he could not rest content with that.

One particular piece of processed text on AIMSX was a telco document known as "Bell South Standard Practice 660-225-104SV Control Office Administration of Enhanced 911 Services for Special Services and Major Account Centers dated March 1988."

Prophet had not been looking for this document. It was merely one among hundreds of similar documents with impenetrable titles. However, having blundered over it in the course of his illicit wanderings through AIMSX, he decided to take it with him as a trophy. It might prove very useful in some future boasting, bragging, and strutting session. So, some time in September 1988, Prophet ordered the AIMSX mainframe computer to copy this document (henceforth called simply "the E911 Document") and to transfer this copy to his home computer.

No one noticed that Prophet had done this. He had "stolen" the E911 Document in some sense, but notions of property in cyberspace can be tricky. BellSouth noticed nothing

> *Prophet decided to take the E911 Document with him as a trophy.*

wrong, because BellSouth still had its original copy. It had not been "robbed" of the document itself. Many people were supposed to copy this document—specifically, people who worked for the nineteen BellSouth "special services and major account centers," scattered throughout the southeastern United States. That was what it was for, why it was present on a computer network in the first place: so that it could be copied and read—by telco employees. But now the data had been copied by someone who wasn't supposed to look at it.

Prophet now had his trophy. But he further decided to store yet another copy of the E911 Document on another person's computer. This unwitting person was a computer enthusiast named Richard Andrews who lived near Joliet, Illinois. Richard Andrews was a UNIX programmer by trade, and ran a powerful UNIX board called Jolnet, in the basement of his house.

Prophet, using the handle "Robert Johnson," had obtained an account on Richard Andrews' computer. And there he stashed the E911 Document, by storing it in his own private section of Andrews' computer.

Why did Prophet do this? If he had eliminated the E911 Document from his own computer and kept it hundreds of miles away, on another machine, under an alias, then he might have been fairly safe from discovery and prosecution—although his sneaky action had certainly put the unsuspecting Richard Andrews at risk.

But, like most hackers, Prophet was a packrat for illicit data. When it came to the crunch, he could not bear to part with his trophy. When Prophet's place in Decatur, Georgia, was raided in July 1989, there was the E911 Document, a smoking gun. And there was Prophet in the hands of the Secret Service, doing his best to "explain."

Our story now takes us away from the raids of the summer of 1989, leaving the Atlanta Three "cooperating fully" with their numerous investigators. And they did cooperate, as their sentencing memorandum from the U.S. District Court of the Northern Division of Georgia explained—just before all three of them were sentenced to various federal prisons in November 1990.

We must now catch up on the other aspects of the war on the Legion of Doom. It was a war on a network—in fact, a network of three networks, which intertwined and interrelated in a complex fashion. The Legion itself, with Atlanta LoD, and its hanger-on Fry Guy, was the first. The second was *Phrack* magazine, with its editors and contributors.

The third network involved the electronic circle around a hacker known as "Terminus."

The war against these hacker networks was carried out by a law enforcement network. Atlanta LoD and Fry Guy were pursued by U.S. Secret Service agents and federal prosecutors in Atlanta, Indiana, and Chicago. Terminus found himself pursued by the Secret Service and federal prosecutors from Baltimore and Chicago. And the war against *Phrack* was almost entirely a Chicago operation.

The investigation of Terminus involved a great deal of energy, mostly from the Chicago Task Force, but it was to be the least known and least publicized of the crackdown operations. Terminus, who lived in Maryland, was a UNIX programmer and consultant, fairly well known (under his given name) in the UNIX community, as an acknowledged expert on AT&T minicomputers. Terminus idolized AT&T, especially Bellcore, and longed for public recognition as a UNIX maven; his highest ambition was to work for Bell Labs.

But Terminus had odd friends and a spotted history. He had once been the subject of an admiring interview in *Phrack* (Volume II, Issue 14, Phile 2—dated May 1987). In this article, *Phrack* co-editor Taran King described Terminus as an electronics engineer, five foot nine inches tall, brown-haired, born in 1959—at twenty-eight years old, quite mature for a hacker.

Terminus had once been sysop of a phreak/hack underground board called MetroNet, which ran on an Apple II. Later he'd replaced MetroNet with an underground board called MegaNet, specializing in IBMs. In his younger days, Terminus had written one of the very first and most elegant code-scanning programs for the IBM-PC. This program had been distributed widely in the underground. Uncounted legions of PC-owning phreaks and hackers had used Terminus' scanner program to rip off telco codes. This feat had not escaped the attention of telco security; it hardly could, because Terminus' earlier handle, "Terminal Technician," was proudly written right on the program.

When he became a full-time computer professional (specializing in telecommunications programming), he adopted the handle Terminus, meant to indicate that he had "reached the final point of being a proficient hacker." He'd moved up to the UNIX-based Netsys board on an AT&T computer, with four phone lines and an impressive 240 megs of storage. Netsys carried complete issues of *Phrack*, and Terminus was quite friendly with its publishers, Taran King and Knight Lightning.

In the early 1980s, Terminus had been a regular on Plovernet, Pirate-80, Sherwood Forest, and Shadowland, all well-known pirate boards, all heavily frequented by the Legion of Doom. As it happened, Terminus was never officially "in LoD," because he'd never been given the official LoD high sign and back slap by Legion maven Lex Luthor. Terminus had never physically met anyone from LoD. But that scarcely mattered much—the Atlanta Three themselves had never been officially vetted by Lex either.

As far as law enforcement was concerned, the issues were clear. Terminus was a full-time, adult computer professional with particular skills at AT&T software and hardware—but Terminus reeked of the Legion of Doom and the underground.

On February 1, 1990—half a month after the Martin Luther

King Day Crash—U.S. Secret Service agents Tim Foley from Chicago and Jack Lewis from the Baltimore office, accompanied by AT&T security officer Jerry Dalton, traveled to Middletown, Maryland. There they grilled Terminus in his home (to the stark terror of his wife and small children) and, in their customary fashion, hauled his computers out the door.

The Netsys machine proved to contain a plethora of arcane UNIX software—proprietary source code formally owned by AT&T. Software such as: UNIX System Five Release 3.2; UNIX SV Release 3.1; UUCP communications software; KORN SHELL; RFS; IWB; WWB; DWB; the C++ programming language; PMON; TOOL CHEST; QUEST; DACT; and S FIND.

In the long-established piratical tradition of the underground, Terminus had been trading this illicitly copied software with a small circle of fellow UNIX programmers. Very unwisely, he had stored seven years of his electronic mail on his Netsys machine, which documented all the friendly arrangements he had made with his various colleagues.

Terminus had not crashed the AT&T phone system on January 15. He was, however, blithely running a not-for-profit AT&T software-piracy ring. This was not an activity AT&T found amusing. AT&T security officer Jerry Dalton valued this "stolen" property at over $300,000.

AT&T's entry into the tussle of free enterprise had been complicated by the new, vague ground rules of the information economy. Until the breakup of Ma Bell, AT&T was forbidden to sell computer hardware or software. Ma Bell was the phone company; Ma Bell was not allowed to use the enormous revenue from telephone utilities in order to finance any entry into the computer market.

AT&T nevertheless invented the UNIX language. And somehow AT&T managed to make UNIX a minor source of income. Weirdly, UNIX was not sold as computer software, but actually retailed under an obscure regulatory exemption allowing sales of surplus equipment and scrap. Any bolder attempt to promote or retail UNIX would have aroused angry legal opposition from computer companies. Instead, UNIX was licensed to universities, at modest rates, where the acids of academic freedom ate away steadily at AT&T's proprietary rights.

Come the breakup, AT&T recognized that UNIX was a potential goldmine. By now, large chunks of UNIX code had been created that were not AT&T's and were being sold by others. An entire rival UNIX-based operating system had arisen in Berkeley, California (one of the world's great founts of ideological hackerdom). Today, hackers commonly consider Berkeley UNIX to be technically superior to AT&T's System V UNIX, but AT&T has not allowed mere technical elegance to intrude on the real-world business of marketing proprietary software. AT&T has made its own code deliberately incompatible with other folks' UNIX and has written code that it can prove is copyrightable, even if that code happens to be somewhat awkward—"kludgey." AT&T UNIX user licenses are serious business agreements, replete with very clear copyright statements and nondisclosure clauses.

AT&T has not exactly kept the UNIX cat in the bag, but it kept a grip on its scruff with some success. By the rampant, explosive standards of software piracy, AT&T UNIX source code is heavily copyrighted, well guarded, well licensed. Traditionally UNIX was run only on mainframe machines, owned by large groups of suit-and-tie professionals, rather than on bedroom machines where people can get up to easy mischief.

And AT&T UNIX source code is serious high-level programming. The number of skilled UNIX programmers with any actual motive to swipe UNIX source code is small. It's tiny, compared to the tens of thousands prepared to rip off, say, entertaining PC games such as "Leisure Suit Larry."

But by 1989, the warez-d00d underground, in the persons of Terminus and his friends, was gnawing at AT&T UNIX. And the property in question was not sold for twenty bucks over the counter at the local branch of Babbage's or Egghead's; this was massive, sophisticated, multiline, multiauthor corporate code worth tens of thousands of dollars.

It must be recognized at this point that Terminus' purported ring of UNIX software pirates had not actually made any money from their suspected crimes. The $300,000 figure bandied about for the contents of Terminus' computer did not mean that Terminus was in actual illicit possession of three hundred thousand of AT&T's dollars. Terminus was shipping software back and forth, privately, person to person, for free. He was not making a commercial business of piracy. He hadn't asked for money; he didn't take money. He lived quite modestly.

They were humble digital drudges, wandering with mop and bucket through the Great Technological Temple of AT&T.

AT&T employees—as well as freelance UNIX consultants, such as Terminus—commonly worked with "proprietary" AT&T software, both in the office and at home on their private machines. AT&T rarely sent security officers out to comb the hard disks of its consultants. Cheap freelance UNIX contractors were quite useful to AT&T; they didn't have health insurance or retirement programs, much less union membership in the Communication Workers of America. They were humble digital drudges, wandering with mop and bucket through the Great Technological Temple of AT&T; but when the Secret Service arrived at their homes, it seemed they were eating with company silverware and sleeping on company sheets! Outrageously, they behaved as if the things they worked with every day belonged to them!

And these were no mere hacker teenagers with their hands full of trash paper and their noses pressed to the corporate windowpane. These guys were UNIX wizards, not only carrying AT&T data in their machines and their heads, but eagerly networking about it, over machines that were far more powerful than anything previously imagined in private hands. How do you keep people disposable, yet assure their awestruck respect for your property? It was a dilemma.

Much UNIX code was public domain, available for free. Much "proprietary" UNIX code had been extensively rewritten, perhaps

THE *DIGITAL UNDERGROUND* ₰₰₰₰₰₰₰₰₰₰₰₰₰₰₰₰₰₰₰₰₰₰₰₰₰₰₰ 123

altered so much that it became an entirely new product—or perhaps not. Intellectual property rights for software developers
were, and are, extraordinarily complex and confused. And software "piracy," like the private copying of videos, is one of the
most widely practiced "crimes" in the world today.

The U.S. Secret Service was not expert in UNIX or familiar
with the customs of its use. The USSS, considered as a body, did
not have one single person in it who could program in a UNIX
environment—no, not even one. The Secret Service *was* making
extensive use of expert help, but the "experts" it had chosen were
AT&T and Bellcore security officials, the very victims of the purported crimes under investigation, the very people whose interest
in AT&T's "proprietary" software was most pronounced.

On February 6, 1990, Terminus was arrested by Agent Lewis.
Eventually Terminus would be sent to prison for his illicit use of a
piece of AT&T software.

The issue of pirated AT&T software would bubble along in the
background during the war on the Legion of Doom. Some half-
dozen of Terminus' on-line acquaintances, including people in
Illinois, Texas, and California, were grilled by the Secret Service
in connection with the illicit copying of software. Except for Terminus, however, none was charged with a crime. None of them
shared his peculiar prominence in the hacker underground.

But that did not mean that these people would, or could, stay
out of trouble. The transferral of illicit data in cyberspace is hazy
and ill-defined business, with paradoxical dangers for everyone
concerned: hackers, signal carriers, board owners, cops, prosecutors, even random passersby. Sometimes well-meant attempts to
avert trouble or punish wrongdoing bring more trouble than
would simple ignorance, indifference, or impropriety.

Terminus' Netsys board was not a common-or-garden bulletin
board system, though it had most of the usual functions of a
board. Netsys was not a stand-alone machine, but part of the
globe-spanning UUCP cooperative network. The UUCP network
uses a set of UNIX software programs called "UNIX-to-UNIX
Copy," which allows UNIX systems to throw data to one another

at high speed through the public telephone network. UUCP is a radically decentralized, not-for-profit network of UNIX computers. There are tens of thousands of these UNIX machines. Some are small, but many are powerful and also link to other networks. UUCP has certain arcane links to major networks such as JANET, EasyNet, BITNET, JUNET, VNET, DASnet, PeaceNet, and FidoNet, as well as the gigantic Internet. (The so-called Internet is not actually a network itself but rather an "internetwork" connections standard that allows several globe-spanning computer networks to communicate with one another. Readers fascinated by the weird and intricate tangles of modern computer networks may enjoy John S. Quarterman's authoritative 719-page explication, *The Matrix*, Digital Press, 1990.)

A skilled user of Terminus' UNIX machine could send and receive electronic mail from almost any major computer network in the world. Netsys was not called a "board" per se, but rather a "node." Nodes were larger, faster, and more sophisticated than mere boards, and for hackers, to hang out on internationally connected nodes was quite the step up from merely hanging out on local boards.

Terminus' Netsys node in Maryland had a number of direct links to other, similar UUCP nodes, run by people who shared his interests and at least something of his free-wheeling attitude. One of these nodes was Jolnet, owned by Richard Andrews, who, like Terminus, was an independent UNIX consultant. Jolnet also ran UNIX and could be contacted at high speed by mainframe machines from all over the world. Jolnet was quite a sophisticated piece of work, technically speaking, but it was still run by an individual, as a private, not-for-profit hobby. Jolnet was used mostly by other UNIX programmers—for mail, storage, and access to networks. Jolnet supplied network access to about two hundred people as well as a local junior college.

Among its various features and services, Jolnet also carried *Phrack* magazine.

For reasons of his own, Richard Andrews had become suspicious of a new user called "Robert Johnson." Andrews took it upon himself to have a look at what "Robert Johnson" was storing in Jolnet. And Andrews found the E911 Document.

"Robert Johnson" was Prophet from the Legion of Doom, and the E911 Document was illicitly copied data from Prophet's raid on the BellSouth computers.

The E911 Document, a particularly illicit piece of digital property, was about to resume its long, complex, and disastrous career.

It struck Andrews as fishy that someone not a telephone employee should have a document referring to the Enhanced 911 System. Besides, the document itself bore an obvious warning.

WARNING: NOT FOR USE OR DISCLOSURE OUTSIDE BELLSOUTH OR ANY OF ITS SUBSIDIARIES EXCEPT UNDER WRITTEN AGREEMENT.

These standard nondisclosure tags are often appended to all sorts of corporate material. Telcos as a species are particularly notorious for stamping most everything in sight as "not for use or disclosure." Still, this particular piece of data *was* about the 911 System. That sounded bad to Rich Andrews.

Andrews was not prepared to ignore this sort of trouble. He thought it would be wise to pass the document along to a friend and acquaintance on the UNIX network, for consultation. So, around September 1988, Andrews sent yet another copy of the E911 Document electronically to an AT&T employee, one Charles Boykin, who ran a UNIX-based node called "attctc" in Dallas, Texas.

Attctc was the property of AT&T and was run from AT&T's Customer Technology Center in Dallas, hence the name "attctc." Attctc was better known as "Killer," the name of the machine that the system was running on. Killer was a hefty, powerful, AT&T 3B2 500 model, a multiuser, multitasking UNIX platform with 32 meg of memory and a mind-boggling 3.2 Gigabytes of storage. When Killer had first arrived in Texas, in 1985, the 3B2 had been one of AT&T's great white hopes for going head-to-head with IBM for the corporate computer-hardware market. Killer had been shipped to the Customer Technology Center in the Dallas Infomart, essentially a high-technology mall, and there it sat, a demonstration model.

Charles Boykin, a veteran AT&T hardware and digital communications expert, was a local technical backup man for the AT&T 3B2 system. As a display model in the Infomart mall, Killer had little to do, and it seemed a shame to waste the system's capacity. So Boykin ingeniously wrote some UNIX bulletin board software for Killer and plugged the machine in to the local phone network. Killer's debut in late 1985 made it the first publicly available UNIX site in the state of Texas. Anyone who wanted to play was welcome.

The machine immediately attracted an electronic community. It joined the UUCP network and offered network links to over eighty other computer sites, all of which became dependent on Killer for their links to the greater world of cyberspace. And it wasn't just for the big guys; personal computer users also stored freeware programs for the Amiga, the Apple, the IBM, and the Macintosh on Killer's vast 3,200 meg archives. At one time, Killer had the largest library of public-domain Macintosh software in Texas.

Eventually, Killer attracted about 1,500 users, all busily communicating, uploading and downloading, getting mail, gossiping, and linking to arcane and distant networks.

Boykin received no pay for running Killer. He considered it good publicity for the AT&T 3B2 system (whose sales were somewhat less than stellar), but he also simply enjoyed the vibrant community his skill had created. He gave away the bulletin board UNIX software he had written, free of charge.

In the UNIX programming community, Charlie Boykin had the reputation of a warm, open-hearted, level-headed kind of guy. In 1989, a group of Texan UNIX professionals voted Boykin "System Administrator of the Year." He was considered a fellow you could trust for good advice.

In September 1988, without warning, the E911 Document came plunging into Boykin's life, forwarded by Richard Andrews. Boykin immediately recognized that the document was hot property. He was not a voice-communications man and knew little about the ins and outs of the Baby Bells, but he certainly knew what the 911 System was, and he was angry to see confidential data about it in the hands of a nogoodnik. This was clearly a matter for telco security. So, on September 21, 1988, Boykin made yet *another* copy of the E911 Document and passed this one along to a professional acquaintance of his, one Jerome Dalton, from AT&T Corporate Information Security. Jerry Dalton was the very fellow who would later raid Terminus' house.

From AT&T's security division, the E911 Document went to Bellcore.

Bellcore (or BELL COmmunications REsearch) had once been the central laboratory of the Bell System. Bell Labs employees had invented the UNIX programming language. Now Bellcore was a quasi-independent, jointly owned company that acted as the research arm for all seven of the Baby Bell RBOCs. Bellcore was in a good

> *Kluepfel recognized the document for what it was: a trophy from a hacker break-in.*

position to coordinate security technology and consultation for the RBOCs, and the gentleman in charge of this effort was Henry M. Kluepfel, a veteran of the Bell System who had worked there for twenty-four years.

On October 13, 1988, Dalton passed the E911 Document to Henry Kluepfel. Kluepfel, a veteran expert witness in telecommunications fraud and computer-fraud cases, had certainly seen worse trouble than this. He recognized the document for what it was: a trophy from a hacker break-in.

However, whatever harm had been done in the intrusion was presumably old news. At this point Kluepfel apparently decided there was little to be done. He made a careful note of the circumstances and shelved the problem for the time being.

Whole months passed.

February 1989 arrived. The Atlanta Three were living it up in Bell South's switches and had not yet met their comeuppance. The Legion was thriving. So was *Phrack* magazine. A good six months had passed since Prophet's AIMSX break-in. Prophet, as hackers will, grew weary of sitting on his laurels. Knight Lightning and Taran King, the editors of *Phrack,* were always begging him for material they could publish. Prophet decided that the heat must be off by this time, and that he could safely brag, boast, and strut.

So he sent a copy of the E911 Document—yet another one— from Rich Andrews' Jolnet machine to Knight Lightning's BITNET account at the University of Missouri.

Let's review the fate of the Document so far.

0. The original E911 Document. This in the AIMSX system on a mainframe computer in Atlanta, available to hundreds of people, but all of them, presumably, BellSouth employees. An unknown number of them may have their own copies of this document, but they are all professionals and all trusted by the phone company.

1. Prophet's illicit copy, at home on his own computer in Decatur, Georgia.

2. Prophet's backup copy, stored on Rich Andrews' Jolnet machine in the basement of Andrews' house near Joliet, Illinois.

3. Charles Boykin's copy on Killer in Dallas, Texas, sent by Rich Andrews from Joliet.

4. Jerry Dalton's copy at AT&T Corporate Information Security in New Jersey, sent by Boykin from Dallas.

5. Henry Kluepfel's copy at Bellcore security headquarters in New Jersey, sent by Dalton.

6. Knight Lightning's copy, sent by Prophet from Rich Andrews' machine, and now in Columbia, Missouri.

We can see that the "security" situation of this proprietary document, once dug out of AIMSX, swiftly became bizarre. Without any money changing hands, without any particular special effort, these data had been reproduced at least six times and had spread itself all over the continent. By far the worst, however, was yet to come.

In February 1989, Prophet and Knight Lightning bargained electronically over the fate of this trophy. Prophet wanted to boast but, at the same time, scarcely wanted to be caught.

For his part, Knight Lightning was eager to publish as much of the document as he could manage. Knight Lightning was a fledgling political science major with a particular interest in freedom-of-information issues. He would gladly publish almost anything that would reflect glory on the prowess of the underground and embarrass the telcos. However, Knight Lightning himself had contacts in telco security, and sometimes consulted them on material he'd received that might be too dicey for publication.

Prophet and Knight Lightning decided to edit the E911 Document so as to delete most of its identifying traits. First of all, its large NOT FOR USE OR DISCLOSURE warning had to go. Then there were other matters. For instance, it listed the office telephone numbers of several BellSouth 911 specialists in Florida. If these phone numbers were published in *Phrack,* the BellSouth employees involved would very likely be hassled by phone phreaks, which would anger BellSouth no end and pose a definite operational hazard for both Prophet and *Phrack.*

So Knight Lightning cut the Document almost in half, removing the phone numbers and some of the touchier and more specific information. He passed it back electronically to Prophet; Prophet was still nervous, so Knight Lightning cut a bit more. They finally agreed that it was ready to go and that it would be published in *Phrack* under the pseudonym "The Eavesdropper."

And this was done on February 25, 1989.

The twenty-fourth issue of *Phrack* featured a chatty interview with coed phone-phreak "Chanda Leir," three articles on

BITNET and its links to other computer networks, an article on 800 and 900 numbers by "Unknown User," "VaxCat's" article on telco basics (slyly entitled "Lifting Ma Bell's Veil of Secrecy,") and the usual "Phrack World News."

The News section, with painful irony, featured an extended account of the sentencing of "Shadowhawk," an eighteen-year-old Chicago hacker who had just been put in federal prison by William J. Cook himself.

And then there were the two articles by The Eavesdropper. The first was the heavily edited E911 Document, now titled "Control Office Administration Of Enhanced 911 Services for Special Services and Major Account Centers." Eavesdropper's second article was a glossary of terms explaining the blizzard of telco acronyms and buzzwords in the E911 Document.

The hapless document was now distributed, in the usual *Phrack* routine, to a good 150 sites. Not 150 *people*, mind you— 150 *sites*, some of them linked to UNIX nodes or bulletin board systems, which themselves had readerships of tens, dozens, even hundreds of people.

This was February 1989. Nothing happened immediately. Summer came, and the Atlanta crew was raided by the Secret Service. Fry Guy was apprehended. Still nothing whatever happened to *Phrack*. Six more issues of *Phrack* came out, thirty in all, more or less on a monthly schedule. Knight Lightning and co-editor Taran King went untouched.

Phrack tended to duck and cover whenever the heat came down. During the summer busts of 1987 (hacker busts tended to cluster in summer, perhaps because hackers were easier to find at home than in college), *Phrack* had ceased publication for several months and laid low. Several LoD hangers-on had been arrested, but nothing had happened to the *Phrack* crew, the premier gossips of the underground. In 1988, *Phrack* had been taken over by a new editor, "Crimson Death," a raucous youngster with a taste for anarchy files.

The year 1989, however, looked like a bounty year for the underground. Knight Lightning and co-editor Taran King took up the reins again, and *Phrack* flourished. Atlanta LoD went down hard in the summer of 1989, but *Phrack* rolled merrily on. Prophet's E911 Document seemed unlikely to cause *Phrack* any trouble. By January 1990, it had been available in *Phrack* for almost a year. Kluepfel and Dalton, officers of Bellcore and AT&T security, had possessed the document for sixteen months—in fact, they'd had it even before Knight Lightning himself and had done nothing in particular to stop its distribution. They hadn't even told Rich Andrews or Charles Boykin to erase the copies from their UNIX nodes, Jolnet and Killer.

But then came the monster Martin Luther King Day Crash of January 15, 1990.

A flat three days later, on January 18, four agents showed up at Knight Lightning's fraternity house. One was Timothy Foley, the second Barbara Golden, both of them Secret Service agents from the Chicago office. Also along was a University of Missouri security officer, and Reed Newlin, a security man from Southwestern Bell, the RBOC having jurisdiction over Missouri.

Foley accused Knight Lightning of causing the nationwide crash of the phone system.

Knight Lightning was aghast at this allegation. On the face of it, the suspicion was not entirely implausible—though Knight Lightning knew that he himself hadn't done it. Plenty of hot-dog hackers had bragged that they could crash the phone system, however. Shadowhawk, for instance, the Chicago hacker whom William Cook had recently put in jail, had several times boasted on boards that he could "shut down AT&T's public switched network."

And now this event, or something that looked just like it, had actually taken place. The crash had lit a fire under the Chicago Task Force. And the former fence-sitters at Bellcore and AT&T were now ready to roll. The consensus among telco security— already horrified by the skill of the BellSouth intruders—was that the digital underground was out of hand. LoD and *Phrack* must go.

And in publishing Prophet's E911 Document, *Phrack* had provided law enforcement with what appeared to be a powerful legal weapon.

Foley confronted Knight Lightning about the E911 Document.

Knight Lightning was cowed. He immediately began "cooperating fully" in the usual tradition of the digital underground.

Knight Lightning was grilled for four hours by Foley and his cohorts. He handed over his electronic mailing list of *Phrack* subscribers. He admitted that Prophet had passed him the E911 Document, and he admitted that he had known it was stolen booty from a hacker raid on a telephone company. Knight Lightning signed a statement to this effect and agreed, in writing, to cooperate with investigators.

Next day—January 19, 1990, a Friday—the Secret Service returned with a search warrant and thoroughly searched Knight Lightning's upstairs room in the fraternity house. Interestingly, they left him in possession of his computer, his floppy disks, and his modem. (The computer had no hard disk, and in Foley's judgment was not a store of evidence.) But this was a very minor bright spot among Knight Lightning's rapidly multiplying troubles. By this time he was in plenty of hot water, not only with federal police, prosecutors, telco investigators, and university security, but with the elders of his own campus fraternity, who were outraged to think that they had been unwittingly harboring a federal computer criminal.

On Monday the 29th, Knight Lightning was summoned to Chicago, where he was further grilled by Foley and USSS veteran agent Barbara Golden, this time with an attorney present. And on February 6, he was formally indicted by a federal grand jury.

The trial of Knight Lightning, which occurred on July 24–27, 1990, was the crucial show trial of the Hacker Crackdown. We will examine the trial at some length in Part Four of this book.

In the meantime, we must continue our dogged pursuit of the E911 Document.

It must have been clear by January 1990 that the E911 Document, in the form *Phrack* had published it back in February 1989, had gone off at the speed of light in at least 150 different directions. To attempt to put this electronic genie back in the bottle was flatly impossible.

And yet, the E911 Document was *still* stolen property, formally and legally speaking. Any electronic transference of this document, by anyone unauthorized to have it, could be interpreted as an act of wire fraud. Interstate transfer of stolen property, including electronic property, was a federal crime.

The Chicago Computer Fraud and Abuse Task Force had been assured that the E911 Document was worth a hefty sum of money. In fact, they had a precise estimate of its worth from BellSouth security personnel: $79,449. A sum of this scale seemed to warrant vigorous prosecution. Even if the damage could not be undone, at least this large sum offered a good legal pretext for stern punishment of the thieves. It seemed likely to impress judges and juries. And it could be used in court to mop up the Legion of Doom.

The Atlanta crowd was already in the bag by the time the Chicago Task Force had gotten around to *Phrack*. But the Legion was a hydra-headed thing. In late 1989, a brand-new Legion of Doom board, Phoenix Project, had gone up in Austin, Texas. Phoenix Project was sysoped by no less a man than the Mentor himself, ably assisted by University of Texas student and hardened Doomster "Erik Bloodaxe."

> *The Mentor was a hacker zealot who regarded computer intrusion as something close to a moral duty.*

As we have seen from his *Phrack* manifesto, Mentor was a hacker zealot who regarded computer intrusion as something close to a moral duty. Phoenix Project was an ambitious effort, intended to revive the digital underground to what Mentor considered the full flower of the early 1980s. The Phoenix board would also boldly bring elite hackers face-to-face with the telco "opposition." On Phoenix, America's cleverest hackers supposedly would shame the telco squareheads out of their stick-in-the-mud attitudes and perhaps convince them that the Legion of Doom elite were really an all-right crew. The premiere of Phoenix Project was heavily trumpeted by *Phrack*, and Phoenix Project carried a complete run of *Phrack* issues, including the E911 Document as *Phrack* had published it.

Phoenix Project was only one of many—possibly hundreds—of nodes and boards all over America that were in guilty possession of the E911 Document. But Phoenix was an outright, unashamed Legion of Doom board. Under Mentor's guidance, it was flaunting itself in the face of telco security personnel. Worse yet, it was actively trying to *win them over* as sympathizers for the digital underground elite. Phoenix had no cards or codes on it. Its hacker elite considered Phoenix at least technically legal. But Phoenix was a corrupting influence, where hacker anarchy was eating away like digital acid at the underbelly of corporate propriety.

The Chicago Computer Fraud and Abuse Task Force now prepared to descend upon Austin, Texas.

Oddly, not one but *two* trails of the task force's investigation led toward Austin. The city of Austin, like Atlanta, had made itself a bulwark of the Sunbelt's Information Age, with a strong university research presence and a number of cutting-edge electronics companies, including Motorola, Dell, CompuAdd, IBM, Sematech, and MCC.

Where computing machinery went, hackers generally followed. Austin boasted not only Phoenix Project, currently LoD's most flagrant underground board, but a number of UNIX nodes.

One of these nodes was Elephant, run by a UNIX consultant named Robert Izenberg. Izenberg, in search of a relaxed southern lifestyle and a lower cost of living, had recently migrated to Austin from New Jersey. In New Jersey, Izenberg had worked for an independent contracting company, programming UNIX code for AT&T itself. Terminus had been a frequent user on Izenberg's privately owned Elephant node.

Having interviewed Terminus and examined the records on

Netsys, the Chicago Task Force was now convinced that it had discovered an underground gang of UNIX software pirates that was demonstrably guilty of interstate trafficking in illicitly copied AT&T source code. Izenberg was swept into the dragnet around Terminus, the self-proclaimed ultimate UNIX hacker.

Izenberg, in Austin, had settled down into a UNIX job with a Texan branch of IBM. He was no longer working as a contractor for AT&T, but he had friends in New Jersey, and he still logged on to AT&T UNIX computers back in New Jersey, more or less whenever it pleased him. Izenberg's activities appeared highly suspicious to the task force. He might well be breaking into AT&T computers, swiping AT&T software, and passing it to Terminus and other possible confederates, through the UNIX node network. And this data was worth, not merely $79,499, but hundreds of thousands of dollars!

On February 21, 1990, Robert Izenberg arrived home from work at IBM to find that all the computers had vanished mysteriously from his Austin apartment. Naturally he assumed that he had been robbed. His Elephant node, his other machines, his notebooks, his disks, his tapes, all gone! However, nothing much else seemed disturbed—the place had not been ransacked.

The puzzle became much stranger some five minutes later. Austin U.S. Secret Service Agent Al Soliz, accompanied by University of Texas campus-security officer Larry Coutorie and the ubiquitous Tim Foley, made their appearance at Izenberg's door. They were in plain clothes: slacks, polo shirts. They came in, and Tim Foley accused Izenberg of belonging to the Legion of Doom.

Izenberg told them that he had never heard of the Legion of Doom. And what about a certain stolen E911 Document, which posed a direct threat to the police emergency lines? Izenberg claimed that he'd never heard of that either.

His interrogators found this difficult to believe. Didn't he know Terminus?

Who?

They gave him Terminus' real name. Oh yes, said Izenberg. He knew *that* guy all right—he was leading discussions on the Internet about AT&T computers, especially the AT&T 3B2.

AT&T had thrust this machine into the marketplace, but, like many of AT&T's ambitious attempts to enter the computing arena, the 3B2 project had something less than a glittering success. Izenberg himself had been a contractor for the division of AT&T that supported the 3B2. The entire division had been shut down.

Nowadays, the cheapest and quickest way to get help with this fractious piece of machinery was to join one of Terminus' discussion groups on the Internet, where friendly and knowledgeable hackers would help you for free. Naturally the remarks within this group were less than flattering about the Death Star . . . was *that* the problem?

Foley told Izenberg that Terminus had been acquiring hot software through his, Izenberg's, machine.

Izenberg shrugged this off. A good eight megabytes of data flowed through his UUCP site every day. UUCP nodes spewed data like fire hoses. Elephant had been directly linked to Netsys— not surprising, since Terminus was a 3B2 expert and Izenberg had been a 3B2 contractor. Izenberg was also linked to attctc and the University of Texas. Terminus was a well-known UNIX expert and might have been up to all manner of hijinks on Elephant. Nothing Izenberg could do about that. That was physically impossible. Needle in a haystack.

In a four-hour grilling, Foley urged Izenberg to come clean and admit that he was in conspiracy with Terminus and a member of the Legion of Doom.

Izenberg denied this. He was no weirdo teenage hacker—he was thirty-two years old and didn't even have a "handle." Izenberg was a former TV technician and electronics specialist who had drifted into UNIX consulting as a full-grown adult. Izenberg had never met Terminus physically. He'd once bought a cheap high-speed modem from him, though.

Foley told him that this modem (a Telebit T2500 that ran at

19.2 kilobaud, and which had just gone out Izenberg's door in Secret Service custody) was likely hot property. Izenberg was taken aback to hear this; but then again, most of Izenberg's equipment, like that of most freelance professionals in the industry, was discounted, passed hand-to-hand through various kinds of barter and gray market. There was no proof that the modem was stolen, and even if it was, Izenberg hardly saw how that gave them the right to take every electronic item in his house.

Still, if the U.S. Secret Service figured it needed his computer for national security reasons—or whatever—then Izenberg would not kick. He figured he would somehow make the sacrifice of his twenty thousand dollars' worth of professional equipment, in the spirit of full cooperation and good citizenship.

Robert Izenberg was not arrested. Izenberg was not charged with any crime. His UUCP node—full of some 140 megabytes of the files, mail, and data of himself and his dozen or so entirely innocent users—went out the door as "evidence." Along with the disks and tapes, Izenberg had lost about 800 megabytes of data.

Six months would pass before Izenberg decided to phone the Secret Service and ask how the case was going. That was the first time that Robert Izenberg would ever hear the name of William Cook. As of January 1992, a full two years after the seizure, Izenberg, still not charged with any crime, would be struggling through the morass of the courts, in hope of recovering his thousands of dollars' worth of seized equipment.

In the meantime, the Izenberg case received absolutely no press coverage. The Secret Service had walked into an Austin home, removed a UNIX bulletin board system, and met with no operational difficulties whatsoever.

Except that word of a crackdown had percolated through the Legion of Doom. The Mentor voluntarily shut down the Phoenix Project. It seemed a pity, especially as telco security employees had, in fact, shown up on Phoenix, just as he had hoped—along with the usual motley crowd of LoD heavies, hangers-on, phreaks, hackers, and wannabes. There was "Sandy" Sandquist from U.S. Sprint security, and some guy named Henry Kluepfel, from

Bellcore itself! Kluepfel had been trading friendly banter with hackers on Phoenix since January 30 (two weeks after the Martin Luther King Day Crash). The presence of such a stellar telco official seemed quite the coup for Phoenix Project.

Still, Mentor could judge the climate. Atlanta in ruins, *Phrack* in deep trouble, something weird going on with UNIX nodes— discretion was advisable. Phoenix Project went off-line.

Kluepfel, of course, had been monitoring this LoD bulletin board for his own purposes—and those of the Chicago unit. As far back as June 1987, Kluepfel had logged on to a Texas underground board called Phreak Klass 2600. There he'd discovered a Chicago youngster named "Shadowhawk," strutting and boasting about rifling AT&T computer files, and bragging of his ambitions to riddle AT&T's Bellcore computers with Trojan horse programs. Kluepfel had passed the news to Cook in Chicago, Shadowhawk's computers had gone out the door in Secret Service custody, and Shadowhawk himself had gone to jail.

Now it was Phoenix Project's turn. Phoenix Project postured about "legality" and "merely intellectual interest," but it reeked of the underground. It had *Phrack* on it. It had the E911 Document. It had a lot of dicey talk about breaking into systems, including some bold and reckless stuff about a supposed "decryption service" that Mentor and friends were planning to run, to help crack encrypted passwords off of hacked systems.

Mentor was an adult. There was a bulletin board at his place of work as well. Kleupfel logged onto this board too and discovered it was called Illuminati. It was run by some company called Steve Jackson Games.

On March 1, 1990, the Austin crackdown went into high gear.

On the morning of March 1—a Thursday—twenty-one-year-old University of Texas student Erik Bloodaxe, co-sysop of Phoenix Project and an avowed member of the Legion of Doom, was wakened by a police revolver leveled at his head.

Bloodaxe watched, jittery, as Secret Service agents appropriated his 300 baud terminal and, rifling his files, discovered his treasured source code for Robert Morris' notorious Internet worm. But Bloodaxe, a wily operator, had suspected that something like this might be coming. All his best equipment had been hidden away elsewhere. The raiders took everything electronic, however, including his telephone. They were stymied by his hefty arcade-style Pac-Man game and left it in place, as it was simply too heavy to move.

Bloodaxe was not arrested. He was not charged with any crime. A good two years later, the police still had what they had taken from him, however.

> *The 21-year-old University of Texas student was wakened by a police revolver leveled at his head.*

The Mentor was less wary. The dawn raid rousted him and his wife from bed in their underwear, and six Secret Service agents, accompanied by an Austin policeman and Henry Kluepfel himself, made a rich haul. Off went the works, into the agents' white Chevrolet minivan: an IBM PC AT clone with 4 meg of RAM and a 120-meg hard disk; a Hewlett-Packard LaserJet II printer; a completely legitimate and highly expensive SCO-Xenix 286 operating system; Pagemaker disks and documentation; and a Microsoft Word word processing program. Mentor's wife had her incomplete academic thesis stored on the hard disk; that went too, and so did the couple's telephone. As of two years later, all this property remained in police custody.

Mentor remained under guard in his apartment as agents prepared to raid Steve Jackson Games. The fact that this was a business headquarters and not a private residence did not deter the agents. It was still very early; no one was at work yet. The agents prepared to break down the door, but Mentor, eavesdropping on the Secret Service walkie-talkie traffic, begged them not to do it and offered his key to the building.

The exact details of the next events are unclear. The agents would not let anyone else into the building. Their search warrant, when produced was unsigned. Apparently they breakfasted from the local Whataburger, as the litter from hamburgers was later found inside. They also sampled extensively a bag of jellybeans kept by an SJG employee. Someone tore a "Dukakis for President" sticker from the wall.

SJG employees, diligently showing up for the day's work, were met at the door and briefly questioned by U.S. Secret Service agents. The employees watched in astonishment as agents wielding crowbars and screwdrivers emerged with captive machines. They attacked outdoor storage units with boltcutters. The agents wore blue nylon windbreakers with SECRET SERVICE stenciled across the back, with running shoes and jeans.

Jackson's company lost three computers, several hard disks, hundreds of floppy disks, two monitors, three modems, a laser printer, various power cords, cables, and adapters (and, oddly, a small bag of screws, bolts, and nuts). The seizure of Illuminati BBS deprived SJG of all the programs, text files, and private e-mail on the board. The loss of two other SJG computers was a severe blow as well, because it caused the loss of electronically stored contracts, financial projections, address directories, mailing lists, personnel files, business correspondence, and, not least, the drafts of forthcoming games and gaming books.

No one at Steve Jackson Games was arrested. No one was accused of any crime. No charges were filed. Everything appropriated was officially kept as "evidence" of crimes never specified.

After the *Phrack* show trial, the Steve Jackson Games scandal was the most bizarre and aggravating incident of the Hacker Crackdown of 1990. This raid by the Chicago Task Force on a science-fiction gaming publisher was to rouse a swarming host of civil liberties issues and gave rise to an enduring controversy that was still recomplicating itself, and growing in the scope of its implications, a full two years later.

The pursuit of the E911 Document stopped with the Steve Jackson Games raid. As we have seen, there were hundreds, perhaps thousands of computer users in America with the E911 Document in their possession. Theoretically, the task force had a perfect legal right to raid any of these people, and legally could have seized the machines of anybody who subscribed to *Phrack*.

However, there was no copy of the E911 Document on Jackson's Illuminati board. And there the Chicago raiders stopped dead; they have not raided anyone since.

It might be assumed that Rich Andrews and Charlie Boykin, who had brought the E911 Document to the attention of telco security, might be spared any official suspicion. But as we have seen, the willingness to "cooperate fully" offers little, if any, assurance against federal antihacker prosecution.

Richard Andrews found himself in deep trouble, thanks to the E911 Document. Andrews lived in Illinois, the native stomping grounds of the Chicago Task Force. On February 3 and 6, both his home and his place of work were raided by USSS. His machines went out the door too, and he was grilled at length (though not arrested). Andrews proved to be in purportedly guilty possession of: UNIX SVR 3.2; UNIX SVR 3.1; UUCP; PMON; WWB; IWB; DWB; NROFF; KORN SHELL '88; C++; and QUEST, among other items. Andrews had received this proprietary code—which AT&T officially valued at well over $250,000—through the UNIX network, much of it supplied to him by Terminus as a personal favor. Perhaps worse yet, Andrews admitted to returning the favor, by passing Terminus a copy of AT&T proprietary STAR-LAN source code.

Even Charles Boykin, himself an AT&T employee, entered some very hot water. By 1990, he'd almost forgotten about the E911 problem he'd reported in September 1988; in fact, since that date, he'd passed two more security alerts to Jerry Dalton, concerning matters that Boykin considered far worse than the E911 Document.

But by 1990, year of the crackdown, AT&T Corporate Information Security was fed up with Killer. This machine offered no direct income to AT&T and was providing aid and comfort to a cloud of suspicious yokels from outside the company, some of them actively malicious toward AT&T, its property, and its corporate interests. Whatever goodwill and publicity had been won among Killer's 1,500 devoted users was considered no longer worth the security risk. On February 20, 1990, Jerry Dalton arrived in Dallas and simply unplugged the phone jacks, to the puzzled alarm of Killer's many Texan users. Killer went permanently off-line, with the loss of vast archives of programs and huge quantities of electronic mail; it was never restored to service. AT&T showed no particular regard for the "property" of these 1,500 people. Whatever "property" the users had been storing on AT&T's computer simply vanished completely.

Boykin, who had himself reported the E911 problem, now found himself under a cloud of suspicion. In a weird private-security replay of the Secret Service seizures, Boykin's own home was visited by AT&T Security and his own machines were carried out the door.

However, there were marked special features in the Boykin case. Boykin's disks and his personal computers were examined swiftly by his corporate employers and returned politely in just two days (unlike Secret Service seizures, which commonly take months or years). Boykin was not charged with any crime or wrongdoing, and he kept his job with AT&T (though he retired in September 1991, at the age of fifty-two).

It's interesting to note that the U.S. Secret Service somehow failed to seize Boykin's Killer node and carry AT&T's own computer out the door. Nor did they raid his home. They seemed perfectly willing to take the word of AT&T Security that AT&T's employee and AT&T's Killer node were free of hacker contraband and on the up-and-up.

It's digital water-under-the-bridge at this point, as Killer's 3,200 megabytes of Texan electronic community were erased in 1990 and Killer itself was shipped out of the state.

But the experiences of Andrews and Boykin, and the users of their systems, remained side issues. They did not begin to assume the social, political, and legal importance that gathered, slowly but inexorably, around the issue of the raid on Steve Jackson Games.

We must now turn our attention to Steve Jackson Games itself, and explain what SJG was, what it really did, and how it had managed to attract this particularly odd and virulent kind of trouble. The reader may recall that this is not the first but the second time that the company has appeared in this narrative; a Steve Jackson game called GURPS was a favorite pastime of Atlanta hacker Urvile, and Urvile's science-fictional gaming notes had been mixed up promiscuously with notes about his actual computer intrusions.

First, Steve Jackson Games, Inc., was *not* a publisher of "computer games." SJG published "simulation games," parlor games that were played on paper, with pencils, and dice, and printed guidebooks full of rules and statistics tables. No computers were involved in the games themselves. When you bought a Steve Jackson Game, you did not receive any software disks. What you got was a plastic bag with some cardboard game tokens, maybe a few maps or a deck of cards. Most of the products were books.

However, computers *were* deeply involved in the Steve Jackson Games business. Like almost all modern publishers, Steve Jackson and his fifteen employees used computers to write text, keep accounts, and run the business generally. They also used a computer to run their official bulletin board system for Steve Jackson Games, a board called Illuminati. On Illuminati, simulation gamers who happened to own computers and modems could associate, trade mail, debate the theory and practice of gaming, and keep up with the company's news and its product announcements.

Illuminati was a modestly popular board, run on a small computer with limited storage, only one phone line, and no ties to large-scale computer networks. It did, however, have hundreds of users, many of them dedicated gamers willing to call from out of state.

Illuminati was *not* an "underground" board. It did not feature hints on computer intrusion, or "anarchy files," or illicitly posted credit card numbers, or long-distance access codes. Some of Illuminati's users, however, were members of the Legion of Doom. And so was one of Steve Jackson's senior employees—the Mentor. Mentor wrote for *Phrack* and also ran an underground board,

Phoenix Project—but Mentor was not a computer professional. Mentor was the managing editor of Steve Jackson Games and a professional game designer by trade. These LoD members did not use Illuminati to help their *hacking* activities. They used it to help their *game-playing* activities—and they were even more dedicated to simulation gaming than they were to hacking.

> *Illuminati involved flying saucers, the CIA, the KGB, the phone companies, the Ku Klux Klan, and the Boy Scouts.*

Illuminati got its name from a card game that Steve Jackson himself, the company's founder and sole owner, had invented. This multiplayer card game was one of Mr. Jackson's best-known, most successful, most technically innovative products. Illuminati was a game of paranoiac conspiracy in which various antisocial cults warred covertly to dominate the world. Illuminati was hilarious, and great fun to play, involving flying saucers, the CIA, the KGB, the phone companies, the Ku Klux Klan, South American Nazis, cocaine cartels, the Boy Scouts, and dozens of other splinter groups from the twisted depths of Mr. Jackson's professionally fervid imagination. For the uninitiated, any public discussion of the Illuminati card game sounded, by turns, utterly menacing or completely insane.

And then there was SJG's Car Wars, in which souped-up armored hot rods with rocket launchers and heavy machine guns did battle on the American highways of the future. The lively Car Wars discussion on the Illuminati board featured many meticulous, painstaking discussions of the effects of grenades, landmines, flamethrowers, and napalm. It sounded like hacker anarchy files run amuck.

Mr. Jackson and his coworkers earned their daily bread by supplying people with make-believe adventures and weird ideas. The more far-out, the better.

Simulation gaming is an unusual hobby, but gamers have not generally had to beg the permission of the Secret Service to exist.

Wargames and role-playing adventures are an old and honored pastime, much favored by professional military strategists. Once little known, these games are now played by hundreds of thousands of enthusiasts throughout North America, Europe, and Japan. Gaming books, once restricted to hobby outlets, now commonly appear in chain stores such as B. Dalton's and Waldenbooks, and sell vigorously.

Steve Jackson Games, Inc., of Austin, Texas, was a games company of the middle rank. In 1989, SJG grossed about a million dollars. Jackson himself had a good reputation in his industry as a talented and innovative designer of rather unconventional games, but his company was something less than a titan of the field—certainly not like the multimillion-dollar TSR Inc., or Britain's gigantic Games Workshop.

SJG's Austin headquarters was a modest two-story brick office suite, cluttered with phones, photocopiers, fax machines, and computers. It bustled with semiorganized activity and was littered with glossy promotional brochures and dog-eared science-fiction novels. Attached to the offices was a large tin-roofed warehouse piled twenty feet high with cardboard boxes of games and books. Despite the weird imaginings that went on within it, the SJG headquarters was quite a quotidian, everyday sort of place. It looked like what it was: a publisher's digs.

Both Car Wars and Illuminati were well-known, popular games. But the mainstay of the Jackson organization was their Generic Universal Role-Playing System, "GURPS." The GURPS system was considered solid and well designed, an asset for players. But perhaps the most popular feature of the GURPS system was that it allowed gaming masters to design scenarios that closely resembled well-known books, movies, and other works of fantasy. Jackson had licensed and adapted works from many science fiction and fantasy authors. There was *GURPS Conan*, *GURPS Riverworld*, *GURPS Horseclans*, *GURPS Witch World*, names eminently familiar to science-fiction readers. And there was *GURPS Special Ops*, from the world of espionage fantasy and unconventional warfare.

And then there was GURPS *Cyberpunk*.

"Cyberpunk" was a term given to certain science-fiction writers who had entered the genre in the 1980s. Cyberpunk, as the label implies, had two general distinguishing features. First, its writers had a compelling interest in information technology, an interest closely akin to science fiction's earlier fascination with space travel. And second, these writers were "punks," with all the distinguishing features that that implies: Bohemian artiness, youth run wild, an air of deliberate rebellion, funny clothes and hair, odd politics, a fondness for abrasive rock and roll; in a word, trouble.

The cyberpunk SF writers were a small group of mostly college-educated white middle-class litterateurs, scattered through the United States and Canada. Only one, Rudy Rucker, a professor of computer science in Silicon Valley, could rank with even the humblest computer hacker. Except for Professor Rucker, the cyberpunk authors were not programmers or hardware experts; they considered themselves artists (as, indeed, did Professor Rucker). However, these writers all owned computers, and took an intense and public interest in the social ramifications of the information industry.

The cyberpunks had a strong following among the global generation that had grown up in a world of computers, multinational networks, and cable television. Their outlook was considered somewhat morbid, cynical, and dark, but then again, so was the outlook of their generational peers. As that generation matured and increased in strength and influence, so did the cyberpunks. As science-fiction writers went, they were doing fairly well for themselves. By the late 1980s, their work had attracted attention from gaming companies, including Steve Jackson Games, which was planning a cyberpunk simulation for the flourishing GURPS gaming system.

The time seemed ripe for such a product, which had already been proven in the marketplace. The first games company out of the gate, with a product boldly called Cyberpunk in defiance of possible infringement-of-copyright suits, had been an upstart group called R. Talsorian. Talsorian's Cyberpunk was a fairly decent game, but the mechanics of the simulation system left a lot to be desired. Commercially, however, the game did very well.

The next cyberpunk game had been the even more successful Shadowrun by FASA Corporation. The mechanics of this game were fine, but the scenario was rendered moronic by sappy fantasy elements such as elves, trolls, wizards, and dragons—all highly ideologically incorrect, according to the hard-edged, high-tech standards of cyberpunk science fiction.

Other game designers were chomping at the bit. Prominent among them was the Mentor, a gentleman who, like most of his friends in the Legion of Doom, was quite the cyberpunk devotee. Mentor reasoned that the time had come for a *real* cyberpunk gaming book—one that the princes of computer-mischief in the Legion of Doom could play without laughing themselves sick. This book, GURPS *Cyberpunk*, would reek of culturally on-line authenticity.

Mentor was particularly well qualified for this task. Naturally, he knew far more about computer intrusion and digital skullduggery than any previously published cyberpunk author. Not only that, but he was good at his work. A vivid imagination combined with an instinctive feeling for the working of systems and, especially, the loopholes within them are excellent qualities for a professional game designer.

By March 1, GURPS *Cyberpunk* was almost complete, ready to print and ship. Steve Jackson expected vigorous sales for this item, which, he hoped, would keep the company financially afloat for several months. GURPS *Cyberpunk*, like the other GURPS "modules," was not a "game" like a Monopoly set, but a *book:* a bound paperback book the size of a glossy magazine, with a slick color cover, and pages full of text, illustrations, tables, and footnotes. It was advertised as a game and was used as an aid to game-playing, but it was a book, with an ISBN number, published in Texas, copyrighted, and sold in bookstores.

And now that book, stored on a computer, had gone out the door in the custody of the Secret Service.

The day after the raid, Steve Jackson visited the local Secret Service headquarters with a lawyer in tow. There he confronted Tim Foley (still in Austin at that time) and demanded his book back. But there was trouble. *GURPS Cyberpunk,* alleged a Secret Service agent to astonished businessman Steve Jackson, was "a manual for computer crime."

"It's science fiction," Jackson said.

"No, this is real." This statement was repeated several times, by several agents. Jackson's ominously accurate game had passed from pure, obscure, small-scale fantasy into the impure, highly publicized, large-scale fantasy of the Hacker Crackdown.

No mention was made of the real reason for the search. According to their search warrant, the raiders had expected to find the E911 Document stored on Jackson's bulletin board system. But that warrant was sealed—a procedure that most law enforcement agencies will use only when lives are demonstrably in danger. The raiders' motives were not discovered until the Jackson search warrant was unsealed by his lawyers many months later. The Secret Service, and the Chicago Computer Fraud and Abuse Task Force, said absolutely nothing to Steve Jackson about any threat to the police 911 System. They said nothing about the Atlanta Three, nothing about *Phrack* or Knight Lightning, nothing about Terminus.

Jackson was left to believe that his computers had been seized because he intended to publish a science-fiction book that law enforcement considered too dangerous to see print.

This misconception was repeated again and again, for months, to an ever-widening public audience. It was not the truth of the case; but as months passed, and this misconception was printed again and again publicly, it became one of the few publicly known "facts" about the mysterious Hacker Crackdown. The Secret Service had seized a computer to stop the publication of a cyberpunk science-fiction book.

The second section of this book, "The Digital Underground," is almost finished now. We have become acquainted with all the major figures of this case who actually belong to the underground milieu of computer intrusion. We have some idea of their history, their motives, their general modus operandi. We now know, I hope, who they are, where they came from, and more or less what they want. In the next section of this book, "Law and Order," we leave this milieu and directly enter the world of America's computer-crime police.

> *The Secret Service had seized a computer to stop the publication of a "cyberpunk" science-fiction book.*

At this point, however, I have another figure to introduce: myself.

My name is Bruce Sterling. I live in Austin, Texas, where I am a science-fiction writer by trade: specifically, a *cyberpunk* science-fiction writer.

Like my cyberpunk colleagues in the United States and Canada, I've never been entirely happy with this literary label—especially after it became a synonym for a computer criminal. But I did once edit a book of stories by my colleagues, called *Mirrorshades: The Cyberpunk Anthology*, and I've long been a writer of literary-critical cyberpunk manifestos. I am not a hacker of any description, though I do have readers in the digital underground.

When the Steve Jackson Games seizure occurred, I naturally took an intense interest. If cyberpunk books were being banned by federal police in my own hometown, I reasonably wondered whether I myself might be next. Would my computer be seized by the Secret Service? At the time, I was in possession of an aging Apple IIe without so much as a hard disk. If I were to be raided as an author of computer-crime manuals, the loss of my feeble word processor would likely provoke more snickers than sympathy.

I'd known Steve Jackson for many years. We knew one another as colleagues, for we frequented the same local science-fiction conventions. I'd played Jackson games and recognized his cleverness; but he certainly had never struck me as a potential mastermind of computer crime.

I also knew a little about computer bulletin board systems. In the mid-1980s I had taken an active role in an Austin board named SMOF-BBS, one of the first boards dedicated to science fiction. I had a modem, and on occasion I'd logged on to Illuminati, which always looked entertainingly wacky but certainly harmless enough.

At the time of the Jackson seizure, I had no experience whatsoever with underground boards. But I knew that no one on Illuminati talked about breaking into systems illegally or about robbing phone companies. Illuminati didn't even offer pirated computer games. Steve Jackson, like many creative artists, was markedly touchy about theft of intellectual property.

It seemed to me that Jackson was either seriously suspected of some crime—in which case, he would be charged soon, and would have his day in court—or else he was innocent, in which case the Secret Service would quickly return his equipment and everyone would have a good laugh. I rather expected the good laugh. The situation was not without its comic side. The raid, known as the "Cyberpunk Bust" in the science-fiction community, was winning a great deal of free national publicity both for Jackson himself and the cyberpunk science-fiction writers generally.

Besides, science-fiction people are used to being misinterpreted. Science fiction is a colorful, disreputable, slipshod occupation, full of unlikely oddballs, which, of course, is why we like it. Weirdness can be an occupational hazard in our field. People who wear Halloween costumes are sometimes mistaken for monsters.

Once upon a time—back in 1939, in New York City—science fiction and the U.S. Secret Service collided in a comic case of mistaken identity. This weird incident involved a literary group quite famous in science fiction, known as "the Futurians," whose membership included such future genre greats as Isaac Asimov, Frederik Pohl, and Damon Knight. The Futurians were every bit as offbeat and wacky as any of their spiritual descendants, includ-

ing the cyberpunks, and were given to communal living, spontaneous group renditions of light opera, and midnight fencing
exhibitions on the lawn. The Futurians didn't have bulletin board
systems, but they did have the technological equivalent in 1939
—mimeographs and a private printing press. These were in steady
use, producing a stream of science-fiction fan magazines, literary
manifestos, and weird articles, which were picked up in ink-sticky
bundles by a succession of strange, gangly, spotty young men in
fedoras and overcoats.

The neighbors grew alarmed at the antics of the Futurians and
reported them to the Secret Service as suspected counterfeiters.
In the winter of 1939, a squad of USSS agents with drawn guns
burst into Futurian House, prepared to confiscate the forged currency and illicit printing presses. There they discovered a slum-
bering science-fiction fan named George Hahn, a guest of the
Futurian commune who had just arrived in New York. Hahn managed to explain himself and his group, and the Secret Service
agents left the Futurians in peace henceforth. (Alas, Hahn died in
1991, just before I had discovered this astonishing historical parallel and just before I could interview him for this book.)

But the Jackson case did not come to a swift and comic end.
No quick answers came his way, or mine; no swift reassurances
that all was right in the digital world, that matters were well in
hand after all. Quite the opposite. In my alternate role as a sometime pop-science journalist, I interviewed Jackson and his staff
for an article for a British magazine. The strange details of the
raid left me more concerned than ever. Without its computers,
the company had been crippled financially and operationally.
Half the SJG workforce, a group of entirely innocent people, had
been fired, deprived of their livelihoods by the seizure. It began to
dawn on me that authors—American writers—might well have
their computers seized, under sealed warrants, without any criminal charge; and that, as Steve Jackson had discovered, there was
no immediate recourse for this. This was no joke; this wasn't
science fiction; this was real.

I determined to put science fiction aside until I had discovered what had happened and where this trouble had come from. It was time to enter the purportedly real world of electronic free expression and computer crime. Hence, this book. Hence, the world of the telcos; and the world of the digital underground; and next, the world of the police.

PART

3

LAW
AND ORDER

Of the various antihacker activities of 1990, Operation Sundevil had by far the highest public profile. The sweeping, nationwide computer seizures of May 8, 1990, were unprecedented in scope and highly, if rather selectively, publicized.

Unlike the efforts of the Chicago Computer Fraud and Abuse Task Force, Operation Sundevil was not intended to combat hacking in the sense of computer intrusion or sophisticated raids on telco switching stations. Nor did it have anything to do with hacker misdeeds with AT&T's software or with Southern Bell's proprietary documents.

Instead, Operation Sundevil was a crackdown on those traditional scourges of the digital underground: credit card theft and telephone code abuse. The ambitious activities out of Chicago, and the somewhat lesser-known but vigorous antihacker actions of the New York State Police in 1990, were never a part of Operation Sundevil per se, which was based in Arizona.

Nevertheless, after the spectacular May 8 raids, the public, misled by police secrecy, hacker panic, and a puzzled national press corps, conflated all aspects of the nationwide crackdown in 1990 under the blanket term Operation Sundevil. "Sundevil" is still the best-known synonym for the crackdown. But the Arizona organizers of Sundevil really did not deserve this reputation—any more, for instance, than all hackers deserve a reputation as hackers.

There was some justice in this confused perception, though. For one thing, the confusion was abetted by the Washington office of the Secret Service, which responded to Freedom of Information Act requests on Operation Sundevil by referring investigators to the publicly known cases of Knight Lightning and the Atlanta Three. And Sundevil was certainly the largest aspect of the crackdown, the most deliberate and the best organized. As a crackdown on electronic fraud, Sundevil lacked the frantic pace of the war on the Legion of Doom; on the contrary, Sundevil's targets were picked out with cool deliberation over an elaborate investigation lasting two full years.

And once again the targets were bulletin board systems.

Boards can be powerful aids to organized fraud. Underground boards carry lively, extensive, detailed, and often quite flagrant "discussions" of lawbreaking techniques and lawbreaking activities. "Discussing" crime in the abstract, or "discussing" the particulars of criminal cases, is not illegal—but there are stern state and federal laws against coldbloodedly conspiring in groups in order to commit crimes.

In the eyes of police, people who actively conspire to break the law are not regarded as "clubs," "debating salons," "users' groups," or "free speech advocates." Rather, such people tend to find themselves formally indicted by prosecutors as "gangs," "racketeers," "corrupt organizations," and "organized crime figures."

What's more, the illicit data contained on outlaw boards goes well beyond mere acts of speech and/or possible criminal conspiracy. As we have seen, it was common practice in the digital underground to post purloined telephone codes on boards, for any phreak or hacker who cared to abuse them. Is posting digital booty of this sort supposed to be protected by the First Amendment? Hardly—though the issue, like most issues in cyberspace, is not entirely resolved. Some theorists argue that merely to *recite* a number publicly is not illegal—only its *use* is illegal. But antihacker police point out that magazines and newspapers (more traditional forms of free expression) never publish stolen telephone codes (even though this might well raise their circulation).

Stolen credit card numbers, being riskier and more valuable, were posted publicly less often on boards—but there is no question that some underground boards carried "carding" traffic, generally exchanged through private mail.

Underground boards also carried handy programs for "scanning" telephone codes and raiding credit card companies, as well as the usual obnoxious galaxy of pirated software, cracked passwords, blue-box schematics, intrusion manuals, anarchy files, porn files, and so forth.

But besides their nuisance potential for the spread of illicit knowledge, bulletin boards have another vitally interesting aspect for the professional investigator. Bulletin boards are cram-full of *evidence*. All that busy trading of electronic mail, all those hacker boasts, brags, and struts, even the stolen codes and cards, can be neat, electronic, real-time recordings of criminal activity.

As an investigator, when you seize a pirate board, you have scored a coup as effective as tapping phones or intercepting mail. However, you have not actually tapped a phone or intercepted a letter. The rules of evidence regarding phone taps and mail interceptions are old, stern, and well understood by police, prosecutors and defense attorneys alike. The rules of evidence regarding boards are new, waffling, and understood by nobody at all.

> *The rules of evidence regarding bulletin boards are understood by nobody at all.*

Sundevil was the largest crackdown on boards in world history. On May 7, 8, and 9, 1990, about forty-two computer systems were seized. Of those forty-two computers, about twenty-five actually were running boards. (The vagueness of this estimate is attributable to the vagueness of [a] what a "computer system" is, and [b] what it actually means to "run a board" with one—or with two—computers, or with three.)

About twenty-five boards vanished into police custody in May 1990. As we have seen, there are an estimated 30,000 boards in America today. If we assume that one board in a hundred is up to no good with codes and cards (which rather flatters the honesty of the board-using community), then that would leave 2,975 outlaw boards untouched by Sundevil. Sundevil seized about one-tenth of 1 percent of all computer bulletin boards in America. Seen objectively, this is something less than a comprehensive assault. In 1990, Sundevil's organizers—the team at the Phoenix Secret Service office and the Arizona attorney general's office— had a list of at least *three hundred* boards that they considered fully deserving of search and seizure warrants. The twenty-five boards actually seized were merely among the most obvious and egregious of this much larger list of candidates. All these boards had been examined beforehand—either by informants, who had passed printouts to the Secret Service, or by Secret Service agents themselves, who not only come equipped with modems but know how to use them.

There were a number of motives for Sundevil. First, it offered a chance to get ahead of the curve on wire-fraud crimes. Tracking back credit card ripoffs to their perpetrators can be appallingly difficult. If these miscreants have any kind of electronic sophistication, they can snarl their tracks through the phone network into a mind-boggling, untraceable mess, while still managing to "reach out and rob someone." Boards, however, full of brags and boasts, codes and cards, offer evidence in the handy congealed form.

Seizures themselves—the mere physical removal of machines —tend to take the pressure off. During Sundevil, a large number of code kids, warez d00dz, and credit card thieves would be deprived of those boards—their means of community and conspiracy—in one swift blow. As for the sysops themselves (commonly among the boldest offenders), they would be stripped directly of their computer equipment, and rendered digitally mute and blind.

And this aspect of Sundevil was carried out with great success. Sundevil seems to have been a complete tactical surprise—unlike the fragmentary and continuing seizures of the war on the Legion of Doom, Sundevil was precisely timed and utterly overwhelming. At least forty "computers" were seized during May 7, 8, and 9, 1990, in Cincinnati, Detroit, Los Angeles, Miami, Newark, Phoenix, Tucson, Richmond, San Diego, San Jose, Pittsburgh, and San Francisco. Some cities saw multiple raids, such as the five separate raids in the New York City environs. Plano, Texas, (essentially a suburb of the Dallas/Fort Worth metroplex and a hub of the telecommunications industry) saw four computer seizures. Chicago, ever in the forefront, saw its own local Sundevil raid, briskly carried out by Secret Service agents Timothy Foley and Barbara Golden.

Many of these raids occurred not in the cities proper, but in associated white middle-class suburbs—places such as Mount Lebanon, Pennsylvania, and Clark Lake, Michigan. There were a few raids on offices; most took place in people's homes, the classic hacker basements and bedrooms.

The Sundevil raids were searches and seizures, not a group of mass arrests. Only four arrests took place. "Tony the Trashman," a longtime teenage bête noire of the Arizona Racketeering unit, was arrested in Tucson on May 9. "Dr. Ripco," sysop of an outlaw

158 aaaaaaaaaaaaaaaaaaaaaaaaaaaaaa THE HACKER CRACKDOWN

board with the misfortune to exist in Chicago itself, was also arrested—on illegal weapons charges. Local units also arrested a nineteen-year-old female phone phreak named "Electra" in Pennsylvania and a male juvenile in California. Federal agents, however, were not seeking arrests, but computers.

Hackers generally are not indicted (if at all) until the evidence in their seized computers is evaluated—a process that can take weeks, months, even years. When hackers are arrested on the spot, it's generally for other reasons. Drugs and/or illegal weapons show up in a good third of antihacker computer seizures. The Sundevil raid in Chicago discovered unregistered handguns; the Californian teenager had illicit drugs.

That scofflaw teenage hackers (or their parents) should have marijuana in their homes is probably not a shocking revelation, but the surprisingly common presence of illegal firearms in hacker dens is a bit disquieting. A personal computer can be a great equalizer for the techno-cowboy—much like that more traditional American "Great Equalizer," the personal sixgun. Maybe it's not all that surprising that some guy obsessed with power through illicit technology would also have a few illicit high-velocity-impact devices around. An element of the digital underground particularly dotes on those "anarchy philes," and this element tends to shade into the crackpot milieu of survivalists, gun nuts, anarcho-leftists, and the ultra-libertarian right wing.

This is not to say that hacker raids to date have uncovered any major crack dens or illegal arsenals; but Secret Service agents do not regard hackers as "just kids." They regard hackers as unpredictable people, bright and slippery. It doesn't help matters that the hacker himself has been "hiding behind his keyboard" all this time. Commonly, police have no idea what he looks like. This makes him an unknown quantity, someone best treated with proper caution.

To date, no hacker has come out shooting, though hackers sometimes do brag on boards that they will do just that. Threats of this sort are taken seriously. Secret Service hacker raids tend to be swift, comprehensive, and well manned (even overmanned); agents generally burst through every door in the home at once, sometimes with drawn guns. Any potential resistance is quelled swiftly. Hacker raids are usually raids on people's homes. It can be a very dangerous business to raid an American home; people can panic when strangers invade their sanctum. Statistically speaking, the most dangerous thing a police officer can do is to enter someone's home. (The second most dangerous thing is to stop a car in traffic.) People have guns in their homes. More cops are hurt in homes than are ever hurt in biker bars or massage parlors.

But in any case, no one was hurt during Sundevil, or indeed during any part of the Hacker Crackdown.

Nor were there any allegations of any physical mistreatment of a suspect. Guns were pointed, interrogations were sharp and prolonged; but no one in 1990 claimed any act of brutality by any crackdown raider.

In addition to the forty or so computers, Sundevil reaped floppy disks in particularly great abundance—an estimated 23,000 of them, which naturally included every manner of illegitimate data: pirated games, stolen codes, hot credit card numbers, the complete text and software of entire pirate bulletin boards. These floppy disks, which remain in police custody today, offer a gigantic, almost embarrassingly rich source of possible criminal indictments. These 23,000 floppy disks also include a thus-far unknown quantity of legitimate computer games, legitimate software, purportedly "private" mail from boards, business records, and personal correspondence of all kinds.

Standard computer-crime search warrants lay great emphasis on seizing written documents as well as computers—specifically including photocopies, computer printouts, telephone bills, address books, logs, notes, memoranda, and correspondence. In practice, this has meant that diaries, gaming magazines, software documentation, nonfiction books on hacking and computer security, sometimes even science-fiction novels have all vanished out the door in police custody. A wide variety of electronic items have been known to vanish as well, including telephones, televisions, answering machines, Sony Walkmans, desktop printers, compact disks, and audiotapes.

No fewer than 150 members of the Secret Service were sent into the field during Sundevil. They frequently were accompanied by squads of local and/or state police. Most of these officers —especially the locals—had never been on an antihacker raid before. (This was one reason, in fact, why so many of them were invited along in the first place.) Also, the presence of a uniformed police officer assures the raidees that the people entering their homes are, in fact, police. Secret Service agents wear plain clothes. So do the telco security experts who commonly accompany the Secret Service on raids (and who make no particular effort to identify themselves as mere employees of telephone companies).

A typical hacker raid goes something like this. First, police storm in rapidly, through every entrance, with overwhelming force, in the assumption that this tactic will keep casualties to a minimum. Second, possible suspects are removed immediately from the vicinity of any and all computer systems, so that they will have no chance to purge or destroy evidence. Suspects are herded into a room without computers, commonly the living room, and kept under guard—not *armed* guard, for the guns are swiftly holstered, but under guard nevertheless. They are presented with the search warrant and warned that anything they say may be held against them. Commonly they have a great deal to say, especially if they are unsuspecting parents.

Somewhere in the house is the "hot spot"—a computer tied to a phone line (possibly several computers and several phones). Commonly it's a teenager's bedroom, but it can be anywhere in the house; there may be several such rooms. This "hot spot" is put in the charge of a two-agent team, the "finder" and the "recorder." The finder is computer-trained, commonly the case agent who actually obtained the search warrant from a judge. He or she understands what is being sought and actually carries out the seizures: unplugs machines, opens drawers, desks, files, floppy-disk containers, and so on. The recorder photographs all the equipment, just as it stands—especially the tangle of wired connections in the back, which can otherwise be a real nightmare to restore. The recorder also commonly photographs every room in the house, lest some wily criminal claim that the police had robbed him during the search. Some recorders also carry video-cams or tape recorders; however, it's more common for the recorder simply to take written notes. Objects are described and numbered as the finder seizes them, generally on standard preprinted police inventory forms.

Even Secret Service agents were not, and are not, expert computer users. They have not made, and do not make, judgments on the fly about potential threats posed by various forms of equipment. They may exercise discretion; they may leave Dad his computer, for instance, but they don't *have* to. Standard computer-crime search warrants, which date back to the early 1980s, use a sweeping language that targets computers, most anything attached to a computer, most anything used to operate a computer—most anything that remotely resembles a computer—plus most any and all written documents surrounding it. Computer-crime investigators have strongly urged agents to seize the works.

In this sense, Operation Sundevil appears to have been a complete success. Boards went down all over America and were shipped en masse to the computer investigation lab of the Secret Service, in Washington, D.C., along with the 23,000 floppy disks and unknown quantities of printed material.

But the seizure of twenty-five boards and the multimegabyte mountains of possibly useful evidence contained in these boards (and in their owners' other computers, also out the door) were far from the only motives for Operation Sundevil. An unprecedented action of great ambition and size, Sundevil's motives can only be described as political. It was a public relations effort, meant to pass certain messages, meant to make certain situations clear: both in the mind of the general public and in the minds of various constituencies of the electronic community.

First—and this motivation was vital—a "message" would be sent from law enforcement to the digital underground. This very message was recited in so many words by Garry M. Jenkins, the assistant director of the U.S. Secret Service, at the Sundevil press conference in Phoenix on May 9, 1990, immediately after the raids. In brief, hackers were mistaken in their foolish belief that they could hide behind the "relative anonymity of their computer terminals." On the contrary, they should fully understand that state and federal cops were actively patrolling the beat in cyberspace—that they were on the watch everywhere, even in those sleazy and secretive dens of cybernetic vice, the underground boards.

> *State and federal cops were actively patrolling the beat in cyberspace.*

This is not an unusual message for police to convey publicly to crooks. The message is a standard message; only the context is new.

In this respect, the Sundevil raids were the digital equivalent of the standard vice-squad crackdown on massage parlors, porno bookstores, head shops, or floating crap games. There may be few or no arrests in a raid of this sort; no convictions, no trials, no interrogations. Police may well walk out the door with many pounds of sleazy magazines, X-rated videotapes, sex toys, gambling equipment, baggies of marijuana . . .

Of course, if something truly horrendous is discovered by the raiders, there will be arrests and prosecutions. Far more likely, however, there will simply be a brief but sharp disruption of the closed and secretive world of the nogoodniks. There will be "street hassle." "Heat." "Deterrence." And, of course, the immediate loss of the seized goods. It is very unlikely that any of this seized material ever will be returned. Whether charged or not, whether convicted or not, the perpetrators will almost surely lack the nerve ever to ask for this stuff to be given back.

Arrests and trials—putting people in jail—may involve all kinds of formal legalities; but dealing with the justice system is far from the only task of police. Police do not simply arrest people. They don't simply put people in jail. That is not how the police perceive their jobs. Police "protect and serve." Police "keep the peace," they "keep public order." Like other forms of public relations, keeping public order is not an exact science. Keeping public order is something of an art form.

If a group of tough-looking teenage hoodlums was loitering on a streetcorner, no one would be surprised to see a street cop arrive and sternly order them to "break it up." On the contrary, the surprise would come if one of these ne'er-do-wells stepped briskly into a phone booth, called a civil rights lawyer, and instituted a civil suit in defense of his constitutional rights of free speech and free assembly. But something much along this line was one of the many anomolous outcomes of the Hacker Crackdown.

Sundevil also carried useful "messages" for other constituents of the electronic community. These messages may not have been read aloud from the Phoenix podium in front of the press corps, but there was little mistaking their meaning. There was a message of reassurance for the primary victims of coding and carding: the telcos and the credit companies. Sundevil was greeted with joy by the security officers of the electronic business community. After years of high-tech harassment and spiraling revenue losses, their complaints of rampant outlawry were being taken seriously by law enforcement. No more head-scratching or dismissive shrugs; no more feeble excuses about "lack of computer-trained officers" or the low priority of "victimless" white-collar telecommunication crimes.

Computer-crime experts have long believed that computer-related offenses are drastically underreported. They regard this as a major open scandal of their field. Some victims are reluctant to come forth, because they believe that police and prosecutors are not computer literate and can and will do nothing. Others are embarrassed by their vulnerabilities and will take strong measures to avoid any publicity; this is especially true of banks, which fear a loss of investor confidence should an embezzlement case or wire-fraud surface. And some victims are so helplessly confused by their own high technology that they never even realize that a crime has occurred—even when they have been fleeced to the bone.

The results of this situation can be dire. Criminals escape apprehension and punishment. The computer-crime units that do exist can't get work. The true scope of computer crime—its size, its real nature, the scope of its threats, and the legal remedies for it—all remain obscured.

Another problem is very little publicized, but it is a cause of genuine concern. Where there is persistent crime but no effective police protection, then vigilantism can result. Telcos, banks, credit companies, the major corporations that maintain extensive computer networks vulnerable to hacking—these organizations are powerful, wealthy, and politically influential. They are disinclined to be pushed around by crooks (or by most anyone else, for that matter). They often maintain well-organized private security forces, commonly run by experienced veterans of military and police units who have left public service for the greener pastures of the private sector. For police, the corporate security manager can be a powerful ally; but if this gentleman finds no allies in the police, and the pressure is on from his board of directors, he may quietly take certain matters into his own hands.

Nor is there any lack of disposable hired help in the corporate security business. Private security agencies—the "security business" generally—grew explosively in the 1980s. Today there are spooky gumshoed armies of "security consultants," "rent-a-cops," "private eyes," "outside experts"—every manner of shady operator who retails in "results" and discretion. Of course, many of these gentlemen and ladies may be paragons of professional and moral rectitude. But as anyone who has read a hard-boiled detective novel knows, police tend to be less than fond of this sort of private-sector competition.

Companies in search of computer security even have been known to hire hackers. Police shudder at this prospect.

Police treasure good relations with the business community. Rarely will you see a police officer so indiscreet as to allege publicly that some major employer in his state or city has succumbed to paranoia and gone off the rails. Nevertheless, police—and computer police in particular—are aware of this possibility. Computer-crime police can and do spend up to half of their business hours just doing public relations: seminars, "dog and pony shows," sometimes with parents' groups or computer users, but generally with their core audience: the likely victims of hacking crimes. These, of course, are telcos, credit card companies, and large computer-equipped corporations. The police strongly urge these people, as good citizens, to report offenses and press criminal charges; they pass the message that there is someone in authority who cares, understands, and, best of all, will take useful action should a computer crime occur.

But reassuring talk is cheap. Sundevil offered action.

The final message of Sundevil was intended for internal consumption by law enforcement. Sundevil was offered as proof that the community of American computer-crime police had come of age. Sundevil was proof that enormous things such as Sundevil itself could now be accomplished. Sundevil was proof that the Secret Service and its local law-enforcement allies could act like a well-oiled machine. It was also proof that the Arizona Organized Crime and Racketeering Unit—the sparkplug of Sundevil— ranked with the best in the world in ambition, organization, and sheer conceptual daring.

And, as a final fillip, Sundevil was a message from the Secret Service to their longtime rivals in the Federal Bureau of Investigation. By congressional fiat, both USSS and FBI formally share jurisdiction over federal computer-crimebusting activities. Neither of these groups has ever been remotely happy with this muddled situation. It seems to suggest that Congress cannot make up its mind as to which of these groups is better qualified. And there is scarcely a Special Agent or a G-man anywhere without a very firm opinion on that topic.

For the neophyte, one of the most puzzling aspects of the crackdown on hackers is why the U.S. Secret Service has anything at all to do with this matter.

The Secret Service is best known for its primary public role: its agents protect the President of the United States. They also guard the President's family, the Vice President and his family, former Presidents, and presidential candidates. They sometimes guard foreign dignitaries who are visiting the United States, especially foreign heads of state, and have been known to accompany American officials on diplomatic missions overseas.

Special Agents of the Secret Service don't wear uniforms, but the USSS also has two uniformed police agencies. There's the former White House Police (now known as the Secret Service Uniformed Division, because they currently guard foreign embassies in Washington as well as the White House itself). And there's the uniformed Treasury Police Force.

The Secret Service has been charged by Congress with a number of little-known duties. It guards the precious metals in Treasury vaults. It guards the most valuable historical documents of the United States: originals of the Constitution, the Declaration of Independence, Lincoln's Second Inaugural Address, an American-owned copy of the Magna Carta, and so forth. Once agents were assigned to guard the *Mona Lisa*, on her American tour in the 1960s.

The entire Secret Service is a division of the Treasury Department. Secret Service Special Agents (there are about 1,900 of them) are bodyguards for the President et al., but they all work for the Treasury. And the Treasury (through its divisions of the U.S. Mint and the Bureau of Engraving and Printing) prints the nation's money.

> *Cash is fading in importance today as money has become electronic.*

As Treasury police, the Secret Service guards the nation's currency; it is the only federal law enforcement agency with direct jurisdiction over counterfeiting and forgery. It analyzes documents for authenticity, and its fight against fake cash is still quite lively (especially since the skilled counterfeiters of Medellín, Colombia, have gotten into the act). Government checks, bonds, and other obligations, which exist in untold millions and are worth untold billions, are common targets for forgery, which the

Secret Service also battles. It even handles forgery of postage stamps.

But cash is fading in importance today as money has become electronic. As necessity beckoned, the Secret Service moved from fighting the counterfeiting of paper currency and the forging of checks, to the protection of funds transferred by wire.

From wire fraud, it was a simple skip-and-jump to what is known formally as "access device fraud." Congress granted the Secret Service the authority to investigate access device fraud under Title 18 of the United States Code (U.S.C. Section 1029).

The term "access device" seems intuitively simple. It's some kind of high-tech gizmo you use to get money with. It makes good sense to put this sort of thing in the charge of counterfeiting and wire-fraud experts.

However, in Section 1029, the term "access device" is defined very generously. An access device is: "any card, plate, code, account number, or other means of account access that can be used, alone or in conjunction with another access device, to obtain money, goods, services, or any other thing of value, or that can be used to initiate a transfer of funds."

"Access device" can therefore be construed to include credit cards themselves (a popular forgery item nowadays). It also includes credit card account *numbers*, those standards of the digital underground. The same goes for telephone charge cards (an increasingly popular item with telcos, which are tired of being robbed of pocket change by phone-booth thieves). And also telephone access *codes*, those *other* standards of the digital underground. (Stolen telephone codes may not "obtain money," but they certainly do obtain valuable "services," which is specifically forbidden by Section 1029.)

We can now see that Section 1029 already pits the U.S. Secret Service directly against the digital underground, without any mention at all of the word "computer."

Standard phreaking devices, such as blue boxes, used to steal phone service from old-fashioned mechanical switches, are unquestionably "counterfeit access devices." Thanks to Section

1029, it is not only illegal to *use* counterfeit access devices, but it is even illegal to *build* them. "Producing," "designing," "duplicating," or "assembling" blue boxes are all federal crimes today, and if you do this, the Secret Service has been charged by Congress to come after you.

Automatic teller machines, which replicated all over America during the 1980s, are definitely "access devices" too, and an attempt to tamper with their punch-in codes and plastic bank cards falls directly under Section 1029.

Section 1029 is remarkably elastic. Suppose you find a computer password in somebody's trash. That password might be a "code"—it's certainly a "means of account access." Now suppose you log on to a computer and copy some software for yourself. You've certainly obtained "service" (computer service) and a "thing of value" (the software). Suppose you tell a dozen friends about your swiped password and let them use it too. Now you're "trafficking in unauthorized access devices." And when Prophet, a member of the Legion of Doom, passed a stolen telephone company document to Knight Lightning at *Phrack* magazine, they were both charged under Section 1029!

There are two limitations on Section 1029. First, the offense must "affect interstate or foreign commerce" in order to become a matter of federal jurisdiction. The term "affect . . . commerce" is not well defined; but you may take it as a given that the Secret Service can take an interest if you've done almost anything that happens to cross a state line. State and local police can be touchy about their jurisdictions and can sometimes be mulish when the feds show up. But when it comes to computer crime, the local police are pathetically grateful for federal help—in fact, they complain that they can't get enough of it. If you're stealing long-distance service, you're almost certainly crossing state lines, and you're definitely affecting the interstate commerce of the telcos. And if you're abusing credit cards by ordering stuff out of glossy catalogs from, say, Vermont, you're in for it.

The second limitation is money. As a rule, the feds don't pursue penny-ante offenders. Federal judges will dismiss cases that appear to waste their time. Federal crimes must be serious; Section 1029 specifies a minimum loss of a thousand dollars.

We now come to the very next section of Title 18, which is Section 1030, "Fraud and related activity in connection with computers." This statute gives the Secret Service direct jurisdiction over acts of computer intrusion. On the face of it, the Secret Service would now seem to command the field. Section 1030, however, is nowhere near so ductile as Section 1029.

The first annoyance is Section 1030(d), which reads:

"(d) The United States Secret Service shall, *in addition to any other agency having such authority,* have the authority to investigate offenses under this section. Such authority of the United States Secret Service shall be exercised in accordance with an agreement which shall be entered into by the Secretary of the Treasury *and the Attorney General.*" (Author's italics.)

The secretary of the treasury is the titular head of the Secret Service, while the attorney general is in charge of the FBI. In Section (d), Congress shrugged off responsibility for the computer-crime turf battle between the Service and the Bureau, and made them fight it out all by themselves. The result was a rather dire one for the Secret Service, for the FBI ended up with exclusive jurisdiction over computer break-ins having to do with national security, foreign espionage, federally insured banks, and U.S. military bases, while retaining joint jurisdiction over all the other computer intrusions. Essentially, when it comes to Section 1030, the FBI not only gets the real glamour stuff for itself, but can peer over the shoulder of the Secret Service and barge in to meddle whenever it suits them.

The second problem has to do with the dicey term "Federal interest computer." Section 1030(a)(2) makes it illegal to "access a computer without authorization" if that computer belongs to a financial institution or an issuer of credit cards (fraud cases, in other words). Congress was quite willing to give the Secret Service jurisdiction over money-transferring computers, but Congress balked at letting the Service investigate any and all computer intrusions. Instead, the USSS had to settle for the money machines and the "Federal interest computers." A "Federal interest computer" is a computer that the government itself owns or is using. Large networks of interstate computers, linked over state lines, are also considered to be of federal interest. (This notion of federal interest is legally rather foggy and has never been clearly defined in the courts. The Secret Service has never yet had its hand slapped for investigating computer break-ins that were *not* of federal interest, but conceivably someday this might happen.)

So the Secret Service's authority over "unauthorized access" to computers covers a lot of territory, but by no means the whole ball of cyberspatial wax. If you are, for instance, a *local* computer retailer, or the owner of a *local* bulletin board system, then a malicious *local* intruder can break in, crash your system, trash your files and scatter viruses, and the U.S. Secret Service cannot do a single thing about it.

At least, it can't do anything *directly*. But the Secret Service will do plenty to help the local people who can.

The tassel-toting Secret Service has ready-and-able hacker-trackers installed in every state in the Union.

The FBI may have dealt itself an ace off the bottom of the deck when it comes to Section 1030; but that's not the whole story; that's not the street. What Congress thinks is one thing, and Congress has been known to change its mind. The *real* turf struggle is out there in the streets where it's happening. If you're a local street cop with a computer problem, the Secret Service wants you to know where you can find the real expertise. While the Bureau crowd are off having their favorite shoes polished (wing tips) and making derisive fun of the Service's favorite shoes ("pansy-ass tassels"), the tassel-toting Secret Service has a crew of ready-and-able hacker-trackers installed in the capital of every state in the Union. Need advice? They'll give you advice, or at least point you in the right direction. Need training? They can see to that too.

If you're a local cop and you call in the FBI, the FBI (as is

widely and slanderously rumored) will order you around like a
coolie, take all the credit for your busts, and mop up every possible scrap of reflected glory. The Secret Service, on the other
hand, doesn't brag a lot. Secret Service agents are quiet types.
Very quiet. Very cool. Efficient. High tech. Mirror shades, icy
stares, radio earplugs, an Uzi machine-pistol tucked somewhere
in that well-cut jacket. American samurai, sworn to give their
lives to protect our President. "The granite agents." Trained in
martial arts, absolutely fearless. Every single one of 'em has a top-
secret security clearance. Something goes a little wrong, you're
not gonna hear any whining and moaning and political buck-
passing out of these guys.

The façade of the granite agent is not, of course, the reality.
Secret Service agents are human beings. And the real glory in
Service work is not in battling computer crime—not yet, anyway
—but in protecting the President. The real glamour of Secret
Service work is in the White House detail. If you're at the President's side, then the kids and the wife see you on television; you
rub shoulders with the most powerful people in the world. That's
the real heart of Service work, the number-one priority. More
than one computer investigation has stopped dead in the water
when Service agents vanished at the President's need.

There's romance in the work of the Service. The intimate access to circles of great power; the esprit-de-corps of a highly
trained and disciplined elite; the high responsibility of defending
the Chief Executive; the fulfillment of a patriotic duty. And as
police work goes, the pay's not bad. But there's squalor in Service
work too. You may get spat upon by protesters howling abuse—
and if they get violent, if they get too close, sometimes you have
to knock one of them down—discreetly.

The real squalor in Service work is drudgery such as "the
quarterlies," traipsing out four times a year, year in, year out, to
interview the various pathetic wretches, many of them in prisons
and asylums, who have seen fit to threaten the President's life.
And then there's the grinding stress of searching all those faces in
the endless bustling crowds, looking for hatred, looking for psy-

chosis, looking for the tight, nervous face of an Arthur Bremer, a Squeaky Fromme, a Lee Harvey Oswald. It's watching all those grasping, waving hands for sudden movements, while your ears strain at your radio headphone for the long-rehearsed cry of "Gun!"

It's poring, in grinding detail, over the biographies of every rotten loser who ever shot at a President. It's the unsung work of the Protective Research Section, which studies scrawled, anonymous death threats with all the meticulous tools of antiforgery techniques.

And it's maintaining the hefty computerized files on anyone who ever threatened the President's life. Civil libertarians have become increasingly concerned at the government's use of computer files to track American citizens—but the Secret Service file of potential presidential assassins, which contains upward of twenty thousand names, rarely causes a peep of protest. If you *ever* state that you intend to kill the President, the Secret Service will want to know and record who you are, where you are, what you are, and what you're up to. If you're a serious threat—if you're officially considered "of protective interest"—then the Secret Service may well keep tabs on you for the rest of your natural life.

Protecting the President has first call on all the Service's resources. But there's a lot more to the Service's traditions and history than standing guard outside the Oval Office.

The Secret Service is the nation's oldest general federal law-enforcement agency. Compared to the Secret Service, the FBI are new-hires and the CIA are temps. The Secret Service was founded way back in 1865, at the suggestion of Hugh McCulloch, Abraham Lincoln's secretary of the treasury. McCulloch wanted a specialized Treasury police to combat counterfeiting. Abraham Lincoln agreed that this seemed a good idea, and, with a terrible irony, Abraham Lincoln was shot that very night by John Wilkes Booth.

The Secret Service originally had nothing to do with protecting

Presidents. They didn't take this on as a regular assignment until after the Garfield assassination in 1881. And they didn't get any congressional money for it until President McKinley was shot in 1901. The Service was originally designed for one purpose: destroying counterfeiters.

There are interesting parallels between the Service's nineteenth-century entry into counterfeiting and America's twentieth-century entry into computer crime.

In 1865, America's paper currency was a terrible muddle. Security was drastically bad. Currency was printed on the spot by local banks in literally hundreds of different designs. No one really knew what the heck a dollar bill was supposed to look like. Bogus bills passed easily. If some joker told you that a one-dollar bill from the Railroad Bank of Lowell, Massachusetts, had a woman leaning on a shield, with a locomotive, a cornucopia, a compass, various agricultural implements, a railroad bridge, and some factories, then you pretty much had to take his word for it. (And in fact he was telling the truth!)

Sixteen hundred local American banks designed and printed their own paper currency, and there were no general standards for security. Like a badly guarded node in a computer network, badly designed bills were easy to fake and posed a security hazard for the entire monetary system.

No one knew the exact extent of the threat to the currency. There were panicked estimates that as much as a third of the entire national currency was faked. Counterfeiters—known as "boodlers" in the underground slang of the time—were mostly technically skilled printers who had gone bad. Many had once worked printing legitimate currency. Boodlers operated in rings and gangs. Technical experts engraved the bogus plates—commonly in basements in New York City. Smooth confidence men passed large wads of high-quality, high-denomination fakes, including the really sophisticated stuff—government bonds, stock certificates, and railway shares. Cheaper, botched fakes were sold or sharewared to low-level gangs of boodler wannabes. (The really cheesy lowlife boodlers merely upgraded real bills by altering face values, changing ones to fives, tens to hundreds, and so on.)

The techniques of boodling were little known and regarded with a certain awe by the mid-nineteenth-century public. The ability to manipulate the system for rip-off seemed diabolically clever. As the skill and daring of the boodlers increased, the situation became intolerable. The federal government stepped in and began offering its own federal currency, which was printed in fancy green ink, but only on the back—the original "greenbacks." And at first, the improved security of the well-designed, well-printed federal greenbacks seemed to solve the problem; but then the counterfeiters caught on. Within a few years things were worse than ever: a *centralized* system where *all* security was bad!

The local police were helpless. The government tried offering blood money to potential informants, but this met with little success. Banks, plagued by boodling, gave up hope of police help and hired private security men instead. Merchants and bankers queued up by the thousands to buy privately printed manuals on currency security, slim little books such as Laban Heath's *Infallible Government Counterfeit Detector*. The back of the book offered Heath's patent microscope for five bucks.

Then the Secret Service entered the picture. The first agents were a rough and ready crew. Their chief was one William P. Wood, a former guerilla in the Mexican War who'd won a reputation busting contractor fraudsters for the War Department during the Civil War. Wood, who was also Keeper of the Capital Prison, had a sideline as a counterfeiting expert, bagging boodlers for the federal bounty money.

Wood was named chief of the new Secret Service in July 1865. There were only ten agents in all: Wood himself, a handful who'd worked for him in the War Department, and a few former private investigators—counterfeiting experts—whom Wood had won over to public service. (The Secret Service of 1865 was much the size of the Chicago Computer Fraud Task Force or the Arizona Racketeering Unit of 1990.) These ten "Operatives" had an additional twenty or so "Assistant Operatives" and "Informants." Besides salary and per diem, each Secret Service employee received a whopping twenty-five dollars for each boodler he captured.

Wood himself publicly estimated that at least *half* of America's currency was counterfeit, a perhaps pardonable perception. Within a year the Secret Service had arrested

> *Wood estimated that at least half of America's currency was counterfeit.*

over two hundred counterfeiters. They busted about two hundred boodlers a year for four years straight.

Wood attributed his success to traveling fast and light, hitting the bad guys hard, and avoiding bureaucratic baggage. "Because my raids were made without military escort and I did not ask the assistance of state officers, I surprised the professional counterfeiter."

Wood's social message to the once-impudent boodlers bore an eerie ring of Sundevil: "It was also my purpose to convince such characters that it would no longer be healthy for them to ply their vocation without being handled roughly, a fact they soon discovered."

William P. Wood, the Secret Service's guerilla pioneer, did not end well. He succumbed to the lure of aiming for the really big score. The notorious Brockway Gang of New York City, headed by William E. Brockway, the "King of the Counterfeiters," had forged a number of government bonds. They'd passed these brilliant fakes on the prestigious Wall Street investment firm of Jay Cooke and Company. The Cooke firm was frantic and offered a huge reward for the forgers' plates.

Laboring diligently, Wood confiscated the plates (though not Mr. Brockway) and claimed the reward. But the Cooke company treacherously reneged. Wood got involved in a down-and-dirty lawsuit with the Cooke capitalists. Wood's boss, Secretary of the Treasury McCulloch, felt that Wood's demands for money and glory were unseemly, and even when the reward money finally came through, McCulloch refused to pay Wood anything. Wood found himself mired in a seemingly endless round of federal suits and congressional lobbying.

Wood never got his money. And he lost his job to boot. He resigned in 1869.

Wood's agents suffered too. On May 12, 1869, the second chief of the Secret Service took over, and almost immediately fired most of Wood's pioneer Secret Service agents: operatives, assistants, and informants alike. The practice of receiving twenty-five dollars per crook was abolished. And the Secret Service began the long, uncertain process of thorough professionalization.

Wood ended badly. He must have felt stabbed in the back. In fact his entire organization was mangled.

On the other hand, William P. Wood *was* the first head of the Secret Service. William Wood was the pioneer. People still honor his name. Who remembers the name of the *second* head of the Secret Service?

As for William Brockway (also known as "Colonel Spencer"), he was finally arrested by the Secret Service in 1880. He did five years in prison, got out, and was still boodling at the age of seventy-four.

Anyone with an interest in Operation Sundevil—or in American computer crime generally—could scarcely miss the presence of Gail Thackeray, Assistant Attorney General of the State of Arizona. Computer-crime training manuals often cited Thackeray's group and her work; she was the highest-ranking state official to specialize in computer-related offenses. Her name had been on the Sundevil press release (though modestly ranked well after the local federal prosecuting attorney and the head of the Phoenix Secret Service office).

As public commentary, and controversy, began to mount about the Hacker Crackdown, this Arizona state official began to achieve a higher and higher public profile. Though uttering almost nothing specific about the Sundevil operation itself, she coined some of the most striking soundbites of the growing propaganda war: "Agents are operating in good faith, and I don't think you can say that for the hacker community" was one. Another was the memorable "I am not a mad dog prosecutor" (*Houston Chronicle*, September 2, 1990). In the meantime, the Secret Service maintained its usual extreme discretion; the Chicago Unit, smarting from the backlash of the Steve Jackson scandal, had gone completely to earth.

As I collated my growing pile of newspaper clippings, Gail Thackeray ranked as a comparative fount of public knowledge on police operations.

I decided that I had to get to know Gail Thackeray. I wrote to her at the Arizona Attorney General's Office. Not only did she kindly reply to me, but, to my astonishment, she knew very well what "cyberpunk" science fiction was.

Shortly after this, Gail Thackeray lost her job. And I temporarily misplaced my own career as a science-fiction writer, to become a full-time computer-crime journalist. In early March 1991, I flew to Phoenix, Arizona, to interview Gail Thackeray for my book on the hacker crackdown.

"Credit cards didn't used to cost anything to get," says Gail Thackeray. "Now they cost forty bucks—and that's all just to cover the costs from *rip-off artists*."

Electronic nuisance criminals are parasites. One by one they're not much harm, no big deal. But they never come just one by one. They come in swarms, heaps, legions, sometimes whole subcultures. And they bite. Every time we buy a credit card today, we lose a little financial vitality to a particular species of bloodsucker.

What, in her expert opinion, are the worst forms of electronic crime, I ask, consulting my notes. Is it credit card fraud? Breaking into ATM bank machines? Phone-phreaking? Computer intrusions? Software viruses? Access-code theft? Records tampering? Software piracy? Pornographic bulletin boards? Satellite TV piracy? Theft of cable service? It's a long list. By the time I reach the end of it I feel rather depressed.

"Oh, no," says Gail Thackeray, leaning forward over the table, her whole body gone stiff with energetic indignation, "the biggest damage is telephone fraud. Fake sweepstakes, fake charities. Boiler-room con operations. You could pay off the national debt with what these guys steal. . . . They target old people, they get hold of credit ratings and demographics, they rip off the old and the weak." The words come tumbling out of her.

It's low-tech stuff, your everyday boiler-room fraud. Grifters, conning people out of money over the phone, have been around for decades. This is where the word "phony" came from!

It's just that it's so much *easier* now, horribly facilitated by advances in technology and the byzantine structure of the modern phone system. The same professional fraudsters do it over and over, Thackeray tells me, hiding behind dense onion shells of fake companies . . . fake holding corporations nine or ten layers deep, registered all over the map. They get a phone installed under a false name in an empty safe house. And then they call-forward everything out of that phone to yet another phone, a phone that may even be in another *state*. And they don't even pay the charges on their phones; after a month or so, they just split. Set up somewhere else in another Podunkville with the same seedy crew of veteran phone crooks. They buy or steal commercial credit card reports, slap them on the PC, have a program pick out people over sixty-five who pay a lot to charities. A whole subculture living off this, merciless folks on the con.

"The 'light bulbs for the blind' people," Thackeray muses, with a special loathing. "There's just no end to them."

We're sitting in a downtown diner in Phoenix, Arizona. It's a tough town, Phoenix. A state capital seeing some hard times. Even to a Texan like myself, Arizona state politics seem rather baroque. There was, and remains, endless trouble over the Martin Luther King holiday, the sort of stiff-necked, foot-shooting incident for which Arizona politics seem famous. There was Evan Mecham, the eccentric Republican millionaire governor who was impeached, after reducing state government to a ludicrous shambles. Then there was the national Keating scandal, involving Arizona savings and loans, in which both of Arizona's U.S. senators, DeConcini and McCain, played sadly prominent roles.

And the very latest is the bizarre AzScam case, in which seven state legislators were videotaped, eagerly taking cash from an informant of the Phoenix city police department, who was posing as a Vegas mobster.

"Oh," Thackeray says cheerfully. "These people are amateurs here, they thought they were finally getting to play with the big boys. They don't have the least idea how to take a bribe! It's not institutional corruption. It's not like back in Philly."

Gail Thackeray was a former prosecutor in Philadelphia. Now she's a former assistant attorney general of the state of Arizona. Since moving to Arizona in 1986, she had worked under the aegis of Steve Twist, her boss in the attorney general's office. Steve Twist wrote Arizona's pioneering computer crime laws and naturally took an interest in seeing them enforced. It was a snug niche, and Thackeray's Organized Crime and Racketeering Unit won a national reputation for ambition and technical knowledgeability . . . until the latest election in Arizona. Thackeray's boss ran for the top job and lost. The victor, the new attorney general, apparently went to some pains to eliminate the bureaucratic traces of his rival, including his pet group—Thackeray's group. Twelve people got their walking papers.

Now Thackeray's painstakingly assembled computer lab sits gathering dust somewhere in the glass-and-concrete Attorney General's HQ on 1275 Washington Street. Her computer-crime books, her painstakingly garnered back issues of phreak and hacker zines—all bought at her own expense—are piled in boxes somewhere. The state of Arizona is simply not particularly interested in electronic racketeering at the moment.

At the moment of our interview, Gail Thackeray, officially unemployed, is working out of the county sheriff's office, living on her savings, and prosecuting several cases—working sixty-hour weeks, just as always—for no pay at all. "I'm trying to train people," she mutters.

Half her life seems to be spent training people—merely pointing out, to the naive and incredulous (such as myself), that this stuff is *actually going on out there*. It's a small world, computer crime. A young world. Gail Thackeray, a trim blond Baby Boomer who favors Grand Canyon white-water rafting to kill some slow time, is one of the world's most senior, most veteran hacker-trackers. Her mentor was Donn Parker, the California think-tank theorist who got it all started way back in the mid-1970s, the "grandfather of the field," "the great bald eagle of computer crime."

And what she has learned, Gail Thackeray teaches. Endlessly. Tirelessly. To anybody. To Secret Service agents and state police, at the Glynco, Georgia, federal training center. To local police, on "roadshows" with her slide projector and notebook. To corporate security personnel. To journalists. To parents.

Sometimes whole crowds of phone phreaks will call Gail Thackeray.

Even *crooks* look to Gail Thackeray for advice. Phone phreaks call her at the office. They know very well who she is. They pump her for information on what the cops are up to, how much they know. Sometimes whole *crowds* of phone phreaks, hanging out on illegal conference calls, will call Gail Thackeray up. They taunt her. And, as always, they boast. Phone phreaks, real stone phone phreaks, simply *cannot shut up*. They natter on for hours.

Left to themselves, they talk mostly about the intricacies of ripping off phones; it's about as interesting as listening to hot-rodders talk about suspension and distributor caps. They also gossip cruelly about each other. And when talking to Gail Thackeray, they incriminate themselves. "I have tapes," Thackeray says coolly.

Phone phreaks just talk like crazy. "Dial-Tone" out in Alabama has been known to spend half an hour simply reading stolen phone codes aloud into voice-mail answering machines. Hundreds, thousands of numbers, recited in a monotone, without a break—an eerie phenomenon. When arrested, it's a rare phone phreak who doesn't inform at endless length on everybody he knows.

Hackers are no better. What other group of criminals, she asks rhetorically, publishes newsletters and holds conventions? She seems deeply nettled by the sheer brazenness of this behavior, though to an outsider, this activity might make one wonder whether hackers should be considered "criminals" at all. Skateboarders have magazines, and they trespass a lot. Hot-rod people have magazines and they break speed limits and sometimes kill people. . . .

I ask her whether it would be any loss to society if phone phreaking and computer hacking, as hobbies, simply dried up and blew away, so that nobody ever did it again.

She seems surprised. "No," she says swiftly. "Maybe a little . . . in the old days . . . the MIT stuff. . . . But there's a lot of wonderful, legal stuff you can do with computers now, you don't have to break into somebody else's just to learn. You don't have that excuse. You can learn all you like."

Did you ever hack into a system? I ask.

The trainees do it at Glynco. Just to demonstrate system vulnerabilities. She's cool to the notion. Genuinely indifferent.

"What kind of computer do you have?"

"A Compaq 286LE," she mutters.

"What kind do you *wish* you had?"

At this question, the unmistakable light of true hackerdom flares in Gail Thackeray's eyes. She becomes tense, animated, the words pour out: "An Amiga 2000 with an IBM card and Mac emulation! The most common hacker machines are Amigas and Commodores. And Apples." If she had the Amiga, she enthuses, she could run a whole galaxy of seized computer-evidence disks on one convenient multifunctional machine. A cheap one too. Not like the old attorney general lab, where they had an ancient CP/M machine, assorted Amiga flavors and Apple flavors, a couple IBMs, all the utility software . . . but no Commodores. The workstations down at the attorney general's are Wang dedicated word processors. Lame machines tied into an office net—though at least they get on-line to the Lexis and Westlaw legal data services.

I don't say anything. I recognize the syndrome, though. This computer fever has been running through segments of our society for years now. It's a strange kind of lust: K hunger, meg hunger; but it's a shared disease; it can kill parties dead, as conversation spirals into the deepest and most deviant recesses of software releases and expensive peripherals. . . . The mark of the hacker beast. I have it too. The whole "electronic community," whatever the hell that is, has it. Gail Thackeray has it. Gail Thackeray is a hacker cop. My immediate reaction is a strong rush of indignant pity: *Why doesn't somebody buy this woman her Amiga?!* It's not like she's asking for a Cray X-MP supercomputer mainframe; an Amiga's a sweet little cookie-box thing. We're losing zillions in organized fraud; prosecuting and defending a single hacker case in court can cost a hundred grand easy. How come nobody can come up with four lousy grand so this woman can do her job? For a hundred grand we could buy every computer cop in America an Amiga. There aren't that many of 'em.

Computers. The lust, the hunger, for computers. The loyalty they inspire, the intense sense of possessiveness. The culture they have bred. I myself am sitting in downtown Phoenix, Arizona, because it suddenly occurred to me that the police might—just *might*—come and take away my computer. The prospect of this, the mere *implied threat*, was unbearable. It literally changed my life. It was changing the lives of many others. Eventually it would change everybody's life.

Gail Thackeray was one of the top computer-crime people in America. And I was just some novelist, and yet I had a better computer than hers. *Practically everybody I knew* had a better computer than Gail Thackeray and her feeble laptop 286. It was like sending the sheriff in to clean up Dodge City and arming her with a slingshot cut from an old rubber tire.

But then again, you don't need a howitzer to enforce the law. You can do a lot just with a badge. With a badge alone, you can basically wreak havoc, take a terrible vengeance on wrongdoers. Ninety percent of "computer crime investigation" is just "crime investigation": names, places, dossiers, modus operandi, search warrants, victims, complainants, informants. . . .

What will computer crime look like in ten years? Will it get better? Did Sundevil send 'em reeling back in confusion?

It'll be like it is now, only worse, she tells me with perfect conviction. Still there in the background, ticking along, changing with the times: the criminal underworld. It'll be

Criminals often are some of the first through the gate of a new technology.

like drugs are. Like our problems with alcohol. All the cops and laws in the world never solved our problems with alcohol. If there's something people want, a certain percentage of them are just going to take it. Fifteen percent of the populace will never steal. Fifteen percent will steal most anything not nailed down. The battle is for the hearts and minds of the remaining 70 percent.

And criminals catch on fast. If there's not "too steep a learning curve"—if it doesn't require a baffling amount of expertise and practice—then criminals often are some of the first through the gate of a new technology. Especially if it helps them to hide. They have tons of cash, criminals. The new communications tech —pagers, cellular phones, faxes, Federal Express—were pioneered by rich corporate people and by criminals. In the early years of pagers and beepers, dope dealers were so enthralled by this technology that owning a beeper was practically prima facie evidence of cocaine dealing. CB radio exploded when the speed limit was reduced to 55 and breaking the highway law became a national pastime. Dope dealers send cash by Federal Express, despite, or perhaps *because of*, the warnings in FedEx offices that tell you never to try this. Fed Ex uses X rays and dogs on its mail, to stop drug shipments. That doesn't work very well.

Drug dealers went wild over cellular phones. There are simple methods of faking IDs on cellular phones, making the location of the call mobile, free of charge, and effectively untraceable. Now victimized cellular companies routinely bring in vast toll lists of calls to Colombia and Pakistan.

Judge Greene's fragmentation of the phone company is driving law enforcement nuts. Four thousand telecommunications companies. Fraud skyrocketing. Every temptation in the world available with a phone and a credit card number. Criminals untraceable. A galaxy of "new neat rotten things to do."

If there was one thing Thackeray would like to have, it would be an effective legal end-run through this new fragmentation minefield.

It would be a new form of electronic search warrant, an "electronic letter of marque" to be issued by a judge. It would create a new category of "electronic emergency." Like a wiretap, its use would be rare, but it would cut across state lines and force swift cooperation from all concerned. Cellular, phone, laser, computer network, PBXes, AT&T, Baby Bells, long-distance entrepreneurs, packet radio. Some document, some mighty court order, that could slice through four thousand separate forms of corporate red tape and get her at once to the source of calls, the source of e-mail threats and viruses, the sources of bomb threats, kidnapping threats. "From now on," she says, "the Lindberg baby will always die."

Something that would make the Net sit still, if only for a moment. Something that would get her up to speed. Seven-league boots. That's what she really needs. "Those guys move in nanoseconds and I'm on the Pony Express."

And then too, there's the coming international angle. Electronic crime has never been easy to localize, to tie to a physical jurisdiction. And phone phreaks and hackers loathe boundaries, they jump them whenever they can. The English. The Dutch. And the Germans, especially the ubiquitous Chaos Computer Club. The Australians. They've all learned phone phreaking from America. It's a growth mischief industry. The multinational networks are global, but governments and the police simply aren't. Neither are the laws. Or the legal frameworks for citizen protection.

One language is global, though—English. Phone phreaks speak English; it's their native tongue even if they're Germans. English may have started in England but now it's the Net language; it might as well be called "CNNese."

Asians just aren't much into phone phreaking. They're the world masters at organized software piracy. The French aren't into phone phreaking either. The French are into computerized industrial espionage.

In the old days of the MIT righteous hackerdom, crashing systems didn't hurt anybody. Not all that much, anyway. Not permanently. Now the players are more venal. Now the consequences are worse. Hacking

> *Hackers in Amtrak computers, or in air-traffic control computers, will kill somebody someday.*

will begin killing people soon. Hackers in Amtrak computers, or in air-traffic control computers, will kill somebody someday. Maybe a lot of people. Gail Thackeray expects it.

And the viruses are getting nastier. The "Scud" virus is the latest one out. It wipes hard disks.

According to Thackeray, the idea that phone phreaks are Robin Hoods is a fraud. They don't deserve this repute. Basically, they pick on the weak. AT&T now protects itself with the fearsome ANI (Automatic Number Identification) trace capability. When AT&T wised up and tightened security generally, the phreaks drifted into the Baby Bells. The Baby Bells lashed out in 1989 and 1990, so the phreaks switched to smaller long-distance entrepreneurs. Today, they are moving into locally owned PBXes and voice-mail systems, which are full of security holes, dreadfully easy to hack. These victims aren't the moneybags Sheriff of Nottingham or Bad King John, but small groups of innocent people who find it hard to protect themselves and who really suffer from these depredations. Phone phreaks pick on the weak. They do it for power. If it was legal, they wouldn't do it. They don't want service, or knowledge, they want the thrill of power-tripping.

There's plenty of knowledge or service around, if you're willing to pay. Phone phreaks don't pay, they steal. It's because it is illegal that it feels like power, that it gratifies their vanity.

I leave Gail Thackeray with a handshake at the door of her office building—a vast International Style office building downtown. The sheriff's office is renting part of it. I get the vague impression that quite a lot of the building is empty—real estate crash.

In a Phoenix sports apparel store, in a downtown mall, I meet the "Sun Devil" himself. He is the cartoon mascot of Arizona State University, whose football stadium, Sundevil, is near the local Secret Service HQ—hence the name Operation Sundevil. The Sun Devil himself is named "Sparky." Sparky the Sun Devil is maroon and bright yellow, the school colors. Sparky brandishes a three-tined yellow pitchfork. He has a small mustache, pointed ears, a barbed tail, and is dashing forward jabbing the air with the pitchfork, with an expression of devilish glee.

Phoenix was the home of Operation Sundevil. The Legion of Doom ran a hacker bulletin board called The Phoenix Project. An Australian hacker named "Phoenix" once burrowed through the Internet to attack Cliff Stoll, then bragged and boasted about it to *The New York Times*. This net of coincidence is both odd and meaningless.

The headquarters of the Arizona attorney general, Gail Thackeray's former workplace, is on 1275 Washington Avenue. Many of the downtown streets in Phoenix are named after prominent American presidents: Washington, Jefferson, Madison. . . .

After dark, all the employees go home to their suburbs. Washington, Jefferson, and Madison—what would be the Phoenix inner city, if there was an inner city in this sprawling automobile-bred town—become the haunts of transients and derelicts. The homeless. The sidewalks along Washington are lined with orange trees. Ripe fallen fruit lies scattered like croquet balls on the sidewalks and gutters. No one seems to be eating them. I try a fresh one. It tastes unbearably bitter.

The attorney general's office, built in 1981 during the Babbitt administration, is a long low two-story building of white cement and wall-size sheets of curtain glass. Behind each glass wall is a lawyer's office, quite open and visible to anyone strolling by. Across the street is a dour government building labeled simply ECONOMIC SECURITY, something that has not been in great supply in the American Southwest lately.

The offices are about twelve feet square. They feature tall wooden cases full of red-spined lawbooks; Wang computer monitors; telephones; Post-it notes galore. Also framed law diplomas and a general excess of bad Western landscape art. Ansel Adams photos are a big favorite, perhaps to compensate for the dismal specter of the parking lot, two acres of striped black asphalt, which features gravel landscaping and some sickly looking barrel cacti.

It has grown dark. Gail Thackeray has told me that the people who work late here are afraid of muggings in the parking lot. It seems cruelly ironic that a woman tracing electronic racketeers across the interstate labyrinth of cyberspace should fear an assault by a homeless derelict in the parking lot of her own workplace.

Perhaps this is less than coincidence. Perhaps these two seemingly disparate worlds are somehow generating one another. The poor and disenfranchised take to the streets, while the rich and computer-equipped, safe in their bedrooms, chatter over their modems. Quite often the derelicts kick the glass out and break in to the lawyers' offices, if they see something they need or want badly enough.

I cross the parking lot to the street behind the attorney general's office. A pair of young tramps are bedding down on flattened sheets of cardboard, under an alcove stretching over the sidewalk. One tramp wears a glitter-covered T-shirt reading CALIFORNIA in Coca-Cola cursive. His nose and cheeks look chafed and swollen; they glisten with what seems to be Vaseline. The other tramp has a ragged long-sleeved shirt and lank brown hair parted in the middle. They both wear blue jeans coated in grime. They are both drunk.

"You guys crash here a lot?" I ask them.

They look at me warily. I am wearing black jeans, a black pin-striped suit jacket, and a black silk tie. I have odd shoes and a funny haircut.

"It's our first time here," says the red-nosed tramp unconvincingly. There is a lot of cardboard stacked here. More than any two people could use.

"We usually stay at the Vinnie's down the street," says the brown-haired tramp, puffing a Marlboro with a meditative air as he sprawls with his head on a blue nylon backpack. "The Saint Vincent's."

"You know who works in that building over there?" I ask, pointing.

The brown-haired tramp shrugs. "Some kind of attorneys, it says."

We urge one another to take it easy. I give them five bucks.

A block down the street I meet a vigorous workman who is wheeling along some kind of industrial trolley; it has what appears to be a tank of propane on it.

We make eye contact. We nod politely. I walk past him. "Hey! Excuse me, sir!" he says.

"Yes?" I say, stopping and turning.

"Have you seen," the guy says rapidly, "a black guy, about six foot seven, scars on both his cheeks like this"—he gestures—"wears a black baseball cap on backward, wandering around here anyplace?"

"Sounds like I don't much *want* to meet him," I say.

"He took my wallet," says my new acquaintance. "Took it this morning. Y'know, some people would be *scared* of a guy like that. But I'm not scared. I'm from Chicago. I'm gonna hunt him down. We do things like that in Chicago."

"Yeah?"

"I went to the cops and now he's got an APB out on his ass," he says with satisfaction. "You run into him, you let me know."

"Okay," I say. "What is your name, sir?"

"Stanley."

"And how can I reach you?"

"Oh," Stanley says, in the same rapid voice, "you don't have to reach, uh, me. You can just call the cops. Go straight to the cops." He reaches into a pocket and pulls out a greasy piece of pasteboard. "See, here's my report on him."

I look. The "report," the size of an index card, is labeled "PRO-ACT: Phoenix Residents Opposing Active Crime Threat." Or is it "Organized Against Crime Threat"? In the darkening street it's hard to read. Some kind of vigilante group? Neighborhood watch? I feel very puzzled.

"Are you a police officer, sir?"

He smiles, seems very pleased by the question.

"No," he says.

"But you are a 'Phoenix Resident'?"

"Would you believe a homeless person," Stanley says.

"Really? But what's with the . . ." For the first time I take a close look at Stanley's trolley. It's a rubber-wheeled thing of industrial metal, but the device I had mistaken for a tank of propane is in fact a water cooler. Stanley also has an army duffel bag, stuffed tight as a sausage with clothing or perhaps a tent, and, at the base of his trolley, a cardboard box and a battered leather briefcase.

"I see," I say, quite at a loss. For the first time I notice that Stanley has a wallet. He has not lost his wallet at all. It is in his back pocket and chained to his belt. It's not a new wallet. It seems to have seen a lot of wear.

"Well, you know how it is, brother," says Stanley. Now that I know that he is homeless—*a possible threat*—my entire perception of him has changed in an instant. His speech, which once seemed just bright and enthusiastic, now seems to have a dangerous tang of mania. "I have to do this!" he assures me. "Track this guy down. . . . It's a thing I do . . . you know . . . to keep myself together!" He smiles, nods, lifts his trolley by its decaying rubber handgrips.

"Gotta work together, y'know," Stanley booms, his face alight with cheerfulness. "The police can't do everything!"

The gentlemen I met in my stroll in downtown Phoenix are

the only computer illiterates in this book. To regard them as irrelevant, however, would be a grave mistake. As computerization spreads across society, the populace at large is subjected to wave after wave of future shock. But, as a necessary converse, the "computer community" itself is subjected to wave after wave of incoming computer illiterates. How will those currently enjoying America's digital bounty regard, and treat, all this teeming refuse yearning to breathe free? Will the electronic frontier be another Land of Opportunity—or an armed and monitored enclave, where the disenfranchised snuggle on their cardboard at the locked doors of our houses of justice?

Some people just don't get along with computers. They can't read. They can't type. They just don't have it in their heads to master arcane instructions from wirebound manuals. Somewhere, the process of computerization of the populace will reach a limit. Some people—quite decent people maybe, who might have thrived in any other situation—will be left irretrievably outside the bounds. What's to be done with these people, in the bright new shiny electroworld? How will they be regarded by the mouse-whizzing masters of cyberspace? With contempt? Indifference? Fear?

In retrospect, it astonishes me to realize how quickly poor Stanley became a perceived threat. Surprise and fear are closely allied feelings. And the world of computing is full of surprises.

I met one character in the streets of Phoenix whose role in this book is supremely and directly relevant. That personage was Stanley's giant thieving scarred phantom. This phantasm is everywhere in this book. He is the specter haunting cyberspace.

Sometimes he's a maniac vandal ready to smash the phone system for no sane reason at all. Sometimes he's a fascist Fed, coldly programming his mighty mainframes to destroy our Bill of Rights. Sometimes he's a telco bureaucrat, covertly conspiring to register all modems in the service of an Orwellian surveillance regime. Mostly, though, this fearsome phantom is a hacker. He's strange, he doesn't belong, he's not authorized, he doesn't smell right, he's not keeping his proper place, he's not one of us. The focus of fear is the hacker, for much the same reasons that Stanley's fancied assailant is black.

Stanley's demon can't go away, because he doesn't exist. Despite singleminded and tremendous effort, he can't be arrested, sued, jailed, or fired. The only constructive way to do *anything* about him is to learn more about Stanley himself. This learning process may be repellent, it may be ugly, it may involve grave elements of paranoiac confusion, but it's necessary. Knowing Stanley requires something more than class-crossing condescension. It requires more than steely legal objectivity. It requires human compassion and sympathy.

To know Stanley is to know his demon. If you know the other guy's demon, then maybe you'll come to know some of your own. You'll be able to separate reality from illusion. And then you won't do your cause, and yourself, more harm than good. Like poor damned Stanley from Chicago did.

The Federal Computer Investigations Committee (FCIC) is the most important and influential organization in the realm of American computer crime. Because the police of other countries have largely taken their computer-crime cues from American methods, the FCIC might well be called the most important computer crime group in the world.

It is also, by federal standards, an organization of great unorthodoxy. State and local investigators mix with federal agents. Lawyers, financial auditors, and computer-security programmers trade notes with street cops. Industry vendors and telco security people show up to explain their gadgetry and plead for protection and justice. Private investigators, think-tank experts, and industry pundits throw in their two cents' worth. The FCIC is the antithesis of a formal bureaucracy.

Members of the FCIC are obscurely proud of this fact; they recognize their group as aberrant but are entirely convinced that this, for them, outright *weird* behavior is nevertheless *absolutely necessary* to get their jobs done.

FCIC regulars—from the Secret Service, the FBI, the Internal

Revenue Service, the Department of Labor, the offices of federal attorneys, state police, the air force, from military intelligence—often attend meetings, held hither and thither across the country, at their own expense. The FCIC doesn't get grants. It doesn't charge membership fees. It doesn't have a boss. It has no head-quarters—just a mail drop in Washington, D.C., at the Fraud Division of the Secret Service. It doesn't have a budget. It doesn't have schedules. It meets three times a year—sort of. Sometimes it issues publications, but the FCIC has no regular publisher, no treasurer, not even a secretary. There are no minutes of FCIC meetings. Nonfederal people are considered "nonvoting mem-bers," but there's not much in the way of elections. There are no badges, lapel pins, or certificates of membership. Everyone is on a first-name basis. There are about forty of them. Nobody knows how many, exactly. People come, people go—sometimes people "go" formally but still hang around anyway. Nobody has ever exactly figured out what "membership" of this "committee" ac-tually entails.

Strange as this may seem to some, to anyone familiar with the social world of computing, the "organization" of the FCIC is very recognizable.

For years now, economists and management theorists have speculated that the tidal wave of the information revolution would destroy rigid, pyramidal bureaucracies, where everything is top-down and centrally controlled. Highly trained "employees" would take on much greater autonomy, being self-starting and self-motivating, moving from place to place, task to task, with great speed and fluidity. "Ad-hocracy" would rule, with groups of people spontaneously knitting together across organizational lines, tackling the problem at hand, applying intense computer-aided expertise to it, and then vanishing whence they came.

This is more or less what has actually happened in the world of federal computer investigation. With the conspicuous exception of the phone companies, which are after all over a hundred years old, practically *every* organization that plays any important role in this book functions just like the FCIC. The Chicago Task Force, the Arizona Racketeering Unit, the Legion of Doom, the *Phrack* crowd, the Electronic Frontier Foundation—they *all* look and act like "tiger teams" or "users' groups." They are all electronic ad-hocracies leaping up spontaneously to attempt to meet a need.

Some are police. Some are, by strict definition, criminals. Some are political interest groups. But every single group has that same quality of apparent spontaneity: "Hey, gang! My uncle's got a barn—let's put on a show!"

Every one of these groups is embarrassed by this "amateur-ism," and, for the sake of their public image in a world of noncomputer people, they all attempt to look as stern and formal and impressive as possible. These electronic frontier dwellers re-semble groups of nineteenth-century pioneers hankering after the respectability of statehood. There are, however, two crucial differ-ences in the historical experience of these "pioneers" of the nine-teenth and twenty-first centuries.

First, powerful information technology *does* play into the hands of small, fluid, loosely organized groups. There have always been pioneers, hobbyists, amateurs, dilettantes, volunteers, movements, users' groups, and blue-ribbon panels of experts around. But a group of this kind—when technically equipped to ship huge amounts of specialized information, at lightning speed, to its members, to government, and to the press—is simply a different kind of animal. It's like the difference between an eel and an electric eel.

The second crucial change is that American society is currently in a state approaching permanent technological revolution. In the world of computers particularly, it is practically impossible *ever* to stop being a "pioneer," unless you either drop dead or deliber-ately jump off the bus. The scene has never slowed down enough to become well institutionalized. And after twenty, thirty, forty years, the "computer revolution" continues to spread, to perme-ate new corners of society. Anything that really works is already obsolete.

If you spend your entire working life as a "pioneer," the word begins to lose its meaning. Your way of life looks less and less like an introduction to "something else" more stable and organized, and more and more like *just the way things are.* A "permanent revolution" is really a contradiction in terms. If "turmoil" lasts long enough, it simply becomes *a new kind of society*—still the same game of history, but new players, new rules.

Apply this to the world of late twentieth-century law enforcement, and the implications are novel and puzzling indeed. Any bureaucratic rulebook you write about computer crime will be flawed when you write it and almost an antique by the time it sees print. The fluidity and fast reactions of the FCIC give it a great advantage in this regard, which explains its success. Even with the best will in the world (which it does not, in fact, possess), it is impossible for an organization the size of the U.S. Federal Bureau of Investigation to get up to speed on the theory and practice of computer crime. If it tried to train all its agents to do this, it

If the FCIC went over a cliff in a bus, the U.S. law enforcement community would be rendered deaf, dumb, and blind in the world of computer crime.

would be *suicidal,* as the Bureau would *never be able to do anything else.*

The FBI does try to train its agents in the basics of electronic crime, at its base in Quantico, Virginia. And the Secret Service, along with many other law enforcement groups, runs quite successful and well attended training courses on wire fraud, business crime, and computer intrusion at the Federal Law Enforcement Training Center (FLETC, pronounced "fletsy") in Glynco, Georgia. But the best efforts of these bureaucracies does not remove the absolute need for a "cutting-edge mess" like the FCIC.

For you see, the FCIC *is* the trainer of the rest of law enforcement. Practically and literally speaking, it is the Glynco computer-crime faculty by another name. If the FCIC went over a cliff on a bus, the U.S. law enforcement community would be rendered deaf, dumb, and blind in the world of computer crime, and would swiftly feel a desperate need to reinvent it. And this is no time to go starting from scratch.

On June 11, 1991, I once again arrived in Phoenix, Arizona, for the latest meeting of the Federal Computer Investigations Committee. This was more or less the twentieth meeting of this stellar group. The count was uncertain, because nobody could figure out whether to include the meetings of "the Colloquy," which is what the FCIC was called in the mid-1980s before it had even managed to obtain the dignity of its own acronym.

Since my last visit to Arizona, in May, the local AzScam bribery scandal had resolved itself in a general muddle of humiliation. The Phoenix chief of police, whose agents had videotaped nine state legislators up to no good, had resigned his office in a tussle with the Phoenix city council over the propriety of his undercover operations. He could now join Gail Thackeray and eleven of her closest associates in the shared experience of politically motivated unemployment. As of June, resignations were still continuing at the Arizona attorney general's office, which could be interpreted as either a New Broom Sweeping Clean or a Night of the Long Knives Part II, depending on your point of view.

The meeting of FCIC was held at the Scottsdale Hilton Resort. Scottsdale is a wealthy suburb of Phoenix, known as "Scottsdull" to scoffing local trendies, but well equipped with posh shopping malls and manicured lawns, while conspicuously undersupplied with homeless derelicts. The Scottsdale Hilton Resort was a sprawling hotel in postmodern crypto-southwestern style. It featured a mission bell tower plated in turquoise tile and vaguely resembling a Saudi minaret.

Inside it was all barbarically striped Santa Fe style decor. There was a health spa downstairs and a large oddly shaped pool in the patio. A poolside umbrella stand offered Ben and Jerry's politically correct Peace Pops.

I registered as a member of FCIC, attaining a handy discount rate, then went in search of the feds. Sure enough, at the back of the hotel grounds came the unmistakable sound of Gail Thackeray holding forth.

Because I had also attended the Computers Freedom and Privacy conference (about which more later), this was the second time I had seen Thackeray in a group of her law enforcement colleagues. Once again I was struck by how simply pleased they seemed to see her. It was natural that she'd get *some* attention, as Gail was one of two women in a group of some thirty men; but there was a lot more to it than that.

Gail Thackeray personifies the social glue of the FCIC. The members could give a damn about her losing her job with the attorney general. They were sorry about it, of course, but hell, they'd all lost jobs. If they were the kind of guys who liked steady boring jobs, they would never have gotten into computer work in the first place.

I wandered into her circle and was immediately introduced to five strangers. The conditions of my visit at FCIC were reviewed. I would not quote anyone directly. I would not tie opinions expressed to the agencies of the attendees. I would not (a purely hypothetical example) report the conversation of a guy from the Secret Service talking quite civilly to a guy from the FBI, as these two agencies *never* talk to each other, and the IRS (also present, also hypothetical) *never talks to anybody.*

Worse yet, I was forbidden to attend the first conference. And I didn't. I have no idea what the FCIC was up to behind closed doors that afternoon. I rather suspect that the members were engaging in a frank and thorough confession of their errors, goof-ups, and blunders, as this has been a feature of every FCIC meeting since their legendary Memphis beer bust of 1986. Perhaps the single greatest attraction of FCIC is that it is a place where you can go, let your hair down, and level completely with people who actually comprehend what you are talking about. Not only do they understand you, but they *really pay attention,* they are *grateful for your insights,* and they *forgive you,* which in nine cases out of ten is something even your boss can't do, because as soon as you start talking "ROM," "BBS," or "T-1 trunk," his eyes glaze over.

I had nothing much to do that afternoon. The FCIC was

beavering away in the conference room. Doors were firmly closed, windows too dark to peer through. I wondered what a real hacker, a computer intruder, would do at a meeting like this.

The answer came at once. He would "trash" the place. Not reduce the place to trash in some orgy of vandalism; that's not the use of the term in the hacker milieu. No, he would quietly *empty the trash baskets* and silently raid any valuable data indiscreetly thrown away.

Journalists have been known to do this. (Journalists hunting information have been known to do almost every single unethical thing that hackers have ever done. They also throw in a few awful techniques all their own.) The legality of "trashing" is somewhat dubious, but it is not in fact flagrantly illegal. It was, however, absurd to contemplate trashing the FCIC. These people knew all about trashing. I wouldn't last fifteen seconds.

The idea sounded interesting, though. I'd been hearing a lot about the practice lately. On the spur of the moment, I decided I would try trashing the office *across the hall* from the FCIC, an area that had nothing to do with the investigators.

The office was tiny: six chairs, a table. . . . Nevertheless, it was open, so I dug around in its plastic trash can.

To my utter astonishment, I came up with the torn scraps of a Sprint long-distance phone bill. More digging produced a bank statement and the scraps of a handwritten letter, along with gum, cigarette ashes, candy wrappers, and a day-old issue of USA To-day.

The trash went back in its receptacle while the scraps of data went into my travel bag. I detoured through the hotel souvenir shop for some Scotch tape and went up to my room.

Coincidence or not, it was quite true. Some poor soul had, in fact, thrown a Sprint bill into the hotel's trash. Date May 1991, total amount due: $252.36. Not a business phone either, but a residential bill, in the name of someone called Evelyn (not her real name). Evelyn's records showed a ** PAST DUE BILL **! Here was her nine-digit account ID. Here was a stern computer-printed warning:

TREAT YOUR FONCARD AS YOU WOULD ANY CREDIT
CARD. TO SECURE AGAINST FRAUD, NEVER GIVE YOUR
FONCARD NUMBER OVER THE PHONE UNLESS YOU INI-
TIATED THE CALL. IF YOU RECEIVE SUSPICIOUS
CALLS PLEASE NOTIFY CUSTOMER SERVICE IMMEDI-
ATELY!

I examined my watch. Still plenty of time left for the FCIC to
carry on. I sorted out the scraps of Evelyn's Sprint bill and reas-
sembled them with fresh Scotch tape. Here was her ten-digit
Foncard number. Didn't seem to have the ID number necessary
to cause real fraud trouble.

I did, however, have Evelyn's home phone number. And the
phone numbers for a whole crowd of Evelyn's long-distance
friends and acquaintances. In San Diego, Folsom, Redondo, Las
Vegas, La Jolla, Topeka, Northampton, Massachusetts. Even
somebody in Australia!

I examined other documents. Here was a bank statement. It
was Evelyn's IRA account down at a bank in San Mateo, California (total balance $1877.20). Here was a charge-card bill for
$382.64. She was paying it off bit by bit.

Driven by motives that were completely unethical and prurient, I now examined the handwritten notes. They had been torn
fairly thoroughly, so much so that it took me almost an entire five
minutes to reassemble them.

They were drafts of a love letter. They had been written on the
lined stationery of Evelyn's employer, a biomedical company.
Probably written at work when she should have been doing something else.

> Dear Bob [not his real name], I guess in everyone's life there
> comes a time when hard decisions have to be made, and this is a
> difficult one for me—very upsetting. Since you haven't called me,
> and I don't understand why, I can only surmise it's because you
> don't want to. I thought I would have heard from you Friday. I did
> have a few unusual problems with my phone and possibly you
> tried, I hope so.
> Robert, you asked me to "let go" . . .

The first note ended. *Unusual problems with her phone?* I looked swiftly at the next note.

> Bob, not hearing from you for the whole weekend has left me very perplexed . . .

Next draft.

> Dear Bob, there is so much I don't understand right now, and I wish I did. I wish I could talk to you, but for some unknown reason you have elected not to call—this is so difficult for me to understand . . .

She tried again.

> Bob, Since I have always held you in such high esteem, I had every hope that we could remain good friends, but now one essential ingredient is missing—respect. Your ability to discard people when their purpose is served is appalling to me. The kindest thing you could do for me now is to leave me alone. You are no longer welcome in my heart or home . . .

Try again.

> Bob, I wrote a very factual note to you to say how much respect I had lost for you, by the way you treat people, me in particular, so uncaring and cold. The kindest thing you can do for me is to leave me alone entirely, as you are no longer welcome in my heart or home. I would appreciate it if you could retire your debt to me as soon as possible—I wish no link to you in any way. Sincerely, Evelyn.

Good heavens, I thought, the bastard actually owes her money! I turned to the next page.

Bob: very simple. GOODBYE! No more mind games—no more
fascination—no more coldness—no more respect for you! It's over
—Finis. Evie

There were two versions of the final brushoff letter, but they read
about the same. Maybe she hadn't sent it. The final item in my
illicit and shameful booty was an envelope addressed to "Bob" at
his home address, but it had no stamp on it and it hadn't been
mailed.

Maybe she'd just been blowing off steam because her rascal
boyfriend had neglected to call her one weekend. Big deal. Maybe
they'd kissed and made up, maybe she and Bob were down at
Pop's Chocolate Shop now, sharing a malted. Sure.

Phone phreaks and hackers deceive people over the phone all the time.

Easy to find out. All I had to
do was call Evelyn up. With a
half-clever story and enough
brass-plated gall I could probably trick the truth out of her.

Phone phreaks and hackers de-
ceive people over the phone all the time. It's called "social engineering." Social engineering is a very common practice in the
underground, and almost magically effective. Human beings are
almost always the weakest link in computer security. The simplest way to learn Things You Are Not Meant To Know is simply
to call up and exploit the knowledgeable people. With social engineering, you use the bits of specialized knowledge you already
have as a key to manipulate people into believing that you are
legitimate. You can then coax, flatter, or frighten them into revealing almost anything you want to know. Deceiving people (especially over the phone) is easy and fun. Exploiting their
gullibility is very gratifying; it makes you feel very superior to
them.

If I'd been a malicious hacker on a trashing raid, I would now
have Evelyn very much in my power. Given all this inside data, it
wouldn't take much effort at all to invent a convincing lie. If I
was ruthless enough, and jaded enough, and clever enough, this

momentary indiscretion of hers—maybe committed in tears, who knows—could cause her a whole world of confusion and grief.

I didn't even have to have a *malicious* motive. Maybe I'd be "on her side" and call up Bob instead, and anonymously threaten to break both his kneecaps if he didn't take Evelyn out for a steak dinner pronto. It was still profoundly *none of my business*. To have gotten this knowledge at all was a sordid act and to use it would be to inflict a sordid injury.

To do all these awful things would require exactly zero high-tech expertise. All it would take was the willingness to do it and a certain amount of bent imagination.

I went back downstairs. The hard-working FCIC members, who had labored forty-five minutes over their schedule, were through for the day and adjourned to the hotel bar. We all had a beer.

I had a chat with a guy about "Isis," or rather IACIS, the International Association of Computer Investigation Specialists. They're into "computer forensics," the techniques of picking computer systems apart without destroying vital evidence. IACIS, currently run out of Oregon, is comprised of investigators in the United States, Canada, Taiwan, and Ireland. "Taiwan and Ireland?" I said. Are *Taiwan* and *Ireland* really in the forefront of this stuff? Well, not exactly, my informant admitted. They just happen to have been the first ones to have caught on by word of mouth. Still, the international angle counts, because this is obviously an international problem. Phone lines go everywhere.

There was a Mountie here from the Royal Canadian Mounted Police. He seemed to be having quite a good time. Nobody had flung this Canadian out because he might pose a foreign security risk. These are cyberspace cops. They still worry a lot about "jurisdictions," but mere geography is the least of their troubles.

NASA had failed to show. NASA suffers a lot from computer intrusions, in particular from Australian raiders and a well-trumpeted Chaos Computer Club case, and in 1990 there was a brief press flurry when it was revealed that one of NASA's Houston branch exchanges had been systematically ripped off by a gang of phone phreaks. But the NASA guys had had their funding cut. They were stripping everything.

Air Force OSI, its Office of Special Investigations, is the *only* federal entity dedicated full time to computer security. It had been expected to show up in force, but some of them had canceled—a Pentagon budget pinch.

As the empties piled up, the guys began joshing around and telling war stories. "These are cops," Thackeray said tolerantly. "If they're not talking shop they talk about women and beer."

I heard the story about the guy who, asked for "a copy" of a computer disk, *photocopied the label on it.* He put the floppy disk onto the glass plate of a photocopier. The blast of static when the copier worked completely erased all the real information on the disk.

Some other poor souls threw a whole bag of confiscated diskettes into the squad-car trunk next to the police radio. The powerful radio signal blasted them too.

We heard a bit about Dave Geneson, the first computer prosecutor, a mainframe system administrator in Dade County turned lawyer. Dave Geneson was one guy who had hit the ground running, a signal virtue in making the transition to computer crime. It generally was agreed that it was easier to learn the world of computers first, then police or prosecutorial work. You could take certain computer people and train 'em to successful police work —but of course they had to have the *cop mentality.* They had to have street smarts. Patience. Persistence. And discretion. You've got to make sure they're not hot shots, showoffs, "cowboys."

Most of the folks in the bar had backgrounds in military intelligence, or drugs, or homicide. In was rudely opined that "military intelligence" was a contradiction in terms, while even the grisly world of homicide was considered cleaner than drug enforcement. One guy had been way undercover doing dope work in Europe for four years straight. "I'm almost recovered now," he said deadpan, with the acid black humor that is pure cop. "Hey, now I can say *fucker* without putting *mother* in front of it."

"In the cop world," another guy said earnestly, "everything is good and bad, black and white. In the computer world everything is gray."

One guy—a founder of the FCIC, who'd been with the group since it was just the Colloquy—described his own introduction to the field. He'd been a Washington, D.C., homicide guy called in on a "hacker" case. From the word "hacker" he naturally assumed he was on the trail of a knife-wielding marauder, and went to the computer center expecting blood and a body. When he finally figured out what was happening there (after loudly demanding, in vain, that the programmers "speak English"), he called headquarters and told them he was clueless about computers. They told him nobody else knew diddly either and to get the hell back to work.

So, he said, he had proceeded by comparisons. By analogy. By metaphor. "Somebody broke in to your computer, huh?" Breaking and entering; I can understand that. How'd he get in? "Over the phone lines." Harassing phone calls, I can understand that! What we need here is a tap and a trace!

It worked. It was better than nothing. And it worked a lot faster when he got hold of another cop who'd done something similar. And then the two of them got another, and another, and pretty soon the Colloquy was a happening thing. It helped a lot that everybody seemed to know Carlton Fitzpatrick, the data-processing trainer in Glynco.

The ice broke big-time in Memphis in 1986. The Colloquy had attracted a bunch of new guys—Secret Service, FBI, military, other feds, heavy guys. Nobody wanted to tell anybody anything. They suspected that if word got back to the home office, they'd all be fired. They passed an uncomfortably guarded afternoon.

The formalities got them nowhere. But after the formal session was over, the organizers brought in a case of beer. As soon as the participants knocked it off with the bureaucratic ranks and turf-fighting, everything changed. "I bared my soul," one veteran reminisced proudly. By nightfall they were building pyramids of empty beer cans and doing everything but composing a team fight song.

FCIC were not the only computer-crime people around. There was DATTA (District Attorneys' Technology Theft Association), though they specialized mostly in chip theft, intellectual property, and black-market cases. There was HTCIA (High Tech Computer Investigators Association), also out in Silicon Valley, a year older than FCIC and featuring brilliant people such as Donald Ingraham. There was LEETAC (Law Enforcement Electronic Technology Assistance Committee) in Florida, and computer-crime units in Illinois and Maryland and Texas and Ohio and Colorado and Pennsylvania. But these were local groups. FCIC were the first to really network nationally and on a federal level.

FCIC people live on the phone lines. Not on bulletin board systems—they know very well what boards are, and they know that boards aren't secure. Everyone in the FCIC has a voice-phone bill like you wouldn't believe. FCIC people have been tight with the telco people for a long time. Telephone cyberspace is their native habitat.

FCIC has three basic subtribes: the trainers, the security people, and the investigators. That's why it's called an "Investigations Committee" with no mention of the term "computer crime"—the dreaded "C-word." FCIC, officially, is "an association of agencies rather than individuals"; unofficially, this field is small enough that the influence of individuals and individual expertise is paramount. Attendance is by invitation only, and most everyone in FCIC considers himself a prophet without honor in his own house.

Again and again I heard this, with different terms but identical sentiments. "I'd been sitting in the wilderness talking to myself." "I was totally isolated." "I was desperate." "FCIC is the best thing there is about computer crime in America." "FCIC is what really works." "This is where you hear real people telling you what's really happening out there, not just lawyers picking nits." "We taught each other everything we knew."

The sincerity of these statements convinces me that this is true. FCIC is the real thing and it is invaluable. It's also very sharply at odds with the rest of the traditions and power structure in American law enforcement. There probably hasn't been anything around as loose and go-getting as the FCIC since the start of the U.S. Secret Service in the 1860s. FCIC people are living like twenty-first-century people in a twenti-eth-century environment, and while there's a great deal to be said for that, there's also a

> *He confessed that later that day he'd arrested a small tree.*

great deal to be said against it, and those against it happen to control the budgets.

I listened to two FCIC guys from Jersey compare life histories. One of them had been a biker in a fairly heavy-duty gang in the 1960s. "Oh, did you know so-and-so?" said the other guy from Jersey. "Big guy, heavyset?"

"Yeah, I knew him."

"Yeah, he was one of ours. He was our plant in the gang."

"Really? Wow! Yeah, I knew him. Helluva guy."

Thackeray reminisced at length about being tear-gassed blind in the November 1969 antiwar protests in Washington Circle, covering them for her college paper. "Oh, yeah I was there," said another cop. "Glad to hear that tear gas hit somethin'. Haw haw haw." He'd been so blind himself, he confessed, that later that day he'd arrested a small tree.

FCIC is an odd group, sifted out by coincidence and necessity, and turned into a new kind of cop. There are a lot of specialized cops in the world—your bunco guys, your drug guys, your tax guys, but the only group that matches FCIC for sheer isolation are probably the child-pornography people. Because they both deal with conspirators who are desperate to exchange forbidden data and also desperate to hide; and because nobody else in law enforcement even wants to hear about it.

FCIC people tend to change jobs a lot. They tend not to get the equipment and training they want and need. And they tend to get sued quite often.

As the night wore on and a band set up in the bar, the talk grew darker. Nothing ever gets done in government, someone opined, until there's a *disaster.* Computing disasters are awful, but there's no denying that they greatly help the credibility of FCIC people. The Internet worm, for instance. "For years we'd been warning about that—but it's nothing compared to what's coming." They expect horrors, these people. They know that nothing will really get done until there is a horror.

Next day we heard an extensive briefing from a guy who'd been a computer cop, gotten into hot water with an Arizona city council, and now installed computer networks for a living (at a considerable raise in pay). He talked about pulling fiber-optic networks apart.

Even a single computer, with enough peripherals, is a literal "network"—a bunch of machines all cabled together, generally with a complexity that puts stereo units to shame. FCIC people invent and publicize methods of seizing computers and maintaining their evidence. Simple things, sometimes, but vital rules of thumb for street cops, who nowadays often stumble across a busy computer in the midst of a drug investigation or a white-collar bust. For instance: Photograph the system before you touch it. Label the ends of all the cables before you detach anything. "Park" the heads on the disk drives before you move them. Get the diskettes. Don't put the diskettes in magnetic fields. Don't write on diskettes with ballpoint pens. Get the manuals. Get the printouts. Get the handwritten notes. Copy data before you look at it, and then examine the copy instead of the original.

Now our lecturer distributed copied diagrams of a typical LAN, or "Local Area Network," which happened to be out of Connecticut. *One hundred and fifty-nine* desktop computers, each with its own peripherals. Three "file servers." Five "star couplers," each with thirty-two ports. One sixteen-port coupler off in the corner office. All these machines talking to each other, distributing electronic mail, distributing software, distributing, quite possibly, criminal evidence. All linked by high-capacity fiber-optic cable. A bad guy—cops talk a lot about "bad guys"—might be lurking on PC #47 or #123 and distributing his ill doings onto some dupe's "personal" machine in another office—or another floor—or, quite possibly, two or three miles away! Or, conceivably, the evidence might be "data-striped"—split up into meaningless slivers stored, one by one, on a whole crowd of different disk drives.

The lecturer challenged us for solutions. I for one was utterly clueless. As far as I could figure, the Cossacks were at the gate; there were probably more disks in this single building than were seized during the entirety of Operation Sundevil.

"Inside informant," somebody said. Right. There's always the human angle, something easy to forget when contemplating the arcane recesses of high technology. Cops are skilled at getting people to talk, and computer people, given a chair and some sustained attention, will talk about their computers till their throats go raw. There's a case on record of a single question— "How'd you do it?"—eliciting a forty-five-minute videotaped confession from a computer criminal who not only completely incriminated himself but drew helpful diagrams.

Computer people talk. Hackers *brag*. Phone phreaks talk *pathologically*—why else are they stealing phone codes, if not to natter for ten hours straight to their friends on an opposite seaboard? Computer-literate people do in fact possess an arsenal of nifty gadgets and techniques that would allow them to conceal all kinds of exotic skullduggery, and if they could only *shut up* about it, they could probably get away with all manner of amazing information crimes. But that's just not how it works—or at least, that's not how it's worked *so far*.

Most every phone phreak ever busted has swiftly implicated his mentors, his disciples, and his friends. Most every white-collar computer criminal, smugly convinced that his clever scheme is bulletproof, swiftly learns otherwise when, for the first time in his life, an actual no-kidding police officer leans over, grabs the front of his shirt, looks him right in the eye, and says: "All right, *asshole*

—you and me are going downtown!" All the hardware in the world will not insulate your nerves from those actual real-life sensations of terror and guilt.

Cops know ways to get from point A to point Z without thumbing through every letter in some smart-ass bad guy's alphabet. Cops know how to cut to the chase. Cops know a lot of things other people don't know.

Hackers know a lot of things other people don't know too. Hackers know, for instance, how to sneak into your computer through the phone lines. But *cops* can show up *right on your doorstep* and carry off *you* and your computer in separate steel boxes. A cop interested in hackers can grab them and grill them. A hacker interested in cops has to depend on hearsay, underground legends, and what cops are willing to publicly reveal. And the Secret Service didn't get named "the *Secret* Service" because they blab a lot.

Some people, our lecturer informed us, were under the mistaken impression that it was "impossible" to tap a fiber-optic line. Well, he announced, he and his son had just whipped up a fiber-optic tap in his workshop at home. He passed it around the audience, along with a circuit-covered LAN plug-in card so we'd all recognize one if we saw it on a case. We all had a look.

The tap was a classic "Goofy Prototype"—a thumb-length rounded metal cylinder with a pair of plastic brackets on it. From one end dangled three thin black cables, each of which ended in a tiny black plastic cap. When you plucked the safety cap off the end of a cable, you could see the glass fiber—no thicker than a pinhole.

Our lecturer informed us that the metal cylinder was a "wavelength division multiplexer." Apparently, what one did was to cut the fiber-optic cable, insert two of the legs into the cut to complete the network again, and then read any passing data on the line by hooking up the third leg to some kind of monitor. Sounded simple enough. I wondered why nobody had thought of it before. I also wondered whether this guy's son back at the workshop had any teenage friends.

We had a break. The guy sitting next to me was wearing a giveaway baseball cap advertising the Uzi submachine gun. We had a desultory chat about the merits of Uzis. Long a favorite of the Secret Service, it seems Uzis went out of fashion with the advent of the Persian Gulf War, our Arab allies taking some offense at Americans toting Israeli weapons. Besides, I was informed by another expert, Uzis jam. The equivalent weapon of choice today is the Heckler & Koch, manufactured in Germany.

The guy with the Uzi cap was a forensic photographer. He also did a lot of photographic surveillance work in computer-crime cases. He used to, that is, until the firings in Phoenix. He was now a private investigator and, with his wife, ran a photography salon specializing in weddings and portrait photos. At—one must repeat—a considerable raise in income.

He was still FCIC. If you were FCIC, and you needed to talk to an expert about forensic photography, well, there he was, willing and able. If he hadn't shown up, people would have missed him.

Our lecturer had raised the point that preliminary investigation of a computer system is vital before any seizure is undertaken. It's vital to understand how many machines are in there, what kinds there are, what kind of operating system they use, how many people use them, where the actual data itself is stored. To simply barge into an office demanding "all the computers" is a recipe for swift disaster.

This entails some discreet inquiries beforehand. In fact, what it entails is basically undercover work. An intelligence operation. *Spying*, not to put too fine a point on it.

In a chat after the lecture, I asked an attendee whether "trashing" might work.

I received a swift briefing on the theory and practice of "trash covers." Police "trash covers," like "mail covers" or like wiretaps, require the agreement of a judge. This obtained, the "trashing" work of cops is just like that of hackers, only more so and much better organized. So much so, I was informed, that mobsters in

Phoenix make extensive use of locked garbage cans picked up by a specialty high-security trash company.

In one case, a tiger team of Arizona cops had trashed a local residence for four months. Every week they showed up on the municipal garbage truck, disguised as garbagemen, and carried the contents of the suspect cans off to a shade tree, where they combed through the garbage—a messy task, especially considering that one of the occupants was undergoing kidney dialysis. All useful documents were cleaned, dried, and examined. A discarded typewriter ribbon was an especially valuable source of data, as its long one-strike ribbon of film contained the contents of every letter mailed out of the house. The letters were neatly retyped by a police secretary equipped with a large desk-mounted magnifying glass.

There is something weirdly disquieting about the whole subject of trashing—an unsuspected and indeed rather disgusting mode of deep personal vulnerability. Things that we pass by every day, that we take utterly for granted, can be exploited with so little work. Once discovered, the knowledge of these vulnerabilities tends to spread.

Take the lowly subject of *manhole covers*. The humble manhole cover reproduces many of the dilemmas of computer security in miniature. Manhole covers are, of course, technological artifacts, access points to our buried urban infrastructure. To the vast majority of us, manhole covers are invisible. They are also vulnerable. For many years now, the Secret Service has made a point of caulking manhole covers along all routes of the presidential motorcade. This is, of course, to deter terrorists from leaping out of underground ambush or, more likely, planting remote-control car-smashing bombs beneath the street.

Lately, manhole covers have seen more and more criminal exploitation, especially in New York City. Recently, a telco in New York City discovered that a cable television service had been sneaking into telco manholes and installing cable service alongside the phone lines—*without paying royalties*. New York companies have also suffered a general plague of (a) underground copper cable theft; (b) dumping of garbage, including toxic waste; and (c) hasty dumping of murder victims.

Industry complaints reached the ears of an innovative New England industrial-security company, and the result was a new product known as "the Intimidator," a thick titanium-steel

> *Quite likely it has never occurred to you to peer under a manhole cover.*

bolt with a precisely machined head that requires a special device to unscrew. All these "keys" have registered serial numbers kept on file with the manufacturer. There are now some thousands of these Intimidator bolts being sunk into American pavements wherever our President passes, like some macabre parody of strewn roses. They are also spreading as fast as steel dandelions around U.S. military bases and many centers of private industry.

Quite likely it has never occurred to you to peer under a manhole cover, perhaps climb down and walk around down there with a flashlight, just to see what it's like. Formally speaking, this might be trespassing, but if you didn't hurt anything, and didn't make an absolute habit of it, nobody would really care. The freedom to sneak under manholes was likely a freedom you never intended to exercise.

You now are rather less likely to have that freedom at all. You may never even have missed it until you read about it here, but if you're in New York City it's gone, and elsewhere it's likely going. This is one of the things that crime, and the reaction to crime, does to us.

The tenor of the meeting now changed as the Electronic Frontier Foundation arrived. The EFF, whose personnel and history will be examined in detail in the next section, is a pioneering civil liberties group that arose in direct response to the Hacker Crackdown of 1990.

Now Mitchell Kapor, the foundation's president, and Michael Godwin, its chief attorney, were confronting federal law enforcement *mano a mano* for the first time ever. Ever alert to the manifold uses of publicity, Mitch Kapor and Mike Godwin had brought their own journalist in tow: Robert Draper, from Austin, whose recent well-received book about *Rolling Stone* magazine was still on the stands. Draper was on assignment for *Texas Monthly*.

The Steve Jackson/EFF civil lawsuit against the Chicago Computer Fraud and Abuse Task Force was a matter of considerable regional interest in Texas. There were now two Austinite journalists here on the case. In fact, counting Godwin (a former Austinite and former journalist), there were three of us. Lunch was like Old Home Week.

Later, I took Draper up to my hotel room. We had a long frank talk about the case, networking earnestly like a miniature freelance-journo version of the FCIC: privately confessing the numerous blunders of journalists covering the story, and trying hard to figure out who was who and what the hell was really going on out there. I showed Draper everything I had dug out of the Hilton trash can. We pondered the ethics of trashing for a while and agreed that they were dismal. We also agreed that finding a Sprint bill on your first time out was a heck of a coincidence.

First I'd "trashed"—and now, mere hours later, I'd bragged to someone else. Having entered the lifestyle of hackerdom, I was now, unsurprisingly, following its logic. Having discovered something remarkable through a surreptitious action, I of course *had* to brag, and to drag the passing Draper into my iniquities. I felt I needed a witness. Otherwise nobody would have believed what I'd discovered. . . .

Back at the meeting, Thackeray cordially, if rather tentatively, introduced Kapor and Godwin to her colleagues. Papers were distributed. Kapor took center stage. The brilliant Bostonian high-tech entrepreneur, normally the hawk in his own administration and quite an effective public speaker, seemed visibly nervous, and frankly admitted as much. He began by saying he considered computer intrusion to be morally wrong and that the EFF was not a "hacker defense fund," despite what had appeared in print. Kapor chatted a bit about the basic motivations of his group, emphasizing their good faith and willingness to listen and seek common ground with law enforcement—when, er, possible.

Then, at Godwin's urging, Kapor suddenly remarked that EFF's own Internet machine had been "hacked" recently and that EFF did not consider this incident amusing.

After this surprising confession, things began to loosen up quite rapidly. Soon Kapor was fielding questions, parrying objections, challenging definitions, and juggling paradigms with something akin to his usual gusto.

Kapor seemed to score quite an effect with his shrewd and skeptical analysis of the merits of telco Caller-ID services. (On this topic, FCIC and EFF have never been at loggerheads, and have no particular established earthworks to defend.) Caller-ID has generally been promoted as a privacy service for consumers, a presentation Kapor described as a "smokescreen," the real point of Caller-ID being to *allow corporate customers to build extensive commercial databases on everybody who phones or faxes them.* Clearly, few people in the room had considered this possibility, except perhaps for two late arrivals from U S West RBOC security, who chuckled nervously.

Mike Godwin then made an extensive presentation entitled "Civil Liberties Implications of Computer Searches and Seizures." Now, at last, we were getting to the real nitty-gritty here, real political horse-trading. The audience listened with close attention, angry mutters rising occasionally: "He's trying to teach us our jobs!" "We've been thinking about this for years! We think about these issues every day!" "If I didn't seize the works, I'd be sued by the guy's victims!" "I'm violating the law if I leave ten thousand disks full of illegal *pirated software* and *stolen codes!*" "It's our job to make sure people don't trash the Constitution— we're the *defenders* of the Constitution!" "We seize stuff when we know it will be forfeited anyway as restitution for the victim!"

"If it's forfeitable, then don't get a search warrant, get a forfeiture warrant," Godwin suggested coolly. He further remarked that most suspects in computer crime don't *want* to see their computers vanish out the door, headed God knew where, for who knows how long. They might not mind a search, even an extensive search, but they want their machines searched on-site.

"Are they gonna feed us?" somebody asked sourly.

"How about if you take copies of the data?" Godwin parried.

"That'll never stand up in court."

"Okay, you make copies, give *them* the copies, and take the originals."

Hmmm.

Godwin championed bulletin board systems as repositories of First Amendment protected free speech. He complained that federal computer-crime training manuals gave boards a bad press, suggesting that they are hotbeds of crime haunted by pedophiles and crooks, whereas the vast majority of the nation's thousands of boards are completely innocuous and nowhere near so romantically suspicious.

People who run boards violently resent it when their systems are seized, and their dozens (or hundreds) of users look on in abject horror. Their rights of free expression are cut short. Their right to associate with other people is infringed. And their privacy is violated as their private electronic mail becomes police property.

Not a soul spoke up to defend the practice of seizing boards. The issue passed in chastened silence. Legal principles aside (and those principles cannot be settled without laws passed or court precedents), seizing bulletin boards has become public-relations poison for American computer police.

And anyway, it's not entirely necessary. If you're a cop, you can get almost everything you need from a pirate board, just by using an inside informant. Plenty of vigilantes—well, *concerned citizens* —will inform police the moment they see a pirate board hit their area (and will tell the police all about it, in such technical detail, actually, that you kinda wish they'd shut up). They will happily supply police with extensive downloads or printouts. It's *impossi-*

ble to keep this fluid electronic information out of the hands of police.

Some people in the electronic community become enraged at the prospect of cops "monitoring" bulletin boards. This does have touchy aspects, as Secret Service people in particular examine bulletin boards with some regularity. But to expect electronic police to be deaf, dumb, and blind in regard to this particular medium rather flies in the face of common sense. Police watch television, listen to radio, read newspapers and magazines; why should the new medium of boards be different? Cops can exercise the same access to electronic information as everybody else. As we have seen, quite a few computer police maintain *their own* bulletin boards, including antihacker sting boards, which have generally proven quite effective.

As a final clincher, their Mountie friends in Canada (and colleagues in Ireland and Taiwan) don't have First Amendment or American constitutional restrictions, but they do have phone lines and can call any bulletin board in America whenever they please. The same technological determinants that play into the hands of hackers, phone phreaks, and software pirates can play into the hands of police. "Technological determinants" don't have *any* human allegiances. They're not black or white, or Establishment or Underground, or pro or anti anything.

Godwin complained at length about what he called "the Clever Hobbyist hypothesis"—the assumption that the hacker you're busting is clearly a technical genius, and must therefore be searched with extreme thoroughness. So: from the law's point of view, why risk missing anything? Take the works. Take the guy's computer. Take his books. Take his notebooks. Take the electronic drafts of his love letters. Take his Walkman. Take his wife's computer. Take his dad's computer. Take his kid sister's computer. Take his employer's computer. Take his compact disks—they *might* be CD-ROM disks, cunningly disguised as pop music. Take his laser printer—he might have hidden something vital in the printer's 5 meg of memory. Take his software manuals and hardware documentation. Take his science-fiction novels and his simulation-gaming books. Take his Nintendo Game-Boy and his Pac-Man arcade game. Take his answering machine, take his telephone out of the wall. Take anything remotely suspicious.

> *It doesn't require an entire computer system and ten thousand disks to prove a case in court.*

Godwin pointed out that most hackers are not, in fact, clever genius hobbyists. Quite a few are crooks and grifters who don't have much in the way of technical sophistication, just some rule-of-thumb rip-off techniques. The same goes for most fifteen-year-olds who've downloaded a code-scanning program from a pirate board. There's no real need to seize everything in sight. It doesn't require an entire computer system and ten thousand disks to prove a case in court.

What if the computer is the instrumentality of a crime? someone demanded.

Godwin admitted quietly that the doctrine of seizing the instrumentality of a crime was pretty well established in the American legal system.

The meeting broke up. Godwin and Kapor had to leave. Kapor was testifying next morning before the Massachusetts Department of Public Utility about ISDN narrowband wide-area networking.

As soon as they were gone, Thackeray seemed elated. She had taken a great risk with this. Her colleagues had not, in fact, torn Kapor's and Godwin's heads off. She was very proud of them, and told them so.

"Did you hear what Godwin said about *instrumentality of a crime?*" she exulted, to nobody in particular. "Wow, that means *Mitch isn't going to sue me.*"

America's computer police are an interesting group. As a social phenomenon they are far more interesting, and far more important, than teenage phone phreaks and computer hackers. First, they're older and wiser; not dizzy hobbyists with leaky morals, but seasoned adult professionals with all the responsibilities of public service. And, unlike hackers, they possess not merely *technical* power alone, but heavy-duty legal and social authority.

And, very interestingly, they are just as much at sea in cyberspace as everyone else. They are not happy about this. Police are authoritarian by nature, and prefer to obey rules and precedents. (Even those police who secretly enjoy a fast ride in rough territory will soberly disclaim any "cowboy" attitude.) But in cyberspace there *are* no rules and precedents. They are groundbreaking pioneers, Cyberspace Rangers, whether they like it or not.

In my opinion, any teenager enthralled by computers, fascinated by the ins and outs of computer security, and attracted by the lure of specialized forms of knowledge and power, would do well to forget all about hacking and set his (or her) sights on becoming a fed. Feds can trump hackers at almost every single thing hackers do, including gathering intelligence, undercover disguise, trashing, phone-tapping, building dossiers, networking, and infiltrating computer systems—*criminal* computer systems. Secret Service agents know more about phreaking, coding, and carding than most phreaks can find out in years, and when it comes to viruses, break-ins, software bombs, and Trojan horses, feds have direct access to red-hot confidential information that is only vague rumor in the underground.

And if it's an impressive public rep you're after, there are few people in the world who can be so chillingly impressive as a well-trained, well-armed U.S. Secret Service agent.

Of course, a few personal sacrifices are necessary in order to obtain that power and knowledge. First, you'll have the galling discipline of belonging to a large organization; but the world of computer crime is still so small, and so amazingly fast moving, that it will remain spectacularly fluid for years to come. The second sacrifice is that you'll have to give up ripping people off. This is not a great loss. Abstaining from the use of illegal drugs, also necessary, will be a boon to your health.

A career in computer security is not a bad choice for a young man or woman today. The field almost certainly will expand drastically in years to come. If you are a teenager today, by the time you become a professional, the pioneers you have read about in this book will be the grand old men and women of the field, swamped by their many disciples and successors. Of course, some of them, like William P. Wood of the 1865 Secret Service, may well be mangled in the whirring machinery of legal controversy; but by the time you enter the computer-crime field, it may have stabilized somewhat, while remaining entertainingly challenging.

But you can't just have a badge. You have to win it. First, there's the federal law enforcement training. And it's hard—it's a challenge. A real challenge—not for wimps and rodents.

Every Secret Service agent must complete grueling courses at the Federal Law Enforcement Training Center. (In fact, Secret Service agents are retrained periodically during their entire careers.)

In order to get a glimpse of what this might be like, in July 1991 I myself traveled to FLETC.

The Federal Law Enforcement Training Center is a 1,500-acre facility on Georgia's Atlantic coast. It's a milieu of marshgrass, seabirds, damp, clinging sea breezes, palmettos, mosquitoes, and bats. Until 1974, it was a navy air base, and still features a working runway, and some WWII vintage blockhouses and officers' quarters. The center has since benefited by a $40 million retrofit, but there's still enough forest and swamp on the facility for the Border Patrol to put in tracking practice.

As a town, Glynco scarcely exists. The nearest real town is Brunswick, a few miles down Highway 17, where I stayed at the aptly named Marshview Holiday Inn. I had Sunday dinner at a seafood restaurant called Jinright's, where I feasted on deep-fried alligator tail. This local favorite was a heaped basket of bite-sized chunks of white, tender, almost fluffy reptile meat, steaming in a peppered batter crust. Alligator makes a culinary experience that's hard to forget, especially when liberally basted with home-made cocktail sauce from a Jinright squeeze bottle.

The crowd of clientele were tourists, fishermen, local black folks in their Sunday best, and white Georgian locals who all seemed to bear an uncanny resemblance to Georgia humorist Lewis Grizzard.

The 2,400 students from 75 federal agencies who make up the FLETC population scarcely seem to make a dent in the low-key local scene. The students look like tourists, and the teachers seem to have taken on much of the relaxed air of the Deep South. My host was Mr. Carlton Fitzpatrick, the program coordinator of the Financial Fraud Institute. Carlton Fitzpatrick is a mustached, sinewy, well-tanned Alabama native somewhere near his late forties, with a fondness for chewing tobacco, powerful computers, and salty, down-home homilies. We'd met before, at FCIC in Arizona.

The Financial Fraud Institute is one of the nine divisions at FLETC. Besides Financial Fraud, there's Driver & Marine, Firearms, and Physical Training. These are specialized pursuits. There are also five general training divisions: Basic Training, Operations, Enforcement Techniques, Legal Division, and Behavioral Science.

Somewhere in this curriculum is everything necessary to turn green college graduates into federal agents. First they're given ID cards. Then they get the rather miserable-looking blue coveralls known as "smurf suits." The trainees are assigned a barracks and a cafeteria, and immediately set on FLETC's bone-grinding physical training routine. Besides the obligatory daily jogging (the trainers run up danger flags beside the track when the humidity rises high enough to threaten heat stroke), there's the Nautilus machines, the martial arts, the survival skills . . .

The eighteen federal agencies that maintain on-site academies at FLETC employ a wide variety of specialized law enforcement units, some of them rather arcane. There's Border Patrol, IRS Criminal Investigation Division, Park Service, Fish and Wildlife,

Customs, Immigration, Secret Service, and the Treasury's uniformed subdivisions . . . If you're a federal cop and you don't work for the FBI, you train at FLETC. This includes people as apparently obscure as the agents of the Railroad Retirement Board Inspector General. Or the Tennessee Valley Authority Police, who are in fact federal police officers, and can and do arrest criminals on the federal property of the Tennessee Valley Authority.

And then there are the computer-crime people. All sorts, all backgrounds. Mr. Fitzpatrick is not jealous of his specialized knowledge. Cops all over, in every branch of service, may feel a need to learn what he can teach. Backgrounds don't matter much. Fitzpatrick himself was originally a border patrol veteran, then became a border patrol instructor at FLETC. His Spanish is still fluent—but he found himself strangely fascinated when the first computers showed up at the training center. Fitzpatrick did have a background in electrical engineering, and though he never considered himself a computer hacker, he somehow found himself writing useful little programs for this new and promising gizmo.

He began looking into the general subject of computers and crime, reading Donn Parker's books and articles, keeping an ear cocked for war stories, useful insights from the field, the up-and-coming people of the local computer-crime and high-technology units. . . . Soon he got a reputation around FLETC as the resident "computer expert," and that reputation alone brought him more exposure, more experience—until one day he looked around, and sure enough he *was* a federal computer-crime expert.

In fact, this unassuming, genial man may be *the* federal computer-crime expert. There are plenty of very good computer people, and plenty of very good federal investigators, but the area where these worlds of expertise overlap is very slim. And Carlton Fitzpatrick has been right at the center of that since 1985, the first year of the Colloquy, a group that owes much to his influence.

He seems quite at home in his modest, acoustic-tiled office, with its Ansel Adams–style Western photographic art, a gold-framed Senior Instructor Certificate, and a towering bookcase crammed with three-ring binders with ominous titles such as *Datapro Reports on Information Security* and *CFCA Telecom Security '90*.

The phone rings every ten minutes; colleagues show up at the door to chat about new developments in locksmithing or to shake their heads over the latest dismal developments in the BCCI global banking scandal.

Carlton Fitzpatrick is a fount of computer-crime war stories, related in an acerbic drawl. He tells me the colorful tale of a hacker caught in California some years back. He'd been raiding systems, typing code without a detectable break, for twenty, twenty-four, thirty-six hours straight. Not just logged on—*typing.* Investigators were baffled. Nobody could do that. Didn't he have to go to the bathroom? Was it some kind of automatic keyboard-whacking device that could actually type code?

A raid on the suspect's home revealed a situation of astonishing squalor. The hacker turned out to be a Pakistani computer-science student who had flunked out of a California university. He'd gone com-

> *The suspect had been sitting in front of his computer for a day and a half straight.*

pletely underground as an illegal electronic immigrant and was selling stolen phone service to stay alive. The place was not merely messy and dirty, but in a state of psychotic disorder. Powered by some weird mix of culture shock, computer addiction, and amphetamines, the suspect had in fact been sitting in front of his computer for a day and a half straight, with snacks and drugs at hand on the edge of his desk and a chamber pot under his chair.

Word about stuff like this gets around in the hacker-tracker community.

Carlton Fitzpatrick takes me for a guided tour by car around the FLETC grounds. One of our first sights is the biggest indoor firing range in the world. There are federal trainees in there, Fitzpatrick assures me politely, blasting away with a wide variety of automatic weapons: Uzis, Glocks, AK-47s. . . . He's willing to take me inside. I tell him I'm sure that's really interesting, but I'd rather see his computers. Carlton Fitzpatrick seems quite surprised and pleased. I'm apparently the first journalist he's ever seen who has turned down the shooting gallery in favor of microchips.

Our next stop is a favorite with touring congressmen: the three-mile-long FLETC driving range. Here trainees of the Driver & Marine Division are taught high-speed pursuit skills, setting and breaking roadblocks, diplomatic security driving for VIP limousines. . . . A favorite FLETC pastime is to strap a passing senator into the passenger seat beside a Driver & Marine trainer, hit a hundred miles an hour, then take it right into "the skid pan," a section of greased track where two tons of Detroit iron can whip and spin like a hockey puck.

Cars don't fare well at FLETC. First they're rifled again and again for search practice. Then they do 25,000 miles of high-speed pursuit training; they get about seventy miles per set of steel-belted radials. Then it's off to the skid pan, where sometimes they roll and tumble headlong in the grease. When they're sufficiently grease-stained, dented, and creaky, they're sent to the roadblock unit, where they're battered without pity. And finally they're sacrificed to the Bureau of Alcohol, Tobacco and Firearms, whose trainees learn the ins and outs of car-bomb work by blowing them into smoking wreckage.

There's a railroad boxcar on the FLETC grounds, and a large grounded boat, and a propless plane; all training grounds for searches. The plane sits forlornly on a patch of weedy tarmac next to an eerie blockhouse known as the "ninja compound," where antiterrorism specialists practice hostage rescues. As I gaze on this creepy paragon of modern low-intensity warfare, my nerves are jangled by a sudden staccato outburst of automatic weapons fire, somewhere in the woods to my right. "Nine-millimeter," Fitzpatrick judges calmly.

Even the eldritch ninja compound pales somewhat compared to the truly surreal area known as "the raid-houses." This is a street lined on both sides with nondescript concrete-block houses with flat pebbled roofs. They were once officers' quarters. Now they are training grounds. The first one to our left, Fitzpatrick tells me, has been specially adapted for computer search-and-seizure practice. Inside it has been wired for video from top to bottom, with eighteen pan-and-tilt remotely controlled video-cams mounted on walls and in corners. Every movement of the trainee agent is recorded live by teachers, for later taped analysis. Wasted movements, hesitations, possibly lethal tactical mistakes —all are gone over in detail.

Perhaps the weirdest single aspect of this building is its front door, scarred and scuffed all along the bottom, from the repeated impact, day after day, of federal shoe leather.

Down at the far end some people are practicing a murder.

Down at the far end of the row of raid-houses some people are practicing a murder. We drive by slowly as some very young and rather nervous-looking federal trainees interview a heavyset bald man on the raid-house lawn. Dealing with murder takes a lot of practice; first you have to learn to control your own instinctive disgust and panic, then you have to learn to control the reactions of a nerve-shredded crowd of civilians, some of whom may have just lost a loved one, some of whom may be murderers—quite possibly both at once.

A dummy plays the corpse. The roles of the bereaved, the morbidly curious, and the homicidal are played, for pay, by local Georgians: waitresses, musicians, most anybody who needs to moonlight and can learn a script. These people, some of whom are FLETC regulars year after year, must surely have one of the strangest jobs in the world.

Something about the scene: "normal" people in a weird situa-

tion, standing around talking in bright Georgia sunshine, unsuc-
cessfully pretending that something dreadful has gone on, while a
dummy lies inside on faked bloodstains. . . . Behind this weird
masquerade, like a nested set of Russian dolls, are grim future
realities of real death, real violence, real murders of real people,
that these young agents will really investigate, many times during
their careers. Over and over. Will those anticipated murders look
like this, feel like this—not as "real" as these amateur actors are
trying to make it seem, but both as "real," and as numbingly
unreal, as watching fake people standing around on a fake lawn?
Something about this scene unhinges me. It seems nightmarish
to me, Kafkaesque. I simply don't know how to take it; my head is
turned around; I don't know whether to laugh, cry, or just shudder.

When the tour is over, Carlton Fitzpatrick and I talk about
computers. For the first time cyberspace seems like quite a comfortable place. It seems very real to me suddenly, a place where I
know what I'm talking about, a place I'm used to. It's real.
"Real." Whatever.

Carlton Fitzpatrick is the only person I've met in cyberspace
circles who is happy with his current equipment. He's got a 5 meg
RAM PC with a 112 meg hard disk; a 660 meg's on the way. He's
got a Compaq 386 desktop and a Zenith 386 laptop with 120
meg. Down the hall is a NEC Multi-Sync 2A with a CD-ROM
drive and a 9600 baud modem with four com lines. There's a
training minicomputer, and a 10 meg local mini just for the Center, and a lab full of student PC clones and half-a-dozen Macs or
so. There's a Data General MV 2500 with 8 meg on board and a
370 meg disk.

Fitzpatrick plans to run a UNIX board on the Data General
when he's finished beta-testing the software for it, which he
wrote himself. It'll have e-mail features, massive files on all manner of computer-crime and investigation procedures, and will follow the computer-security specifics of the Department of
Defense "Orange Book." He thinks it will be the biggest BBS in
the federal government.

Will it have *Phrack* on it? I ask wryly.

Sure, he tells me. *Phrack, TAP, Computer Underground Digest,* all that stuff. With proper disclaimers, of course.

I ask him if he plans to be the sysop. Running a system that size is very time-consuming, and Fitzpatrick teaches two three-hour courses every day.

No, he says seriously, FLETC has to get its money's worth out of the instructors. He thinks he can get a local volunteer to do it, a high school student.

He says a bit more, something I think about an Eagle Scout law-enforcement liaison program, but my mind has rocketed off in disbelief.

"You're going to put a *teenager* in charge of a federal security BBS?" I'm speechless. It hasn't escaped my notice that the FLETC Financial Fraud Institute is the *ultimate* hacker-trashing target; there is stuff in here, stuff of such utter and consummate cool by every standard of the digital underground. . . . I imagine the hackers of my acquaintance fainting dead-away from forbidden-knowledge greed fits at the mere prospect of cracking the superultra top-secret computers used to train the Secret Service in computer crime.

"Uhm, Carlton," I babble, "I'm sure he's a really nice kid and all, but that's a terrible temptation to set in front of somebody who's, you know, into computers and just starting out."

"Yeah," he says, "that did occur to me." For the first time I begin to suspect that he's pulling my leg.

He seems proudest when he shows me an ongoing project called "JICC," Joint Intelligence Control Council. It's based on the services provided by EPIC, the El Paso Intelligence Center, which supplies data and intelligence to the Drug Enforcement Administration, the Customs Service, the Coast Guard, and the state police of the four southern border states. Certain EPIC files can now be accessed by drug-enforcement police of Central America, South America, and the Caribbean, who can also trade information among themselves. Using a telecom program called "White Hat," written by two brothers named Lopez from the

Dominican Republic, police can now network internationally on inexpensive PCs. Carlton Fitzpatrick is teaching a class of drug-war agents from the Third World, and he's very proud of their progress. Perhaps soon the sophisticated smuggling networks of the Medellín Cartel will be matched by a sophisticated computer network of the Medellín Cartel's sworn enemies. They'll track boats, contraband, the international drug lords who now leap over borders with great ease, defeating the police through the clever use of fragmented national jurisdictions.

JICC and EPIC must remain beyond the scope of this book. They seem to me to be very large topics fraught with complications that I am not fit to judge. I do know, however, that the international, computer-assisted networking of police, across national boundaries, is something that Carlton Fitzpatrick considers very important, a harbinger of a desirable future. I also know that networks by their nature ignore physical boundaries. And I also know that where you put communications you put a community, and that when those communities become self-aware they will fight to preserve themselves and to expand their influence. I make no judgments whether this is good or bad. It's just cyberspace; it's just the way things are.

I asked Carlton Fitzpatrick what advice he would have for a twenty-year-old who wanted to shine someday in the world of electronic law enforcement.

He told me that the number-one rule was simply not to be scared of computers. You don't need to be an obsessive "computer weenie," but you mustn't be buffaloed just because some machine looks fancy. The advantages computers give smart crooks are matched by the advantages they give smart cops. Cops in the future will have to enforce the law "with their heads, not their holsters." Today you can make good cases without ever leaving your office. In the future, cops who resist the computer revolution will never get far beyond walking a beat.

I asked Carlton Fitzpatrick if he had some single message for the public, some single thing that he would most like the American public to know about his work.

He thought about it for a while. "Yes," he said finally. *"Tell* me the rules, and I'll *teach* those rules!" He looked me straight in the eye. "I do the best that I can."

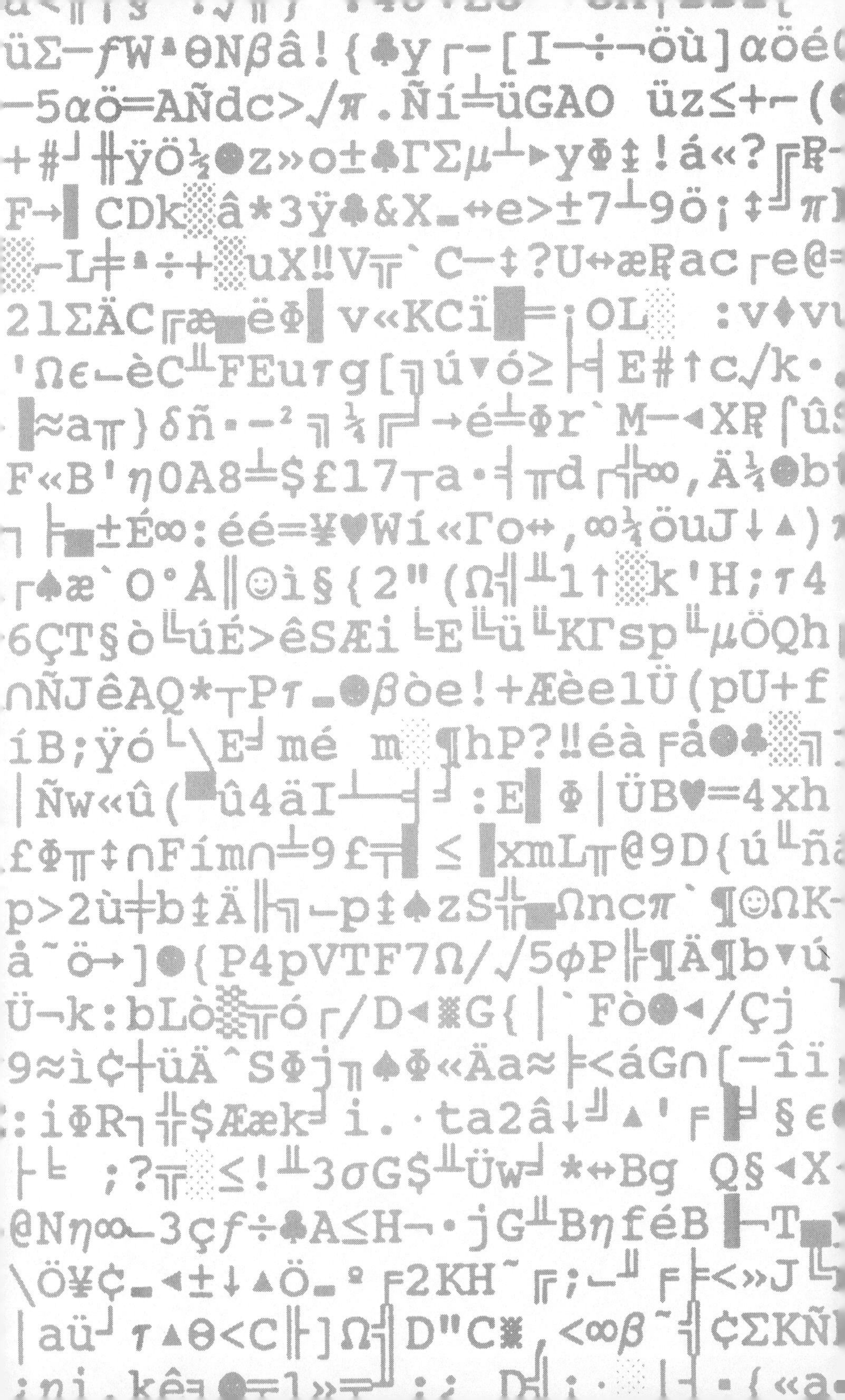

PART
4

THE CIVIL
LIBERTARIANS

$\mathbf{T}$he story of the Hacker Crack-
down, as we have followed it thus far, has been technological,
subcultural, criminal, and legal. The story of the civil libertarians,
though it partakes of all those other aspects, is profoundly and
thoroughly *political*.

In 1990, the obscure, long-simmering struggle over the ownership and nature of cyberspace became loudly and irretrievably
public. People from some of the oddest corners of American society suddenly found themselves public figures. Some of these people found this situation much more than they had ever bargained
for. They backpedaled and tried to retreat back to the mandarin

obscurity of their cozy subcultural niches. This was generally to prove a mistake.

But the civil libertarians seized the day. They found themselves organizing, propagandizing, podium-pounding, persuading, touring, negotiating, posing for publicity photos, submitting to interviews, squinting in the limelight as they tried a tentative, but growingly sophisticated, buck-and-wing upon the public stage.

It's not hard to see why the civil libertarians should have this competitive advantage.

The hackers of the digital underground are a hermetic elite. They find it hard to make any remotely convincing case for their actions in front of the general public. Actually, hackers roundly despise the "ignorant" public, and have never trusted the judgment of "the system." Hackers do propagandize, but only among themselves, mostly in giddy, badly spelled manifestos of class warfare, youth rebellion, or naive techie utopianism. Hackers must strut and boast in order to establish and preserve their underground reputations. But if they speak out too loudly and publicly, they will break the fragile surface tension of the underground, and they will be harassed or arrested. Over the longer term, most hackers stumble, get busted, get betrayed, or simply give up. As a political force, the digital underground is hamstrung.

The telcos, for their part, are an ivory tower under protracted siege. They have plenty of money with which to push their calculated public image, but they waste much energy and goodwill attacking one another with slanderous and demeaning ad campaigns. The telcos have suffered at the hands of politicians, and, like hackers, they don't trust the public's judgment. And this distrust may be well founded. Should the general public of the high-tech 1990s come to understand its own best interests in telecommunications, the situation might well pose a grave threat to the specialized technical power and authority that the telcos have relished for over a century. The telcos do have strong advantages: loyal employees, specialized expertise, influence in the halls of power, tactical allies in law enforcement, and unbelievably vast amounts of money. But politically speaking, they lack genuine grassroots support. They simply don't seem to have many friends.

Cops know a lot of things other people don't know. But cops willingly reveal only those aspects of their knowledge that they feel will meet their institutional purposes and further public order. Cops have respect, they have responsibilities, they have power in the streets and even power in the home, but cops don't do particularly well in limelight. When pressed, they will step out in the public gaze to threaten bad guys, or to cajole prominent citizens, or perhaps to sternly lecture the naive and misguided. But then they retreat to their time-honored fortresses: the station house, the courtroom, and the rule book.

The electronic civil libertarians, however, have proven to be born political animals. They seemed to grasp very early on the postmodern truism that communication is power. Publicity is power. Soundbites are power. The ability to shove one's issue onto the public agenda— and *keep it there*—is power. Fame is power. Simple personal fluency and eloquence can be power, if you can somehow catch the public's eye and ear.

> *The ability to shove one's issue onto the public agenda and keep it there is power.*

The civil libertarians had no monopoly on "technical power"— though they all owned computers, most were not particularly advanced computer experts. They had a good deal of money, but nowhere near the earthshaking wealth and the galaxy of resources possessed by telcos or federal agencies. They had no ability to arrest people. They carried out no phreak and hacker covert dirty tricks.

But they really knew how to network.

Unlike the other groups in this book, the civil libertarians have operated very much in the open, more or less right in the public hurly-burly. They have lectured audiences galore and talked to countless journalists, and have learned to refine their spiels. They've kept the cameras clicking, kept those faxes humming, swapped that e-mail, run those photocopiers on overtime, licked envelopes, and spent small fortunes on airfare and long distance. In an information society, this open, overt, obvious activity has proven to be a profound advantage.

In 1990, the civil libertarians of cyberspace assembled out of nowhere in particular, at warp speed. This "group" (actually, a networking gaggle of interested parties that scarcely deserves even that loose term) has almost nothing in the way of formal organization. Those formal civil libertarian organizations that did take an interest in cyberspace issues, mainly the Computer Professionals for Social Responsibility and the American Civil Liberties Union, were carried along by events in 1990, and acted mostly as adjuncts, underwriters, or launching pads.

The civil libertarians nevertheless enjoyed the greatest success of any of the groups in the Crackdown of 1990. At this writing, their future looks rosy and the political initiative is firmly in their hands. This should be kept in mind as we study the highly unlikely lives and lifestyles of the people who actually made this happen.

In June 1989, Apple Computer, Inc., of Cupertino, California, had a problem. Someone illicitly had copied a small piece of Apple's proprietary software, software that controlled an internal chip driving the Macintosh screen display. This Color QuickDraw source code was a closely guarded piece of Apple's intellectual property. Only trusted Apple insiders were supposed to possess it.

But the "NuPrometheus League" wanted things otherwise. This person (or persons) made several illicit copies of this source code, perhaps as many as two dozen. He (or she, or they) then put those illicit floppy disks into envelopes and mailed them to people all over America: people in the computer industry who were associated with, but not directly employed by, Apple Computer.

The NuPrometheus caper was a complex, highly ideological, and very hackerlike crime. Prometheus, it will be recalled, stole the fire of the gods and gave this potent gift to the general ranks of downtrodden mankind. A similar god-in-the-manger attitude was implied for the corporate elite of Apple Computer, while the "Nu" Prometheus had himself cast in the role of rebel demigod. The illicitly copied data was given away for free.

The new Prometheus, whoever he was, escaped the fate of the ancient Greek Prometheus, who was chained to a rock for centuries by the vengeful gods while an eagle tore and ate his liver. On the other hand, NuPrometheus chickened out somewhat by comparison with his role model. The small chunk of Color Quick-Draw code he had filched and replicated was more or less useless to Apple's industrial rivals (or, in fact, to anyone else). Instead of giving fire to mankind, it was more as if NuPrometheus had photocopied the schematics for part of a Bic lighter. The act was not a genuine work of industrial espionage. It was best interpreted as a symbolic, deliberate slap in the face for the Apple corporate hierarchy.

Apple's internal struggles were well known in the industry. Apple's founders, Jobs and Wozniak, had both taken their leave long since. Their raucous core of senior employees had been a barnstorming crew of 1960s Californians, many of them markedly less than happy with the new button-down multimillion-dollar regime at Apple. Many of the programmers and developers who had invented the Macintosh model in the early 1980s had also left the company. It was they, not the current masters of Apple's corporate fate, who had invented the stolen Color QuickDraw code. The NuPrometheus stunt was well calculated to wound company morale.

Apple called the FBI. The Bureau takes an interest in high-profile intellectual-property theft cases, industrial espionage, and theft of trade secrets. These were likely the right people to call, and rumor has it that the entities responsible were in fact discovered by the FBI and then quietly squelched by Apple management. NuPrometheus was never publicly charged with a crime, prosecuted, or jailed. But there were no further illicit releases of Macintosh internal software. Eventually the painful issue of NuPrometheus was allowed to fade.

In the meantime, however, a large number of puzzled bystanders found themselves entertaining surprise guests from the FBI.

One of these people was John Perry Barlow. Barlow is a most unusual man, difficult to describe in conventional terms. He is perhaps best known as a songwriter for the Grateful Dead, for he composed lyrics for "Hell in a Bucket," "Picasso Moon," "Mexicali Blues," "I Need a Miracle," and many more; he has been writing for the band since 1970.

> *A large number of puzzled bystanders found themselves entertaining surprise guests from the FBI.*

Before we tackle the vexing question as to why a rock lyricist should be interviewed by the FBI in a computer-crime case, it might be well to say a word or two about the Grateful Dead. The Grateful Dead are perhaps the most successful and long-lasting of the numerous cultural emanations from the Haight-Ashbury district of San Francisco, in the glory days of Movement politics and lysergic transcendence. The Grateful Dead are a nexus, a veritable whirlwind, of appliqué decals, psychedelic vans, tie-dyed T-shirts, earth-color denim, frenzied dancing, and open and unashamed drug use. The symbols, and the realities, of Californian freak power surround the Grateful Dead like knotted macrame.

The Grateful Dead and their thousands of Deadhead devotees are radical Bohemians. This much is widely understood. Exactly what this implies in the 1990s is rather more problematic.

The Grateful Dead are among the world's most popular and wealthy entertainers: number twenty, according to *Forbes* magazine, right between M.C. Hammer and Sean Connery. In 1990, this jeans-clad group of purported raffish outcasts earned $17 million. They have been earning sums much along this line for quite some time now.

And while the Dead are not investment bankers or three-piece-suit tax specialists—they are, in point of fact, hippie musicians—this money has not been squandered in senseless Bohemian excess. The Dead have been quietly active for many years, funding various worthy activities in their extensive and widespread cultural community.

The Grateful Dead are not conventional players in the American power establishment. They nevertheless are something of a force to be reckoned with. They have a lot of money and a lot of friends in many places, both likely and unlikely.

The Dead may be known for back-to-the-earth environmentalist rhetoric, but this hardly makes them antitechnological Luddites. On the contrary, like most rock musicians, the Grateful Dead have spent their entire adult lives in the company of complex electronic equipment. They have funds to burn on any sophisticated tool and toy that might happen to catch their fancy. And their fancy is quite extensive.

The Deadhead community boasts any number of recording engineers, lighting experts, rock video mavens, electronic technicians of all descriptions. And the drift goes both ways. Steve Wozniak, Apple's co-founder, used to throw rock festivals. Silicon Valley rocks out.

These are the 1990s, not the 1960s. Today, for a surprising number of people all over America, the supposed dividing line between Bohemian and technician simply no longer exists. People of this sort may have a set of windchimes and a dog with a knotted kerchief 'round its neck, but they're also quite likely to own a multimegabyte Macintosh running MIDI synthesizer software and trippy fractal simulations. These days, even Timothy Leary himself, prophet of LSD, does virtual-reality computer-graphics demos in his lecture tours.

John Perry Barlow is not a member of the Grateful Dead. He is, however, a ranking Deadhead.

Barlow describes himself as a "techno-crank." A vague term such as "social activist" might not be far from the mark either. But Barlow might be better described as a "poet"—if one keeps in mind Percy Shelley's archaic definition of poets as "unacknowledged legislators of the world."

Barlow once made a stab at acknowledged legislator status. In

1987, he narrowly missed the Republican nomination for a seat in the Wyoming State Senate. Barlow is a Wyoming native, the third-generation scion of a well-to-do cattle-ranching family. He is in his early forties, married and the father of three daughters.

Barlow is not much troubled by other people's narrow notions of consistency. In the late 1980s, this Republican rock lyricist cattle rancher sold his ranch and became a computer telecommunications devotee.

The free-spirited Barlow made this transition with ease. He genuinely enjoyed computers. With a beep of his modem, he leapt from small-town Pinedale, Wyoming, into electronic contact with a large and lively crowd of bright, inventive, technological sophisticates from all over the world. Barlow found the social milieu of computing attractive: its fast-lane pace, its blue-sky rhetoric, its open-endedness. Barlow began dabbling in computer journalism, with marked success, as he was a quick study, and both shrewd and eloquent. He frequently traveled to San Francisco to network with Deadhead friends. There Barlow made extensive contacts throughout the Californian computer community, including friendships among the wilder spirits at Apple.

He had to explain the nature of computer crime to a head-scratching local FBI man who specialized in cattle rustling.

In May 1990, Barlow received a visit from a local Wyoming agent of the FBI. The NuPrometheus case had reached Wyoming.

Barlow was troubled to find himself under investigation in an area of his interests once quite free of federal attention. He had to struggle to explain the very nature of computer crime to a head-scratching local FBI man who specialized in cattle rustling. Barlow, chatting helpfully and demonstrating the wonders of his modem to the puzzled fed, was alarmed to find all hackers generally under FBI suspicion as an evil influence in the electronic community. The FBI, in pursuit of a hacker called

NuPrometheus, was tracing attendees of a suspect group called the Hackers Conference.

The Hackers Conference, which had been started in 1984, was a yearly Californian meeting of digital pioneers and enthusiasts. The hackers of the Hackers Conference had little if anything to do with the hackers of the digital underground. On the contrary, the hackers of this conference were mostly well-to-do Californian high-tech CEOs, consultants, journalists, and entrepreneurs. (This group of hackers were the exact sort of "hackers" most likely to react with militant fury at any criminal degradation of the term.)

Barlow, though he was not arrested or accused of a crime, and though his computer had certainly not gone out the door, was very troubled by this anomaly. He carried the word to the Well.

Like the Hackers Conference, "the Well" was an emanation of the Point Foundation. Point Foundation, the inspiration of a wealthy Californian 1960s radical named Stewart Brand, was to be a major launchpad of the civil libertarian effort.

Point Foundation's cultural efforts, like those of their fellow Bay Area Californians the Grateful Dead, were multifaceted and multitudinous. Rigid ideological consistency had never been a strong suit of the *Whole Earth Catalog*. This Point publication had enjoyed a strong vogue during the late 1960s and early 1970s, when it offered hundreds of practical (and not so practical) tips on communitarian living, environmentalism, and getting back to the land. The *Whole Earth Catalog*, and its sequels, sold two and a half million copies and won a National Book Award.

With the slow collapse of American radical dissent, the *Whole Earth Catalog* had slipped to a more modest corner of the cultural radar; but in its magazine incarnation, *CoEvolution Quarterly*, the Point Foundation continued to offer a magpie potpourri of "access to tools and ideas."

CoEvolution Quarterly, which started in 1974, was never a widely popular magazine. Despite periodic outbreaks of millennarian fervor, *CoEvolution Quarterly* failed to revolutionize Western civilization and replace leaden centuries of history with bright new California paradigms. Instead, this propaganda arm of Point Foundation cakewalked a fine line between impressive brilliance and New Age flakiness. *CoEvolution Quarterly* carried no advertising, cost a lot, and came out on cheap newsprint with modest black-and-white graphics. It was poorly distributed, and spread mostly by subscription and word of mouth.

It could not seem to grow beyond 30,000 subscribers. And yet —it never seemed to shrink much either. Year in, year out, decade in, decade out, some strange demographic minority accreted to support the magazine. The enthusiastic readership did not seem to have much in the way of coherent "politics" or "ideals." It was sometimes hard to understand what held them together (if the often bitter debate in the letter columns could be described as "togetherness").

But if the magazine did not flourish, it was resilient; it got by. Then, in 1984, the birth-year of the Macintosh computer, *CoEvolution Quarterly* suddenly hit the rapids. Point Foundation had discovered the computer revolution. Out came the *Whole Earth Software Catalog* of 1984, arousing head-scratching doubts among the tie-dyed faithful and rabid enthusiasm among the nascent cyberpunk milieu, present company included. Point Foundation started its yearly Hackers Conference and began to take an extensive interest in the strange new possibilities of digital counterculture. *CoEvolution Quarterly* folded its teepee, replaced by *Whole Earth Software Review* and eventually by *Whole Earth Review* (the magazine's present incarnation, currently under the editorship of virtual-reality maven Howard Rheingold).

The year 1985 saw the birth of the "WELL"—the "Whole Earth 'Lectronic Link." The Well was Point Foundation's bulletin board system.

As boards went, the Well was an anomaly from the beginning, and remained one. It was local to San Francisco. It was huge, with multiple phone lines and enormous files of commentary. Its complex UNIX-based software might be most charitably described as "user-opaque." It was run on a mainframe out of the rambling offices of a nonprofit cultural foundation in Sausalito. And it was crammed with fans of the Grateful Dead.

Though the Well was peopled by chattering hipsters of the Bay Area counterculture, it was by no means a "digital underground" board. Teenagers were fairly scarce; most Well users (known as "Wellbeings") were thirty- and forty-something Baby Boomers. They tended to work in the information industry: hardware, software, telecommunications, media, entertainment. Librarians, academics, and journalists were especially common on the Well, attracted by Point Foundation's open-handed distribution of "tools and ideas."

There were no anarchy files on the Well, scarcely a dropped hint about access codes or credit card theft. No one used handles. Vicious "flame-wars" were held to a comparatively civilized rumble. Debates were sometimes sharp, but no Wellbeing ever claimed that a rival had disconnected his phone, trashed his house, or posted his credit card numbers.

The Well grew slowly as the 1980s advanced. It charged a modest sum for access and storage, and lost money for years—but not enough to hamper the Point Foundation, which was nonprofit anyway. By 1990, the Well had about five thousand users. These users wandered about a gigantic cyberspace smorgasbord of "Conferences," each conference consisting of a welter of "topics," each topic containing dozens, sometimes hundreds of comments, in a tumbling, multiperson debate that could last for months or years on end.

In 1991, the Well's list of conferences looked like this:

CONFERENCES ON THE WELL

WELL ''Screenzine'' Digest (g zine)

Best of the WELL-vintage material (g best)

Index listing of new topics in all
conferences (g newtops)

Business Education

Apple Library Users Group	(g alug)	Agriculture	(g agri)
Brainstorming	(g brain)	Classifieds	(g cla)
Computer Journalism	(g cj)	Consultants	(g consult)
Comsumers	(g cons)	Design	(g design)
Desktop Publishing	(g desk)	Disability	(g disability)
Education	(g ed)	Energy	(g energy¶l)
Entrepreneurs	(g entre)	Homeowners	(g home)
Indexing	(g indexing)	Investments	(g invest)
Kids¶l	(g kids)	Legal	(g legal)
One Person Business	(g one)	Periodical/ newsletter	(g per)
Telecomm Law	(g tcl)	The Future	(g fut)
Translators	(g trans)	Travel	(g tra)
Work	(g work)		

Electronic Frontier Foundation (g eff)
Computers, Freedom & Privacy (g cfp)
Computer Professionals for Social Responsibility (g cpsr)

Social Political Humanities

Aging	(g gray)	AIDS	(g aids)
Amnesty International	(g amnesty)	Archives	(g arc)
Berkeley	(g berk)	Buddhist	(g wonderland)
Christian	(g cross)	Couples	(g couples)
Current Events	(g curr)	Dreams	(g dream)
Drugs	(g dru)	East Coast	(g east)
Emotional Health ****	(g private)	Erotica	(g eros)
Environment	(g env)	Firearms	(g firearms)
First Amendment	(g first)	Fringes of Reason	(g fringes)
Gay	(g gay)	Gay (Private)#	(g gaypriv)

Geography	(g geo)	German	(g german)
Gulf War	(g gulf)	Hawaii	(g aloha)
Health	(g heal)	History	(g hist)
Holistic	(g holi)	Interview	(g inter)
Italian	(g ital)	Jewish	(g jew)
Liberty	(g liberty)	Mind	(g mind)
Miscellane-ous	(g misc)	Men on the WELL**	(g mow)
Network In-tegration	(g origin)	Nonprofits	(g non)
North Bay	(g north)	Northwest	(g nw)
Pacific Rim	(g pacrim)	Parenting	(g par)
Peace	(g pea)	Peninsula	(g pen)
Poetry	(g poetry)	Philosophy	(g phi)
Politics	(g pol)	Psychology	(g psy)
Psychother-apy	(g therapy)	Recovery##	(g recovery)
San Fran-cisco	(g sanfran)	Scams	(g scam)
Sexuality	(g sex)	Singles	(g singles)
Southern	(g south)	Spanish	(g spanish)
Spiritual-ity	(g spirit)	Tibet	(g tibet)
Transporta-tion	(g transport)	True Confes-sions	(g tru)
Unclear	(g unclear)	WELL Writer's Work-shop***	(g www)
Whole Earth	(g we)	Women on the WELL*	(g wow)
Words	(g words)	Writers	(g wri)

****Private Conference - mail wooly for entry
***Private conference - mail sonia for entry
**Private conference - mail flash for entry
*Private conference - mail reva for entry
#Private Conference - mail hudu for entry
##Private Conference - mail dhawk for entry

Arts Recreation Entertainment

ArtCom Elec-tronic Net	(g acen)	Audio-Video-philia	(g aud)
Bicycles	(g bike)	Bay Area To-night**	(g bat)
Boating	(g wet)	Books	(g books)

CD's	(g cd)	Comics	(g comics)
Cooking	(g cook)	Flying	(g flying)
Fun	(g fun)	Games	(g games)
Gardening	(g gard)	Kids	(g kids)
Nightowls*	(g owl)	Jokes	(g jokes)
MIDI	(g midi)	Movies	(g movies)
Motorcy-cling	(g ride)	Motoring	(g car)
Music	(g mus)	On Stage	(g onstage)
Pets	(g pets)	Radio	(g rad)
Restaurant	(g rest)	Science Fic-tion	(g sf)
Sports	(g spo)	Star Trek	(g trek)
Television	(g tv)	Theater	(g theater)
Weird	(g weird)	Zines/Fact-sheet Five	(g f5)

* Open from midnight to 6am
** Updated daily

Grateful Dead

Grateful Dead	(g gd)	Deadplan*	(g dp)
Deadlit	(g deadlit)	Feedback	(g feedback)
GD Hour	(g gdh)	Tapes	(g tapes)
Tickets	(g tix)	Tours	(g tours)

* Private conference - mail tnf for entry

Computers

AI/Forth/Realtime	(g realtime)	Amiga	(g amiga)
Apple	(g app)	Computer Books	(g cbook)
Art& Graphics	(g gra)	Hacking	(g hack)
HyperCard	(g hype)	IBM PC	(g ibm)
LANs	(g lan)	Laptop	(g lap)
Macintosh	(g mac)	Mactech	(g mactech)
Microtimes	(g microx)	Muchomedia	(g mucho)
NeXt	(g next)	OS/2	(g os2)
Printers	(g print)	Program-mer's Net	(g net)

Siggraph	(g siggraph)	Software De- sign	(g sdc)
Software/ Program- ming	(software)	Software Support	(g ssc)
Unix	(g unix)	Windows	(g windows)
Word Pro- cessing	(g word)		

Technical Communications

Bioinfo	(g bioinfo)	Info	(g boing)
Media	(g media)	NAPLPS	(g naplps)
Netweaver	(g netweaver)	Networld	(g networld)
Packet Radio	(g packet)	Photography	(g pho)
Radio	(g rad)	Science	(g science)
Technical Writers	(g tec)	Telecommu- nications	(g tele)
Usenet	(g usenet)	Video	(g vid)
Virtual Re- ality	(g vr)		

The WELL Itself

Deeper	(g deeper)	Entry	(g ent)
General	(g gentech)	Help	(g help)
Hosts	(g hosts)	Policy	(g policy)
System News	(g news)	Test	(g test)

The list itself is dazzling, bringing to the untutored eye a dizzying impression of a bizarre milieu of mountain-climbing Hawaiian holistic photographers trading true-life confessions with bisexual word-processing Tibetans.

But this confusion is more apparent than real. Each of these conferences was a little cyberspace world in itself, comprising dozens and perhaps hundreds of subtopics. Each conference commonly was frequented by a fairly small, fairly like-minded community of perhaps a few dozen people. It was humanly impossible to encompass the entire Well (especially because access to the Well's mainframe computer was billed by the hour). Most long-time users contented themselves with a few favorite topical neighborhoods, with the occasional foray elsewhere for a taste of exotica. But especially important news items, and hot topical debates, could catch the attention of the entire Well community.

Like any community, the Well had its celebrities, and John Perry Barlow, the silver-tongued and silver-modemed lyricist of the Grateful Dead, ranked prominently among them. It was here on the Well that Barlow posted his true-life tale of computer-crime encounter with the FBI.

The story, as might be expected, created a great stir. The Well was already primed for hacker controversy. In December 1989, *Harper's* magazine had hosted a debate on the Well about the ethics of illicit computer intrusion. While over forty various computer mavens took part, Barlow proved a star in the debate. So did "Acid Phreak" and "Phiber Optik," a pair of young New York hacker-phreaks whose skills at telco switching-station intrusion were matched only by their apparently limitless hunger for fame. The advent of these two boldly swaggering outlaws in the precincts of the Well created a sensation akin to that of Black Panthers at a cocktail party for the radically chic.

Phiber Optik in particular was to seize the day in 1990. A devotee of the *2600* circle and stalwart of the New York hackers' group "Masters of Deception," Phiber Optik was a splendid exemplar of the computer intruder as committed dissident. The eighteen-year-old Optik, a high school dropout and part-time computer repairman, was young, smart, and ruthlessly obsessive, a sharp-dressing, sharp-talking digital dude who was utterly and airily contemptuous of anyone's rules but his own. By late 1991, Phiber Optik had appeared in *Harper's, Esquire, The New York Times*, in countless public debates and conventions, even on a television show hosted by Geraldo Rivera.

Treated with gingerly respect by Barlow and other Well mavens, Phiber Optik swiftly became a Well celebrity. Strangely, despite his thorny attitude and utter singlemindedness, Phiber Optik seemed to arouse strong protective instincts in most of the people who met him. He was great copy for journalists, always fearlessly ready to swagger and, better yet, actually to *demonstrate* some off-the-wall digital stunt. He was a born media darling.

Even cops seemed to recognize that there was something peculiarly unworldly and uncriminal about this particular troublemaker. He was so bold, so flagrant, so young, and so obviously doomed that even those who strongly disapproved of his actions grew anxious for his welfare and began to flutter about him as if he were an endangered seal pup.

In January 24, 1990 (nine days after the Martin Luther King Day Crash), Phiber Optik, Acid Phreak, and a third NYC scofflaw named "Scorpion" were raided by the Secret Service and the New York State Police. Their computers went out the door, along with the usual blizzard of papers, notebooks, compact disks, answering machines, Sony Walkmans, and the like. Both Acid Phreak and Phiber Optik were accused of having caused the crash.

The mills of justice ground slowly. Phiber had lost his machinery in the raid, but no charges were filed against him for over a year. His predicament was extensively publicized on the Well, where it caused much resentment for police tactics. It's one thing to merely hear about a hacker raided or busted; it's another to see the police attacking someone you've come to know personally, and who has explained his motives at length. Through the *Harper's* debate on the Well, it had become clear to the Wellbeings that Phiber Optik was not in fact going to "hurt anything." In their own salad days, many Wellbeings had tasted tear-gas in pitched street battles with police. They were inclined to indulgence for acts of civil disobedience.

Wellbeings were also startled to learn of the draconian thoroughness of a typical hacker search-and-seizure. It took no great stretch of imagination for them to envision themselves suffering much the same treatment.

As early as January 1990, sentiment on the Well had already begun to sour, and people had begun to grumble that "hackers" were getting a raw deal from the ham-handed powers-that-be. The resultant issue of *Harper's* magazine posed the question as to whether computer intrusion was a "crime" at all. As Barlow put it later: "I've begun to wonder if we wouldn't also regard spelunkers as desperate criminals if AT&T owned all the caves."

In February 1991, more than a year after the raid on his home, Phiber Optik was finally arrested and was charged with first-degree Computer Tampering and Computer Trespass, New York state offenses. He was also charged with a theft-of-service misde-meanor, involving a complex free-call scam to a 900 number. Phiber Optik pled guilty to the misdemeanor charge and was sentenced to thirty-five hours of community service.

This passing harassment from the unfathomable world of straight people seemed to bother Optik little if at all. Deprived of his computer by the January search-and-seizure, he simply bought himself a portable computer so the cops could no longer monitor the phone where he lived with his mom, and he went right on with his depredations, sometimes on live radio or in front of television cameras.

The crackdown raid may have done little to dissuade Phiber Optik, but its galling effect on the Wellbeings was profound. As 1990 rolled on, the slings and arrows mounted: the Knight Light-ning raid, the Steve Jackson raid, the nation-spanning Operation Sundevil. The rhetoric of law enforcement made it clear that there was, in fact, a concerted crackdown on hackers in progress.

The hackers of the Hackers Conference, the Wellbeings, and their ilk did not really mind the occasional public misapprehen-sion of "hacking"; if anything, this membrane of differentiation from straight society made the "computer community" feel dif-ferent, smarter, better. They had never before been confronted, however, by a concerted vilification campaign.

Barlow's central role in the counterstruggle was one of the major anomalies of 1990. Journalists investigating the controversy often stumbled over the truth about Barlow, but they commonly dusted themselves off and hurried on as if nothing had happened. It was as if it were *too much to believe* that a 1960s freak from the Grateful Dead had taken on a federal law enforcement operation head-to-head and actually *seemed to be winning!*

Barlow had no easily detectable power base for a political struggle of this kind. He had no formal legal or technical credentials. Barlow was, however, a computer networker of truly stellar brilliance. He had a poet's gift of concise, colorful phrasing. He also had a journalist's shrewdness, an off-the-wall, self-deprecating wit, and a phenomenal wealth of simple personal charm.

The kind of influence Barlow possessed is fairly common currency in literary, artistic, or musical circles. A gifted critic can wield great artistic influence simply through defining the temper of the times, by coining the catchphrases and the terms of debate that become the common currency of the period. (And as it happened, Barlow *was* a part-time art critic, with a special fondness for the Western art of Frederic Remington.)

Barlow was the first commentator to adopt novelist William Gibson's striking science-fictional term "cyberspace" as a synonym for the present-day nexus of computer

> *Cyberspace demanded a new set of metaphors, rules, and behaviors.*

and telecommunications networks. Barlow was insistent that cyberspace should be regarded as a qualitatively new world, a "frontier." According to Barlow, the world of electronic communications, now made visible through the computer screen, could no longer be usefully regarded as just a tangle of high-tech wiring. Instead, it had become a *place*, cyberspace, which demanded a new set of metaphors, a new set of rules and behaviors. The term, as Barlow employed it, struck a useful chord, and this concept of cyberspace was picked up by *Time, Scientific American,* computer police, hackers, and even constitutional scholars. "Cyberspace" now seems likely to become a permanent fixture of the language.

Barlow was very striking in person: a tall, craggy-faced, bearded, deep-voiced Wyomingan in a dashing Western ensemble of jeans, jacket, cowboy boots, a knotted throat kerchief, and an ever-present Grateful Dead cloisonné lapel pin.

Armed with a modem, however, Barlow was truly in his element. Formal hierarchies were not Barlow's strong suit; he rarely missed a chance to belittle the "large organizations and their drones," with their uptight, institutional mindset. Barlow was very much of the free-spirit persuasion, deeply unimpressed by brass hats and jacks-in-office. But when it came to the digital grapevine, Barlow was a cyberspace ad-hocrat par excellence.

There was not a mighty army of Barlows. There was only one Barlow, and he was a fairly anomolous individual. However, the situation only seemed to *require* a single Barlow. In fact, after 1990, many people must have concluded that a single Barlow was far more than they'd ever bargained for.

Barlow's querulous miniessay about his encounter with the FBI struck a strong chord on the Well. A number of other free spirits on the fringes of Apple Computing had come under suspicion, and they liked it not one whit better than he did.

One of these was Mitchell Kapor, the co-inventor of the spreadsheet program "Lotus 1-2-3" and the founder of Lotus Development Corporation. Kapor had written off the passing in-dignity of being fingerprinted down at his own local Boston FBI headquarters, but Barlow's essay made the full national scope of the FBI's dragnet clear to him. The issue now had Kapor's full attention. As the Secret Service swung into antihacker operation nationwide in 1990, Kapor watched every move with deep skepticism and growing alarm.

As it happened, Kapor had already met Barlow, who had inter-viewed him for a California computer journal. Like most people who met Barlow, Kapor had been very taken with him. Now Kapor took it upon himself to drop in on Barlow for a heart-to-heart talk about the situation.

Kapor was a regular on the Well. Kapor had been a devotee of the *Whole Earth Catalog* since the beginning, and treasured a complete run of the magazine. And Kapor not only had a mo-dem, but a private jet. In pursuit of the scattered high-tech investments of Kapor Enterprises Inc., his personal, multimillion-dollar holding company, Kapor commonly crossed state lines with about as much thought as one might give to faxing a letter.

The Kapor-Barlow council of June 1990, in Pinedale, Wyoming, was the start of the Electronic Frontier Foundation. Barlow swiftly wrote a manifesto, "Crime and Puzzlement," which announced his and Kapor's intention to form a political organization to "raise and disburse funds for education, lobbying, and litigation in the areas relating to digital speech and the extension of the Constitution into Cyberspace."

Furthermore, proclaimed the manifesto, the foundation would "fund, conduct, and support legal efforts to demonstrate that the Secret Service has exercised prior restraint on publications, limited free speech, conducted improper seizure of equipment and data, used undue force, and generally conducted itself in a fashion which is arbitrary, oppressive, and unconstitutional."

"Crime and Puzzlement" was distributed far and wide through computer networking channels and also printed in the *Whole Earth Review*. The sudden declaration of a coherent, politicized counterstrike from the ranks of hackerdom electrified the community. Steve Wozniak (perhaps a bit stung by the Nu-Prometheus scandal) swiftly offered to match any funds Kapor offered the foundation.

John Gilmore, one of the pioneers of Sun Microsystems, immediately offered his own extensive financial and personal support. Gilmore, an ardent libertarian, was to prove an eloquent advocate of electronic privacy issues, especially freedom from governmental and corporate computer-assisted surveillance of private citizens.

A second meeting in San Francisco rounded up further allies: Stewart Brand of the Point Foundation, virtual-reality pioneers Jaron Lanier and Chuck Blanchard, network entrepreneur and venture capitalist Nat Goldhaber. At this dinner meeting, the activists settled on a formal title: the Electronic Frontier Foundation, Incorporated. Kapor became its president. A new EFF Conference was opened on the Point Foundation's Well, and the Well was declared "the home of the Electronic Frontier Foundation."

Press coverage was immediate and intense. Like their nine-teenth-century spiritual ancestor, Alexander Graham Bell, the high-tech computer entrepreneurs of the 1970s and 1980s—people such as Wozniak, Jobs, Kapor, Gates, and Texas billionaire H. Ross Perot, who had raised themselves by their bootstraps to dominate a glittering new industry—had always made very good copy.

But while the Wellbeings rejoiced, the press in general seemed nonplussed by the self-declared "civilizers of cyberspace." EFF's insistence that the war against "hackers" involved grave constitutional civil liberties issues seemed somewhat farfetched, especially because none of EFF's organizers were lawyers or established politicians. The business press in particular found it easier to seize on the apparent core of the story—that high-tech entrepreneur Mitchell Kapor had established a "defense fund for hackers." Was EFF a genuinely important political development, or merely a clique of wealthy eccentrics, dabbling in matters better left to the proper authorities? The jury was still out.

But the stage was now set for open confrontation. And the first and the most critical battle was the hacker show trial of Knight Lightning.

It has been my practice throughout this book to refer to hackers only by their "handles." There is little to gain by giving the real names of these people, many of whom are juveniles, many of whom have never been convicted of any crime, and many of whom had unsuspecting parents who have since suffered enough.

But the trial of Knight Lightning on July 24–27, 1990, made this particular hacker a nationally known public figure. It can do no particular harm to him or his family if I repeat the long-established fact that his name is Craig Neidorf (pronounced NYE-dorf).

Neidorf's jury trial took place in the United States District Court, Northern District of Illinois, Eastern Division, with the Honorable Nicholas J. Bua presiding. The United States of America was the plaintiff, the defendant Mr. Neidorf. The defendant's attorney was Sheldon T. Zenner of the Chicago firm of Katten, Muchin and Zavis.

The prosecution was led by the stalwarts of the Chicago Computer Fraud and Abuse Task Force: William J. Cook, Colleen D. Coughlin, and David A. Glockner, all assistant United States attorneys. The Secret Service case agent was Timothy M. Foley.

It will be recalled that Neidorf was the co-editor of an underground hacker "magazine" called *Phrack*. As mentioned, *Phrack* was an entirely electronic publication, distributed through bulletin boards and over electronic networks. It was an amateur publication given away for free. Neidorf had never made any money for his work in *Phrack*. Neither had his unindicted co-editor, Taran King, or any of the numerous *Phrack* contributors.

The Chicago Computer Fraud and Abuse Task Force, however, had decided to prosecute Neidorf as a fraudster. To formally admit that *Phrack* was a "magazine" and Neidorf a "publisher" was to open a prosecutorial Pandora's Box of First Amendment issues. To do this was to play into the hands of Zenner and his EFF advisors, which now included a phalanx of prominent New York civil rights lawyers as well as the formidable legal staff of Katten, Muchin and Zavis. Instead, the prosecution relied heavily on the issue of computer fraud and abuse, wire fraud and interstate transportation of stolen property. Section 1029 of Title 18, the section from which the Secret Service drew its most direct jurisdiction over computer crime.

Neidorf's alleged crimes centered around the E911 Document. He was accused of having entered into a fraudulent scheme with the Prophet, who, it will be recalled, was the Atlanta LoD member who had illicitly copied the E911 Document from the Bell-South AIMSX system.

Prophet himself was also a co-defendant in the Neidorf case, part and parcel of the alleged "fraud scheme" to "steal" Bell-South's E911 Document (and to pass the document across state lines, which helped establish the Neidorf trial as a federal case). Prophet, in the spirit of full cooperation, had agreed to testify against Neidorf.

In fact, all three of the Atlanta crew stood ready to testify against Neidorf. Their own federal prosecutors in Atlanta had charged the Atlanta Three with: (a) conspiracy, (b) computer fraud, (c) wire fraud, (d) access device fraud, and (e) interstate transportation of stolen property (Title 18, Sections 371, 1030, 1343, 1029, and 2314).

Faced with this blizzard of trouble, Prophet and Leftist had ducked any public trial and had pled guilty to reduced charges— one conspiracy count apiece. Urvile had pled guilty to that odd bit of Section 1029 which makes it illegal to possess "fifteen or more" illegal access devices (in his case, computer passwords). And their sentences were scheduled for September 14, 1990— well after the Neidorf trial. As witnesses, they presumably could be relied upon to behave.

Neidorf, however, was pleading innocent. Most everyone else caught up in the crackdown had "cooperated fully" and pled guilty in hope of reduced sentences. (Steve Jackson was a notable exception, of course, and had strongly protested his innocence from the very beginning. But Steve Jackson could not get a day in court—Steve Jackson had never been charged with any crime in the first place.)

Neidorf had been urged to plead guilty. But Neidorf was a political science major and was disinclined to go to jail for "fraud" when he had not made any money, had not broken into any computer, and had been publishing a magazine that he considered protected under the First Amendment. Neidorf's trial was the *only* legal action of the entire crackdown that actually involved bringing the issues at hand out for a public test in front of a jury of American citizens.

Neidorf too had cooperated with investigators. He had voluntarily handed over much of the evidence that had led to his own indictment. He had already admitted in writing that he knew that the E911 Document had been stolen before he had "published" it in *Phrack*—or, from the prosecution's point of view, *illegally transported stolen property by wire* in something purporting to be a "publication."

But even if the "publication" of the E911 Document was not held to be a crime, that wouldn't let Neidorf off the hook. Neidorf had still *received* the E911 Document when Prophet had transferred it to him from Rich Andrews' Jolnet node. On *that* occasion, it certainly hadn't been "published"—it was hacker booty, pure and simple, transported across state lines.

The Chicago Task Force led a Chicago grand jury to indict Neidorf on a set of charges that could have put him in jail for thirty years. When some of these charges were challenged successfully before Neidorf actually went to trial, the task force rearranged his indictment so that he faced a possible jail term of over sixty years! As a first offender, it was very unlikely that Neidorf would in fact receive a sentence so drastic; but the Chicago Task Force clearly intended to see him put in prison and his conspiratorial "magazine" put permanently out of commission. This was a federal case, and Neidorf was charged with the fraudulent theft of property worth almost $80,000.

William Cook was a strong believer in high-profile prosecutions with symbolic overtones. He often published articles on his work in the security trade press, arguing that "a clear message had to be sent to the public at large and the computer community in particular that unauthorized attacks on computers and the theft of computerized information would not be tolerated by the courts."

The issues were complex, the prosecution's tactics somewhat unorthodox, but the Chicago Task Force had proved sure-footed to date. Shadowhawk had been bagged on the wing in 1989 by the task force, and sentenced to nine months in prison, and a $10,000 fine. The Shadowhawk case involved charges under Section 1030, the "federal interest computer" section.

Shadowhawk had not in fact been a devotee of "federal-interest" computers per se. On the contrary, Shadowhawk, who owned an AT&T home computer, seemed to cherish a special aggression toward AT&T. He had bragged on the underground boards Phreak Klass 2600 and Dr. Ripco of his skills at raiding AT&T and of his intention to crash AT&T's national phone system. Shadowhawk's brags were noticed by Henry Kluepfel of Bellcore Security, scourge of the outlaw boards, whose relations with the Chicago Task Force were long and intimate.

The task force successfully established that Section 1030 ap-
plied to the teenage Shadowhawk, despite the objections of his
defense attorney. Shadowhawk had entered a computer "owned"
by U.S. Missile Command and merely "managed" by AT&T. He
had also entered an AT&T computer located at Robbins Air
Force Base in Georgia. Attacking AT&T was of "federal interest"
whether Shadowhawk had intended it or not.

The task force also convinced the court that a piece of AT&T
software that Shadowhawk had illicitly copied from Bell Labs, the
"Artificial Intelligence C5 Expert System," was worth a cool $1
million. Shadowhawk's attorney had argued that his client had
not sold the program and had made no profit from the illicit
copying. And in point of fact, the C5 Expert System was experimental software and had no established market value because it
had never been on the market in the first place. AT&T's own
assessment of a "$1 million" figure for its own intangible property
was accepted without challenge by the court, however. And
the court concurred with the government prosecutors that
Shadowhawk showed clear "intent to defraud" whether he'd gotten any money or not. Shadowhawk went to jail.

The task force's other best-known triumph had been the conviction and jailing of "Kyrie." Kyrie, a true denizen of the digital
criminal underground, was a thirty-six-year-old Canadian woman,
convicted and jailed for telecommunications fraud in Canada.
After her release from prison, she had fled the wrath of Canada
Bell and the Royal Canadian Mounted Police and eventually settled, very unwisely, in Chicago.

Kyrie, who also called herself "Long Distance Information,"
specialized in voice-mail abuse. She assembled large numbers of
hot long-distance codes, then read them aloud into a series of
corporate voice-mail systems. Kyrie and her friends were electronic squatters in corporate voice-mail systems, using them
much as if they were pirate bulletin boards, then moving on when
their vocal chatter clogged the system and the owners necessarily
wised up. Kyrie's camp followers were a loose tribe of some 150

phone phreaks, who followed her trail of piracy from machine to machine, ardently begging for her services and expertise.

Kyrie's disciples passed her stolen credit card numbers in exchange for her stolen "long-distance information." Some of Kyrie's clients paid her off in cash, by scamming credit card cash advances from Western Union.

Kyrie traveled incessantly, mostly through airline tickets and hotel rooms that she scammed through stolen credit cards. Tiring of this, she found refuge with a fellow female

Kyrie's camp followers were a loose tribe of some 150 phone phreaks.

phone phreak in Chicago. Kyrie's hostess, like a surprising number of phone phreaks, was blind. She was also physically disabled. Kyrie allegedly made the best of her new situation by applying for, and receiving, state welfare funds under a false identity as a qualified caretaker for the handicapped.

(Sadly, Kyrie's two children by an earlier marriage had also vanished underground with her; these preteen digital refugees had no legal American identity and had never spent a day in school.)

Kyrie was addicted to technical mastery and enthralled by her own cleverness and the ardent worship of her teenage followers. This foolishly led her to phone up Gail Thackeray in Arizona, to boast, brag, strut, and offer to play informant. Thackeray, however, had already learned far more than enough about Kyrie, whom she roundly despised as an adult criminal corrupting minors, a "female Fagin." Thackeray passed her tapes of Kyrie's boasts to the Secret Service.

Kyrie was raided and arrested in Chicago in May 1989. She confessed at great length and pled guilty.

In August 1990, Cook and his task force colleague Colleen Coughlin sent Kyrie to jail for twenty-seven months, for computer and telecommunications fraud. This was a markedly severe sentence by the usual wrist-slapping standards of hacker busts.

Seven of Kyrie's foremost teenage disciples were also indicted and convicted. The Kyrie "high-tech street gang," as Cook described it, had been crushed. Cook and his colleagues had been the first ever to put someone in prison for voice-mail abuse. Their pioneering efforts had won them attention and kudos.

In his article on Kyrie, Cook drove the message home to the readers of *Security Management* magazine, a trade journal for corporate security professionals. The case, Cook said, and Kyrie's stiff sentence, "reflect a new reality for hackers and computer crime victims in the '90s. . . . Individuals and corporations who report computer and telecommunications crimes can now expect that their cooperation with federal law enforcement will result in meaningful punishment. Companies and the public at large must report computer-enhanced crimes if they want prosecutors and the courts to protect their rights to the tangible and intangible property developed and stored on computers."

Cook had made it his business to construct this "new reality for hackers." He'd also made it his business to police corporate property rights to the intangible.

Had the Electronic Frontier Foundation been a hacker defense fund, as that term was generally understood, it presumably would have stood up for Kyrie. Her 1990 sentence did indeed send a "message" that federal heat was coming down on hackers. But Kyrie found no defenders at EFF, or anywhere else, for that matter. EFF was not a bailout fund for electronic crooks.

The Neidorf case paralleled the Shadowhawk case in certain ways. The victim once again was allowed to set the value of the "stolen" property. Once again Kluepfel was both investigator and technical advisor. Once again no money had changed hands, but the "intent to defraud" was central.

The prosecution's case showed signs of weakness early on. The task force had originally hoped to prove Neidorf the center of a nationwide Legion of Doom criminal conspiracy. The *Phrack* editors threw physical get-togethers every summer, which attracted hackers from across the country—generally two dozen or so of the magazine's favorite contributors and readers. (Such conventions were common in the hacker community; 2600 *Magazine*, for instance, held public meetings of hackers in New York every month.) LoD heavy dudes were always a strong presence at these *Phrack*-sponsored "SummerCons."

In July 1988, an Arizona hacker named "Dictator" attended SummerCon in Neidorf's home town of St. Louis. Dictator was one of Gail Thackeray's underground informants; Dictator's underground board in Phoenix was a sting operation for the Secret Service. Dictator brought an undercover crew of Secret Service agents to SummerCon. The agents bored spyholes through the wall of his hotel room in St. Louis and videotaped the frolicking hackers through a one-way mirror. As it happened, however, nothing illegal had occurred on videotape, other than the guzzling of beer by a couple of minors. SummerCons were social events, not sinister cabals. The tapes showed fifteen hours of raucous laughter, pizza-gobbling, in jokes, and back-slapping.

Neidorf's lawyer, Sheldon Zenner, saw the Secret Service tapes before the trial. Zenner was shocked by the complete harmlessness of this meeting, which Cook had earlier characterized as a sinister interstate conspiracy to commit fraud. Zenner wanted to show the SummerCon tapes to the jury. It took protracted maneuverings by the task force to keep the tapes from the jury as "irrelevant."

The E911 Document was also proving a weak reed. It had originally been valued at $79,449. Unlike Shadowhawk's arcane Artificial Intelligence booty, the E911 Document was not software—it was written in English. Computer-knowledgeable people found this value—for a twelve-page bureaucratic document— frankly incredible. In his "Crime and Puzzlement" manifesto for EFF, Barlow commented: "We will probably never know how this figure was reached or by whom, though I like to imagine an appraisal team consisting of Franz Kafka, Joseph Heller, and Thomas Pynchon."

As it happened, Barlow was unduly pessimistic. The EFF did,

in fact, eventually discover *exactly* how this figure was reached, and by whom—but only in 1991, long after the Neidorf trial was over.

Kimberly Megahee, a Southern Bell security manager, had arrived at the document's value by simply adding up the "costs associated with the production" of the E911 Document. Those "costs" were as follows:

1. A technical writer had been hired to research and write the E911 Document: 200 hours of work, at $35 an hour, cost $7,000. A project manager had overseen the technical writer: 200 hours, at $31 an hour, made $6,200.

2. A week of typing had cost $721 dollars. A week of formatting had cost $721. A week of graphics formatting had cost $742.

3. Two days of editing cost $367.

4. A box of order labels cost $5.

5. Preparing a purchase order for the Document, including typing and the obtaining of an authorizing signature from within the BellSouth bureaucracy, cost $129.

6. Printing cost $313. Mailing the Document to fifty people took fifty hours by a clerk, and cost $858.

7. Placing the Document in an index took two clerks an hour each, totaling $43.

Bureaucratic overhead alone, therefore, was alleged to have cost a whopping $17,099. According to Ms. Megahee, the typing of a twelve-page document had taken a full week. Writing it had taken five weeks, including an overseer who apparently did nothing else but watch the author for five weeks. Editing twelve pages had taken two days. Printing and mailing an electronic document (which was already available on the Southern Bell Data Network to any telco employee who needed it) had cost over a thousand dollars.

But this was just the beginning. There were also the *hardware expenses.* Eight hundred fifty dollars for a VT220 computer monitor. *Thirty-one thousand dollars* for a sophisticated VAXstation II computer. Six thousand dollars for a computer printer. *Twenty-two thousand dollars* for a copy of "Interleaf" software. Two thousand five hundred dollars for VMS software. All this to create the twelve-page Document.

Plus 10 percent of the cost of the software and the hardware, for maintenance. (Actually, the 10 percent maintenance costs, though mentioned, had been left off the final $79,449 total, apparently through a merciful oversight.)

Ms. Megahee's letter had been mailed directly to William Cook himself, at the office of the Chicago federal attorneys. The United States Government accepted these telco figures without question.

As incredulity mounted, the value of the E911 Document was officially revised downward. This time, Robert Kibler of BellSouth Security estimated the value of the twelve pages as a mere $24,639.05—based, purportedly, on "R&D costs." But this specific estimate, right down to the nickel, did not move the skeptics at all; in fact, it provoked open scorn and a torrent of sarcasm.

The financial issues concerning theft of proprietary information have always been peculiar. It could be argued that BellSouth had not "lost" its E911 Document at all in the first place and therefore had not suffered any monetary damage from this "theft." And Sheldon Zenner did in fact argue this at Neidorf's trial—that Prophet's raid had not been "theft" but was better understood as illicit copying.

The money, however, was not central to anyone's true purposes in this trial. It was not Cook's strategy to convince the jury that the E911 Document was a major act of theft and should be punished for that reason alone. His strategy was to argue that the E911 Document was *dangerous.* It was his intention to establish that the E911 Document was "a road-map" to the Enhanced 911

System. Neidorf had deliberately and recklessly distributed a dangerous weapon. Neidorf and Prophet did not care (or perhaps even gloated at the sinister idea) that the E911 Document could be used by hackers to disrupt 911 service, "a life line for every person certainly in the Southern Bell region of the United States, and indeed, in many communities throughout the United States," in Cook's own words. Neidorf had put people's lives in danger.

In pretrial maneuverings, Cook had established that the E911 Document was too hot to appear in the public proceedings of the Neidorf trial. The *jury itself* would not be allowed to ever see this Document, lest it slip into the official court records and thus into the hands of the general public and, thus, somehow, to malicious hackers who might lethally abuse it.

Hiding the E911 Document from the jury may have been a clever legal maneuver, but it had a severe flaw. There were, in point of fact, hundreds, perhaps thousands, of people already in possession of the Document, just as *Phrack* had published it. Its true nature was already obvious to a wide section of the interested public (all of whom, by the way, were, at least theoretically, party to a gigantic wire-fraud conspiracy). Most everyone in the electronic community who had a modem and any interest in the Neidorf case *already* had a copy of the Document. It had already been available in *Phrack* for over a year.

People, even quite normal people without any particular prurient interest in forbidden knowledge, did not shut their eyes in terror at the thought of beholding a "dangerous" document from a telephone company. On the contrary, they tended to trust their own judgment and simply read the document for themselves. And they were not impressed.

One such person was John Nagle. Nagle was a forty-one-year-old professional programmer with a master's degree in computer science from Stanford. He had worked for Ford Aerospace, where he had invented a computer-networking technique known as the "Nagle Algorithm," and for the prominent Californian computer-graphics firm Autodesk, where he was a major stockholder.

Nagle was also a prominent figure on the Well, much respected for his technical knowledgeability.

Nagle had followed the civil-liberties debate closely, for he was an ardent telecommunicator. He was no particular friend of computer intruders, but he believed electronic publishing had a great deal to offer society at large, and attempts to restrain its growth, or to censor free electronic expression, strongly roused his ire.

The Neidorf case and the E911 Document were both being discussed in detail on the Internet, in an electronic publication called *Telecom Digest*. Nagle, a longtime Internet maven, was a regular reader of *Telecom Digest*. Nagle had never seen a copy of *Phrack*, but the implications of the case disturbed him.

While in a Stanford bookstore hunting books on robotics, Nagle happened across a book called *The Intelligent Network*. Thumbing through it at random, Nagle came across an entire chapter meticulously detailing the workings of E911 police emergency systems. This extensive text was being sold openly, and yet in Illinois a young man was in danger of going to prison for publishing a thin six-page document about 911 service.

Nagle made an ironic comment to this effect in *Telecom Digest*. From there, Nagle was put in touch with Mitch Kapor, and then with Neidorf's lawyers.

Sheldon Zenner was delighted to find a computer telecommunications expert willing to speak up for Neidorf, one who was not a wacky teenage "hacker." Nagle was fluent, mature, and respectable; he'd once had a federal security clearance.

Nagle was asked to fly to Illinois to join the defense team.

Having joined the defense as an expert witness, Nagle read the entire E911 Document for himself. He made his own judgment about its potential for menace.

The time has now come for you, the reader, to have a look at the edited E911 Document yourself. This six-page piece of work was the pretext for a federal prosecution that could have sent an electronic publisher to prison for thirty, or even sixty, years. It was the pretext for the search and seizure of Steve Jackson Games, a legitimate publisher of printed books. It was also the formal pretext for the search and seizure of the Mentor's bulletin board, Phoenix Project, and for the raid on the home of Erik Bloodaxe. It also had much to do with the seizure of Richard Andrews' Jolnet node and the shutdown of Charles Boykin's AT&T node. The E911 Document was the single most important piece of evidence in the Hacker Crackdown. There can be no real and legitimate substitute for the Document itself.

Phrack Inc.

Volume Two, Issue 24, File 5 of 13

Control Office Administration
Of Enhanced 911 Services For
Special Services And Major Account Centers

By The Eavesdropper

March, 1988

Description of Service
~~~~~~~~~~~
The control office for Emergency 911 service is assigned in accordance with the existing standard guidelines to one of the following centers:

- Special Services Center (SSC)
- Major Accounts Center (MAC)
- Serving Test Center (STC)
- Toll Control Center (TCC)

The SSC/MAC designation is used in this document interchangeably for any of these four centers. The Special Services Centers (SSCs) or Major Account Centers (MACs) have been designated as the trouble reporting contact for all E911 customer (PSAP) reported troubles. Subscribers who have trouble on an E911 call will continue to contact local repair service (CRSAB) who will refer the trouble to the SSC/MAC, when appropriate.

Due to the critical nature of E911 service, the control and timely repair of troubles is demanded. As the primary E911 customer contact, the SSC/MAC is in the unique position to monitor the status of the trouble and insure its resolution.

System Overview
~~~~~~~
The number 911 is intended as a nationwide universal telephone number which provides the public with direct access to a Public Safety Answering Point (PSAP). A PSAP is also referred to as an Emergency Service Bureau (ESB). A PSAP is an agency or facility which is authorized by a municipality to receive and respond to police, fire and/or ambulance services. One or more attendants are located at the PSAP facilities to receive and handle calls of an emergency nature in accordance with the local municipal requirements.

An important advantage of E911 emergency service is improved (reduced) response times for emergency services. Also close coordination among agencies providing various emergency services is a valuable capability provided by E911 service.

1A ESS is used as the tandem office for the E911 network to route all 911 calls to the correct (primary) PSAP designated to serve the calling station. The E911 feature was developed primarily to provide routing to the correct PSAP for all 911 calls. Selective routing allows a 911 call originated from a particular station located in a particular district, zone, or town, to be routed to the primary PSAP designated to serve that customer station regardless of wire center boundaries. Thus, selective routing eliminates the problem of wire center boundaries not coinciding with district or other political boundaries.

The services available with the E911 feature include:

Forced Disconnect   Default Routing
Alternative Routing   Night Service

Selective Routing   Automatic Number Identification (ANI)
Selective Transfer   Automatic Location Identification (ALI)

Preservice/Installation Guidelines
~~~~~~~~~~~~~~~~~~
When a contract for an E911 system has been signed, it is the responsibility of Network Marketing to establish an implementation/cutover committee which should include a representative from the SSC/MAC. Duties of the E911 Implementation Team include coordination of all phases of the E911 system deployment and the formation of an on-going E911 maintenance subcommittee.

Marketing is responsible for providing the following customer specific information to the SSC/MAC prior to the start of call through testing:

- All PSAP's (name, address, local contact)
- All PSAP circuit ID's
- 1004 911 service request including PSAP details on each PSAP (1004 Section K, L, M)
- Network configuration
- Any vendor information (name, telephone number, equipment)

The SSC/MAC needs to know if the equipment and sets at the PSAP are maintained by the BOCs, an independent company, or an outside vendor, or any combination. This information is then entered on the PSAP profile sheets and reviewed quarterly for changes, additions and deletions.

Marketing will secure the Major Account Number (MAN) and provide this number to Corporate Communications so that the initial issue of the service orders carry the MAN and can be tracked by the SSC/MAC via CORDNET. PSAP circuits are official services by definition.

All service orders required for the installation of the E911 system should include the MAN assigned to the city/county which has purchased the system.

In accordance with the basic SSC/MAC strategy for provisioning, the SSC/MAC will be Overall Control Office (OCO) for all Node to PSAP circuits (official services) and any other services for this customer. Training must be scheduled for all SSC/MAC involved personnel during the pre-service stage of the project.

The E911 Implementation Team will form the on-going maintenance subcommittee prior to the initial implementation of the E911 system. This subcommittee will establish post implementation quality assurance procedures to ensure that the E911 system continues to provide quality service to the customer. Customer/ Company training, trouble reporting interfaces for the customer, telephone company and any involved independent telephone companies needs to be addressed and implemented prior to E911 cutover. These functions can be best addressed by the formation of a subcommittee of the E911 Implementation Team to set up guidelines for and to secure service commitments of interfacing organizations. A SSC/MAC supervisor should chair this subcommittee and include the following organizations:

1) Switching Control Center
   - E911 translations
   - Trunking
   - End office and Tandem office hardware/software
2) Recent Change Memory Administration Center
   - Daily RC update activity for TN/ESN translations
   - Processes validity errors and rejects
3) Line and Number Administration
   - Verification of TN/ESN translations
4) Special Service Center/Major Account Center
   - Single point of contact for all PSAP and Node to host troubles
   - Logs, tracks & statusing of all trouble reports
   - Trouble referral, follow up, and escalation
   - Customer notification of status and restoration
   - Analyzation of "chronic" troubles
   - Testing, installation and maintenance of E911 circuits
5) Installation and Maintenance (SSIM/I&M)
   - Repair and maintenance of PSAP equipment and Telco owned sets

6) Minicomputer Maintenance Operations Center
 - E911 circuit maintenance (where applicable)
7) Area Maintenance Engineer
 - Technical assistance on voice (CO-PSAP) network related
   E911 troubles

Maintenance Guidelines
~~~~~~~~~~~~
The CCNC will test the Node circuit from the 202T at the Host
site to the 202T at the Node site. Since Host to Node (CCNC to
MMOC) circuits are official company services, the CCNC will
refer all Node circuit troubles to the SSC/MAC. The SSC/MAC is
responsible for the testing and follow up to restoration of these
circuit troubles.

Although Node to PSAP circuit are official services, the MMOC
will refer PSAP circuit troubles to the appropriate SSC/MAC. The
SSC/MAC is responsible for testing and follow up to restoration of
PSAP circuit troubles.

The SSC/MAC will also receive reports from CRSAB/IMC(s) on
subscriber 911 troubles when they are not line troubles. The SSC/
MAC is responsible for testing and restoration of these troubles.

Maintenance responsibilities are as follows:

SCC*   Voice Network (ANI to PSAP)
           *SCC responsible for tandem switch
SSIM/I&M   PSAP Equipment (Modems, CIU's, sets)
Vendor   PSAP Equipment (when CPE)
SSC/MAC   PSAP to Node circuits, and tandem to PSAP voice
           circuits
(EMNT)
MMOC   Node site (Modems, cables, etc)

Note: All above work groups are required to resolve troubles by interfacing
with appropriate work groups for resolution.

The Switching Control Center (SCC) is responsible for E911/
1AESS translations in tandem central offices. These translations
route E911 calls, selective transfer, default routing, speed calling,

etc., for each PSAP. The SCC is also responsible for troubleshooting on the voice network (call originating to end office tandem equipment).

For example, ANI failures in the originating offices would be a responsibility of the SCC.

Recent Change Memory Administration Center (RCMAC) performs the daily tandem translation updates (recent change) for routing of individual telephone numbers.

Recent changes are generated from service order activity (new service, address changes, etc.) and compiled into a daily file by the E911 Center (ALI/DMS E911 Computer).

SSIM/I&M is responsible for the installation and repair of PSAP equipment. PSAP equipment includes ANI Controller, ALI Controller, data sets, cables, sets, and other peripheral equipment that is not vendor owned. SSIM/I&M is responsible for establishing maintenance test kits, complete with spare parts for PSAP maintenance. This includes test gear, data sets, and ANI/ALI Controller parts.

Special Services Center (SSC) or Major Account Center (MAC) serves as the trouble reporting contact for all (PSAP) troubles reported by customer. The SSC/MAC refers troubles to proper organizations for handling and tracks status of troubles, escalating when necessary. The SSC/MAC will close out troubles with customer. The SSC/MAC will analyze all troubles and tracks "chronic" PSAP troubles.

Corporate Communications Network Center (CCNC) will test and refer troubles on all node to host circuits. All E911 circuits are classified as official company property.

The Minicomputer Maintenance Operations Center (MMOC) maintains the E911 (ALI/DMS) computer hardware at the Host site. This MMOC is also responsible for monitoring the system and reporting certain PSAP and system problems to the local MMOC's, SCC's or SSC/MAC's. The MMOC personnel also operate software programs that maintain the TN data base under the direction of the E911 Center. The maintenance of the NODE computer (the interface between the PSAP and the ALI/DMS computer) is a function of the MMOC at the NODE site. The MMOC's at the NODE sites may also be involved in the testing of NODE to Host circuits. The MMOC will also assist on Host to PSAP and data network related troubles not resolved through standard trouble clearing procedures.

Installation And Maintenance Center (IMC) is responsible for referral of E911 subscriber troubles that are not subscriber line problems. E911 Center—Performs the role of System Administration and is responsible for overall operation of the E911 computer software. The E911 Center does A-Z trouble analysis and provides statistical information on the performance of the system.

This analysis includes processing PSAP inquiries (trouble reports) and referral of network troubles. The E911 Center also performs daily processing of tandem recent change and provides information to the RCMAC for tandem input. The E911 Center is responsible for daily processing of the ALI/DMS computer data base and provides error files, etc. to the Customer Services department for investigation and correction. The E911 Center participates in all system implementations and on-going maintenance effort and assists in the development of procedures, training and education of information to all groups.

Any group receiving a 911 trouble from the SSC/MAC should close out the trouble with the SSC/MAC or provide a status if the trouble has been referred to another group. This will allow the SSC/MAC to provide a status back to the customer or escalate as appropriate.

Any group receiving a trouble from the Host site (MMOC or CCNC) should close the trouble back to that group.

The MMOC should notify the appropriate SSC/MAC when the Host, Node, or all Node circuits are down so that the SSC/MAC can reply to customer reports that may be called in by the PSAPs. This will eliminate duplicate reporting of troubles.

On complete outages the MMOC will follow escalation procedures for a Node after two (2) hours and for a PSAP after four (4) hours. Additionally the MMOC will notify the appropriate SSC/ MAC when the Host, Node, or all Node circuits are down.

The PSAP will call the SSC/MAC to report E911 troubles. The person reporting the E911 trouble may not have a circuit I.D. and will therefore report the PSAP name and address. Many PSAP troubles are not circuit specific. In those instances where the caller cannot provide a circuit I.D., the SSC/MAC will be required to determine the circuit I.D. using the PSAP profile. Under no circumstances will the SSC/MAC Center refuse to take the trouble. The E911 trouble should be handled as quickly as possible, with the SSC/MAC providing as much assistance as possible while taking the trouble report from the caller.

The SSC/MAC will screen/test the trouble to determine the appropriate handoff organization based on the following criteria:

PSAP equipment problem: SSIM/I&M
Circuit problem: SSC/MAC
Voice network problem: SCC (report trunk group number)
Problem affecting multiple PSAPs (No ALI report from all PSAPs):
    Contact the MMOC to check for NODE or Host computer
    problems before further testing.

The SSC/MAC will track the status of reported troubles and escalate as appropriate. The SSC/MAC will close out customer/company reports with the initiating contact. Groups with specific maintenance responsibilities, defined above, will investigate "chronic" troubles upon request from the SSC/MAC and the ongoing maintenance subcommittee.

All "out of service" E911 troubles are priority one type reports. One link down to a PSAP is considered a priority one trouble and should be handled as if the PSAP was isolated.

The PSAP will report troubles with the ANI controller, ALI controller or set equipment to the SSC/MAC.

NO ANI: Where the PSAP reports NO ANI (digital display screen is blank) ask if this condition exists on all screens and on all calls. It is important to differentiate between blank screens and screens displaying 911-00XX, or all zeroes.

When the PSAP reports all screens on all calls, ask if there is any voice contact with callers. If there is no voice contact the trouble should be referred to the SCC immediately since 911 calls are not getting through which may require alternate routing of calls to another PSAP.

When the PSAP reports this condition on all screens but not all calls and has voice contact with callers, the report should be referred to SSIM/I&M for dispatch. The SSC/MAC should verify with the SCC that ANI is pulsing before dispatching SSIM.

When the PSAP reports this condition on one screen for all calls (others work fine) the trouble should be referred to SSIM/I&M for dispatch, because the trouble is isolated to one piece of equipment at the customer premise.

An ANI failure (i.e. all zeroes) indicates that the ANI has not been received by the PSAP from the tandem office or was lost by the PSAP ANI controller. The PSAP may receive "02" alarms which can be caused by the ANI controller logging more than three all zero failures on the same trunk. The PSAP has been instructed to report this condition to the SSC/MAC since it could indicate an equipment trouble at the PSAP which might be affecting all subscribers calling into the PSAP. When all zeroes are being received on all calls or "02" alarms continue, a tester should analyze the condition to determine the appropriate action to be taken. The tester must perform cooperative testing with the SCC when there appears to be a problem on the Tandem-PSAP trunks before requesting dispatch.

When an occasional all zero condition is reported, the SSC/MAC should dispatch SSIM/I&M to routine equipment on a "chronic" troublesweep.

The PSAPs are instructed to report incidental ANI failures to the BOC on a PSAP inquiry trouble ticket (paper) that is sent to the Customer Services E911 group and forwarded to E911 center when required. This usually involves only a particular telephone number and is not a condition that would require a report to the SSC/MAC. Multiple ANI failures which are from the same end office (XX denotes end office), indicate a hard trouble condition may exist in the end office or end office tandem trunks. The PSAP will report this type of condition to the SSC/MAC and the SSC/MAC should refer the report to the SCC responsible for the tandem office. NOTE: XX is the ESCO (Emergency Service Number) associated with the incoming 911 trunks into the tandem. It is important that the C/MAC tell the SCC what is displayed at the PSAP (i.e. 911-0011) which indicates to the SCC which end office is in trouble.

Note: It is essential that the PSAP fill out inquiry form on every ANI failure.

The PSAP will report a trouble any time an address is not received on an address display (screen blank) E911 call. (If a record is not in the 911 data base or an ANI failure is encountered, the screen will provide a display noticing such condition.) The SSC/MAC should verify with the PSAP whether the NO ALI condition is on one screen or all screens.

When the condition is on one screen (other screens receive ALI information) the SSC/MAC will request SSIM/I&M to dispatch.

If no screens are receiving ALI information, there is usually a circuit trouble between the PSAP and the Host computer. The SSC/MAC should test the trouble and refer for restoral.

Note: If the SSC/MAC receives calls from multiple PSAP's, all of which are receiving NO ALI, there is a problem with the Node or Node to Host circuits or the Host computer itself. Before referring the trouble the SSC/MAC should call the MMOC to inquire if the Node or Host is in trouble.

Alarm conditions on the ANI controller digital display at the PSAP are to be reported by the PSAP's. These alarms can indicate various trouble conditions so the SSC/MAC should ask the PSAP if any portion of the E911 system is not functioning properly.

The SSC/MAC should verify with the PSAP attendant that the equipment's primary function is answering E911 calls. If it is, the SSC/MAC should request a dispatch SSIM/I&M. If the equipment is not primarily used for E911, then the SSC/MAC should advise PSAP to contact their CPE vendor.

Note: These troubles can be quite confusing when the PSAP has vendor equipment mixed in with equipment that the BOC maintains. The Marketing representative should provide the SSC/MAC information concerning any unusual or exception items where the PSAP should contact their vendor. This information should be included in the PSAP profile sheets.

ANI or ALI controller down: When the host computer sees the PSAP equipment down and it does not come back up, the MMOC will report the trouble to the SSC/MAC; the equipment is down at the PSAP, a dispatch will be required.

PSAP link (circuit) down: The MMOC will provide the SSC/MAC with the circuit ID that the Host computer indicates in trouble. Although each PSAP has two circuits, when either circuit is down the condition must be treated as an emergency since failure of the second circuit will cause the PSAP to be isolated.

Any problems that the MMOC identifies from the Node location to the Host computer will be handled directly with the appropriate MMOC(s)/CCNC.

Note: The customer will call only when a problem is apparent to the PSAP. When only one circuit is down to the PSAP, the customer may not be aware there is a trouble, even though there is one link down, notification should appear on the PSAP screen. Troubles called into the SSC/MAC from the MMOC or other company employee should not be closed out by calling the PSAP since it may result in the customer responding that they do not have a trouble. These reports can only be closed out by receiving information that the trouble was fixed and by checking with the company employee that reported the trouble. The MMOC personnel will be able to verify that the trouble has cleared by reviewing a printout from the host.

When the CRSAB receives a subscriber complaint (i.e., cannot dial 911) the RSA should obtain as much information as possible while the customer is on the line.

For example, what happened when the subscriber dialed 911? The report is automatically directed to the IMC for subscriber line testing. When no line trouble is found, the IMC will refer the trouble condition to the SSC/MAC. The SSC/MAC will contact Customer Services E911 Group and verify that the subscriber should be able to call 911 and obtain the ESN. The SSC/MAC will verify the ESN via 2SCCS. When both verifications match, the SSC/MAC will refer the report to the SCC responsible for the 911 tandem office for investigation and resolution. The MAC is responsible for tracking the trouble and informing the IMC when it is resolved.

For more information, please refer to E911 Glossary of Terms.
End of Phrack File

The reader is forgiven if he or she was entirely unable to read this document. John Perry Barlow had a great deal of fun at its expense, in "Crime and Puzzlement." "Bureaucrat-ese of surpassing opacity. . . . To read the whole thing straight through without entering coma requires either a machine or a human who has too much practice thinking like one. Anyone who can understand it fully and fluidly had altered his consciousness beyond the ability to ever again read Blake, Whitman, or Tolstoy. . . . The document contains little of interest to anyone who is not a student of advanced organizational sclerosis."

With the Document itself to hand, however, exactly as it was published in *Phrack*, you may be able to verify a few statements of fact about its nature. First, there is no software, no computer code, in the Document. It is not computer-programming language like UNIX or C++, it is English; all the sentences have nouns and verbs and punctuation. It does not explain how to break into the E911 system. It does not suggest ways to destroy or damage the E911 system.

There are no access codes in the Document. There are no computer passwords. It does not explain how to steal long-distance service. It does not explain how to break in to telco switching stations. There is nothing in it about using a personal computer or a modem for any purpose at all, good or bad.

Close study will reveal that this Document is not about machinery. The E911 Document is about *administration*. It describes how one creates and administers certain units of telco bureaucracy: Special Service Centers and Major Account Centers (SSC/MAC). It describes how these centers should distribute responsibility for the E911 service, to other units of telco bureaucracy, in a chain of command, a formal hierarchy. It describes who answers customer complaints, who screens calls, who reports equipment failures, who answers those reports, who handles maintenance, who chairs subcommittees, who gives orders, who follows orders, *who* tells *whom* what to do. The Document is not a "roadmap" to computers. The Document is a roadmap to *people.*

As an aid to breaking into computer systems, the Document is *useless.* As an aid to harassing and deceiving telco people, however, the Document might prove handy (especially with its glossary, which I have not included). An intense and protracted study of this Document and its glossary, combined with many other such documents, might teach one to speak like a telco employee. And telco people live by *speech*—they live by phone communication. If you can mimic their language over the phone, you can "social-engineer" them. If you can con telco people, you can wreak havoc among them. You can force them no longer to trust one another; you can break the telephonic ties that bind their community; you can make them paranoid. And people will fight harder to defend their community than they will fight to defend their individual selves.

If you can con telco people, you can wreak havoc among them.

This was the genuine, gut-level threat posed by *Phrack* magazine. The real struggle was over the control of telco language, the control of telco knowledge. It was a struggle to defend the social "membrane of differentiation" that forms the walls of the telco community's ivory tower—the special jargon that allows telco professionals to recognize one another and to exclude charlatans, thieves, and upstarts. And the prosecution brought out this fact. It repeatedly made reference to the threat posed to telco professionals by hackers using "social engineering."

However, Craig Neidorf was not on trial for learning to speak like a professional telecommunications expert. Craig Neidorf was on trial for wire fraud and transportation of stolen property. He was on trial for stealing a document that was purportedly highly sensitive and purportedly worth tens of thousands of dollars.

John Nagle read the E911 Document. He drew his own conclusions. And he presented Zenner and his defense team with an overflowing box of similar material, drawn mostly from Stanford University's engineering libraries. During the trial, the defense team—Zenner, half-a-dozen other attorneys, Nagle, Neidorf, and computer-security expert Dorothy Denning, all pored over the E911 Document line-by-line.

On the afternoon of July 25, 1990, Zenner began to cross-examine a woman named Billie Williams, a service manager for Southern Bell in Atlanta. Ms. Williams had been responsible for the E911 Document. (She was not its author—its original "author" was a Southern Bell staff manager named Richard Helms. However, Mr. Helms should not bear the entire blame; many telco staff people and maintenance personnel had amended the Document. It had not been so much "written" by a single author as built by committee out of concrete blocks of jargon.)

Ms. Williams had been called as a witness for the prosecution and had gamely tried to explain the basic technical structure of the E911 system, aided by charts.

Now it was Zenner's turn. He first established that the "proprietary stamp" that BellSouth had used on the E911 Document was stamped on *every single document* that BellSouth wrote—*thousands* of documents. "We do not publish anything other than for our own company," Ms. Williams explained. "Any company document of this nature is considered proprietary." Nobody was in charge of singling out special high-security publications for special high-security protection. They were *all* special, no matter how trivial, no matter what their subject matter—the stamp was put on as soon as any document was written, and the stamp was never removed.

Zenner now asked whether the charts she had been using to explain the mechanics of E911 system were "proprietary" too. Were they *public information*, these charts, all about PSAPs, ALIs, nodes, local end switches? Could he take the charts out in the street and show them to anybody, "without violating some proprietary notion that BellSouth has?"

Ms. Williams showed some confusion, but finally agreed that the charts were, in fact, public.

"But isn't this what you said was basically what appeared in *Phrack?*"

Ms. Williams denied this.

Zenner now pointed out that the E911 Document as published in *Phrack* was only half the size of the original E911 Document (as Prophet had purloined it). Half of it had been deleted —edited by Neidorf.

Ms. Williams countered that "Most of the information that is in the text file is redundant."

Zenner continued to probe. Exactly what bits of knowledge in the Document were, in fact, unknown to the public? Locations of E911 computers? Phone numbers for telco personnel? Ongoing maintenance subcommittees? Hadn't Neidorf removed much of this?

Then he pounced. "Are you familiar with Bellcore Technical Reference Document TR-TSY-000350?" It was, Zenner explained, officially titled "E911 Public Safety Answering Point Interface Between 1-1AESS Switch and Customer Premises Equipment." It contained highly detailed and specific technical information about the E911 System. It was published by Bellcore and publicly available for about $20.

He showed the witness a Bellcore catalog that listed thousands of documents from Bellcore and from all the Baby Bells, BellSouth included. The catalog, Zenner pointed out, was free. Anyone with a credit card could call the Bellcore toll-free 800 number and simply order any of these documents, which would be shipped to any customer without question. Including, for instance, "BellSouth E911 Service Interfaces to Customer Premises Equipment at a Public Safety Answering Point."

Zenner gave the witness a copy of "BellSouth E911 Service Interfaces," which cost, as he pointed out, $13, straight from the catalog. "Look at it carefully," he urged Ms. Williams, "and tell

me if it doesn't contain about twice as much detailed information about the E911 system of BellSouth than appeared anywhere
in *Phrack*."

"You want me to . . ." Ms. Williams trailed off. "I don't understand."

"Take a careful look," Zenner persisted. "Take a look at that
document, and tell me when you're done looking at it if, indeed,
it doesn't contain much more detailed information about the
E911 system than appeared in *Phrack*."

"*Phrack* wasn't taken from this," Ms Williams said.

"Excuse me?" said Zenner.

"*Phrack* wasn't taken from this."

"I can't hear you," Zenner said.

"*Phrack* was not taken from this document. I don't understand
your question to me."

"I guess you don't," Zenner said.

At this point, the prosecution's case had been gutshot.
Ms. Williams was distressed.
Her confusion was quite genuine. *Phrack* had not been taken
from any publicly available
Bellcore document. *Phrack*'s E911 Document had been stolen
from her own company's computers, from her own company's
text files, which her own colleagues had written, and revised, with
much labor.

The value of the Document had been blown to smithereens.

But the "value" of the Document had been blown to smithereens. It wasn't worth eighty grand. According to Bellcore it was
worth thirteen bucks. And the looming menace that it supposedly
posed had been reduced in instants to a scarecrow. Bellcore itself
was selling material far more detailed and "dangerous," to anybody with a credit card and a phone.

Actually, Bellcore was not giving this information to just anybody. They gave it to *anybody who asked*, but not many did ask.
Not many people knew that Bellcore had a free catalog and an
800 number. John Nagle knew, but certainly the average teenage

phreak didn't know. "Tuc," a friend of Neidorf's and sometime *Phrack* contributor, knew, and Tuc had been very helpful to the defense, behind the scenes. But the Legion of Doom didn't know —otherwise, they would never have wasted so much time raiding dumpsters. Cook didn't know. Foley didn't know. Kluepfel didn't know. The right hand of Bellcore knew not what the left hand was doing. The right hand was battering hackers without mercy, while the left hand was distributing Bellcore's intellectual property to anybody who was interested in telephone technical trivia —apparently, a pathetic few.

The digital underground was so amateurish and poorly organized that it had never discovered this heap of unguarded riches. The ivory tower of the telcos was so wrapped up in the fog of its own technical obscurity that it had left all the windows open and flung open the doors. No one had even noticed.

Zenner sank another nail in the coffin. He produced a printed issue of *Telephone Engineer & Management,* a prominent industry journal that comes out twice a month and costs $27 a year. This particular issue of *TE&M,* called "Update on 911," featured a galaxy of technical details on 911 service and a glossary far more extensive than *Phrack's.*

The trial rumbled on, somehow, through its own momentum. Tim Foley testified about his interrogations of Neidorf. Neidorf's written admission that he had known the E911 Document was pilfered was officially read into the court record.

An interesting side issue came up: Terminus had once passed Neidorf a piece of UNIX AT&T software, a log-in sequence, that had been cunningly altered so that it could trap passwords. The UNIX software itself was illegally copied AT&T property, and the alterations Terminus had made to it had transformed it into a device for facilitating computer break-ins. Terminus himself would eventually plead guilty to theft of this piece of software, and the Chicago group would send Terminus to prison for it. But it was of dubious relevance in the Neidorf case. Neidorf hadn't written the program. He wasn't accused of ever having used it.

And Neidorf wasn't being charged with software theft or owning a password trapper.

On the next day, Zenner took the offensive. The civil libertarians now had their own arcane, untried legal weaponry to launch into action—the Electronic Communications Privacy Act of 1986 (ECPA), 18 U.S. Code, Section 2701 et seq. Section 2701 makes it a crime intentionally to access without authorization a facility in which an electronic communication service is provided—it is, at heart, an antibugging and antitapping law, intended to carry the traditional protections of telephones into other electronic channels of communication. While providing penalties for amateur snoops, however, Section 2703 of the ECPA also lays some formal difficulties on the bugging and tapping activities of police.

The Secret Service, in the person of Tim Foley, had served Richard Andrews with a federal grand jury subpoena, in their pursuit of Prophet, the E911 Document, and the Terminus software ring. But according to the Electronic Communications Privacy Act, a "provider of remote computing service" was legally entitled to "prior notice" from the government if a subpoena was used. Richard Andrews and his basement UNIX node, Jolnet, had not received any "prior notice." Tim Foley had purportedly violated the ECPA and committed an electronic crime! Zenner now sought the judge's permission to cross-examine Foley on the topic of Foley's own electronic misdeeds.

Cook argued that Richard Andrews' Jolnet was a privately owned bulletin board, and not within the purview of ECPA. Judge Bua granted the motion of the government to prevent cross-examination on that point, and Zenner's offensive fizzled. This, however, was the first direct assault on the legality of the actions of the Computer Fraud and Abuse Task Force itself—the first suggestion that the Task Force itself had broken the law and might, perhaps, be called to account.

Zenner, in any case, did not really need the ECPA. Instead, he grilled Foley on the glaring contradictions in the supposed value of the E911 Document. He also brought up the embarrassing fact that the supposedly red-hot E911 Document had been sitting around for months, in Jolnet, with Kluepfel's knowledge, while Kluepfel had done nothing about it.

In the afternoon, Prophet was brought in to testify for the prosecution. (Prophet, it will be recalled, had also been indicted in the case as partner in a fraud scheme with Neidorf.) In Atlanta, Prophet had already pled guilty to one charge of conspiracy, one charge of wire fraud, and one charge of interstate transportation of stolen property. The wire fraud charge and the stolen property charge were both directly based on the E911 Document.

The twenty-year-old Prophet proved a sorry customer, answering questions politely but in a barely audible mumble, his voice trailing off at the ends of sentences. He was constantly urged to speak up.

Cook, examining Prophet, forced him to admit that he had once had a "drug problem," abusing amphetamines, marijuana, cocaine, and LSD. This may have established to the jury that hackers are, or can be, seedy lowlife characters, but it also may have damaged Prophet's credibility somewhat. Zenner later suggested that drugs might have damaged Prophet's memory. The interesting fact also surfaced that Prophet had never physically met Craig Neidorf. He didn't even know Neidorf's last name—at least, not until the trial.

Prophet confirmed the basic facts of his hacker career. He was a member of the Legion of Doom. He had abused codes, he had broken into switching stations and rerouted calls, he had hung out on pirate bulletin boards. He had raided the BellSouth AIMSX computer, copied the E911 Document, stored it on Jolnet, mailed it to Neidorf. He and Neidorf had edited it, and Neidorf had known where it came from.

Zenner, however, had Prophet confirm that Neidorf was not a member of the Legion of Doom and had not urged Prophet to break into BellSouth computers. Neidorf had never urged Prophet to defraud anyone or to steal anything. Prophet also admitted that he had never known Neidorf to break in to any computer.

Prophet said that no one in the Legion of Doom considered Craig Neidorf a hacker at all. Neidorf was not a UNIX maven and simply lacked the necessary skill and ability to break into computers. Neidorf just published a magazine.

On Friday, July 27, 1990, the case against Neidorf collapsed. Cook moved to dismiss the indictment, citing "information currently available to us that was not available to us at the inception of the trial." Judge Bua praised the prosecution for this action, which he described as "very responsible," then dismissed a juror and declared a mistrial.

Neidorf was a free man. His defense, however, had cost himself and his family dearly. Months of his life had been consumed in anguish; he had seen his closest friends shun him as a federal criminal. He owed his lawyers over $100,000, despite a generous payment to the defense by Mitch Kapor.

Neidorf was not found innocent. The trial was simply dropped. Nevertheless, on September 9, 1991, Judge Bua granted Neidorf's motion for the "expungement and sealing" of his indictment record. The U.S. Secret Service was ordered to delete and destroy all fingerprints, photographs, and other records of arrest or processing relating to Neidorf's indictment, including their paper documents and their computer records.

Craig Neidorf went back to school, blazingly determined to become a lawyer. Having seen the justice system at work, he lost much of his enthusiasm for merely technical power. At this writing, he is working in Washington as a salaried researcher for the Electronic Frontier Foundation.

The outcome of the Neidorf trial changed the Electronic Frontier Foundation from voices in the wilderness to the media darlings of the new frontier.

Legally speaking, the Neidorf case was not a sweeping triumph for anyone concerned. No constitutional principles had been established. The issues of "freedom of the press" for electronic publishers remained in legal limbo. There were public misconceptions about the case. Many people thought Neidorf had been found innocent and relieved of all his legal debts by Kapor. The truth was that the government had simply dropped the case, and Neidorf's family had gone deeply into hock to support him.

But the Neidorf case did provide a single, devastating, public soundbite: *The feds said it was worth eighty grand, and it was only worth thirteen bucks.*

This is the Neidorf case's single most memorable element. No serious report of the case missed this particular element. Even cops could not read this without a wince and a shake of the head. It left the public credibility of the crackdown agents in tatters.

The crackdown, in fact, continued, however. Those two charges against Prophet, which had been based on the E911 Document, were quietly forgotten at his sentencing—even though Prophet had already pled guilty to them. Georgia federal prosecutors strongly argued for jail time for the Atlanta Three, insisting on "the need to send a message to the community," "the message that hackers around the country need to hear."

The Atlanta Three were sent to prison.

There was a great deal in their sentencing memorandum about the awful things that various other hackers had done (though the Atlanta Three themselves had not, in fact, actually committed these crimes). There was also much speculation about the awful things that the Atlanta Three *might* have done and *were capable* of doing (even though they had not, in fact, actually done them). The prosecution's argument carried the day. The Atlanta Three were sent to prison: Urvile and Leftist both got fourteen months each, while Prophet (a second offender) got twenty-one months.

The Atlanta Three were also assessed staggering fines as "restitution": $233,000 each. BellSouth claimed that the defendants had "stolen" "approximately $233,880 worth" of "proprietary computer access information"—specifically, $233,880 worth of computer passwords and connect addresses. BellSouth's astonishing claim of the extreme value of its own computer passwords and addresses was accepted at face value by the Georgia court.

Furthermore (as if to emphasize its theoretical nature), this enormous sum was not divvied up among the Atlanta Three, but each of them had to pay all of it.

A striking aspect of the sentence was that the Atlanta Three were specifically forbidden to use computers, except for work or under supervision. Depriving hackers of home computers and modems makes some sense if one considers hackers as "computer addicts," but EFF, filing an amicus brief in the case, protested that this punishment was unconstitutional—it deprived the Atlanta Three of their rights of free association and free expression through electronic media.

Terminus, the "ultimate hacker," was finally sent to prison for a year through the dogged efforts of the Chicago Task Force. His crime, to which he pled guilty, was the transfer of the UNIX password trapper, which was officially valued by AT&T at $77,000, a figure that aroused intense skepticism among those familiar with UNIX "login.c" programs.

The jailing of Terminus and the Atlanta Legionnaires of Doom, however, did not cause the EFF any sense of embarrassment or defeat. On the contrary, the civil libertarians were rapidly gathering strength.

An early and potent supporter was Senator Patrick Leahy, Democrat from Vermont who had been a Senate sponsor of the Electronic Communications Privacy Act. Even before the Neidorf trial, Leahy had spoken out in defense of hacker power and freedom of the keyboard: "We cannot unduly inhibit the inquisitive 13-year-old who, if left to experiment today, may tomorrow develop the telecommunications or computer technology to lead the United States into the 21st century. He represents our future and our best hope to remain a technologically competitive nation."

It was a handsome statement, rendered perhaps rather more effective by the fact that the crackdown raiders *did not have* any senators speaking out for *them*. On the contrary, their highly secretive actions and tactics, all "sealed search warrants" here and "confidential ongoing investigations" there, might have won them a burst of glamorous publicity at first, but were crippling them in the ongoing propaganda war. Gail Thackeray was reduced to unsupported bluster: "Some of these people who are loudest on the bandwagon may just slink into the background," she predicted in *Newsweek*—meaning when all the facts came out and the cops were vindicated.

But all the facts did not come out. Those facts that did were not very flattering. And the cops were not vindicated. And Gail Thackeray lost her job. By the end of 1991, William Cook had also left public employment.

The year 1990 had belonged to the crackdown, but by 1991 its agents were in severe disarray and the libertarians were on a roll. People were flocking to the cause.

A particularly interesting ally had been Mike Godwin of Austin, Texas. Godwin was an individual almost as difficult to describe as Barlow; he had been editor of the student newspaper of the University of Texas, and a computer salesman, and a programmer, and in 1990 was back in law school, looking for a law degree.

Godwin was also a bulletin board maven. He was very well-known in the Austin board community under his handle "Johnny Mnemonic," which he adopted from a cyberpunk science-fiction story by William Gibson. Godwin was an ardent cyberpunk science-fiction fan. As a fellow Austinite of similar age and similar interests, I myself had known Godwin socially for many years. When William Gibson and I had been writing our collaborative SF novel, *The Difference Engine,* Godwin had been our technical advisor in our effort to link our Apple word processors from Austin to Vancouver. Gibson and I were so pleased by his generous expert help that we named a character in the novel "Michael Godwin" in his honor.

The handle "Mnemonic" suited Godwin very well. His erudition and his mastery of trivia were impressive to the point of stupor; his ardent curiosity seemed insatiable, and his desire to debate and argue seemed the central drive of his life. Godwin had even started his own Austin debating society, wryly known as the

"Dull Men's Club." In person, Godwin could be overwhelming: a flypaper-brained polymath who could not seem to let any idea go. On bulletin boards, however, Godwin's closely reasoned, highly grammatical, erudite posts suited the medium well, and he became a local board celebrity.

Mike Godwin was the man most responsible for the public national exposure of the Steve Jackson case. The Izenberg seizure in Austin had received no press coverage at all. The March 1 raids on Mentor, Bloodaxe, and Steve Jackson Games had received a brief front-page splash in the *Austin American-Statesman,* but it was confused and ill informed: the warrants were sealed, and the Secret Service wasn't talking. Steve Jackson seemed doomed to obscurity. Jackson had not been arrested; he was not charged with any crime; he was not on trial. He had lost some computers in an ongoing investigation—so what? Jackson tried hard to attract attention to the true extent of his plight, but he was drawing a blank; no one in a position to help him seemed able to get a mental grip on the issues.

Godwin, however, was uniquely, almost magically, qualified to carry Jackson's case to the outside world. Godwin was a board enthusiast, a science-fiction fan, a former journalist, a computer salesman, a lawyer-to-be, and an Austinite. Through a coincidence yet more amazing, in his last year of law school Godwin had specialized in federal prosecutions and criminal procedure. Acting entirely on his own, Godwin made up a press packet that summarized the issues and provided useful contacts for reporters. Godwin's behind-the-scenes effort (which he carried out mostly to prove a point in a local board debate) broke the story again in the *Austin American-Statesman* and then in *Newsweek.*

Life was never the same for Mike Godwin after that. As he joined the growing civil liberties debate on the Internet, it was obvious to all parties involved that here was one guy who, in the midst of complete murk and confusion, *genuinely understood everything he was talking about.* The disparate elements of Godwin's dilettantish existence suddenly fell together as neatly as the facets of a Rubik's Cube.

When the time came to hire a full-time EFF staff attorney, Godwin was the obvious choice. He took the Texas bar exam, left Austin, moved to Cambridge, became a full-time, professional computer civil libertarian, and was soon touring the nation on behalf of EFF, delivering well-received addresses on the issues to crowds as disparate as academics, industrialists, science-fiction fans, and federal cops.

Michael Godwin is currently the chief legal counsel of the Electronic Frontier Foundation in Cambridge, Massachusetts.

Another early and influential participant in the controversy was Dorothy Denning. Dr. Denning was unique among investigators of the computer underground in that she did not enter the debate with any set of politicized motives. She was a professional cryptographer and computer security expert whose primary interest in hackers was *scholarly.* She had a B.A. and M.A. in mathematics and a Ph.D. in computer science from Purdue. She had worked for SRI International, the California think tank that was also the home of computer-security maven Donn Parker, and had authored an influential text called *Cryptography and Data Security.* In 1990, Dr. Denning was working for Digital Equipment Corporation in their Systems Research Center. Her husband, Peter Denning, was also a computer security expert, working for NASA's Research Institute for Advanced Computer Science. He had edited the well-received *Computers Under Attack: Intruders, Worms and Viruses.*

Denning took it upon herself to contact the digital underground, more or less with an anthropological interest. There she discovered that these computer-intruding hackers, who had been characterized as unethical, irresponsible, and a serious danger to society, did in fact have their own subculture and their own rules. They were not particularly well-considered rules, but they were, in fact, rules. Basically, they didn't take money and they didn't break anything.

Her dispassionate reports on her researches did a great deal to influence serious-minded computer professionals—the sort of people who merely rolled their eyes at the cyberspace rhapsodies of a John Perry Barlow.

For young hackers of the digital underground, meeting Dorothy Denning was a genuinely mind-boggling experience. Here was this neatly coiffed, conservatively dressed, dainty little personage, who reminded most hackers of their moms or their aunts. And yet she was an IBM systems programmer with profound expertise in computer architectures and high-security information flow, who had personal friends in the FBI and the National Security Agency.

Dorothy Denning was a shining example of the American mathematical intelligentsia, a genuinely brilliant person from the central ranks of the computer-science elite. And here she was, gently questioning twenty-year-old hairy-eyed phone phreaks over the deeper ethical implications of their behavior.

Here she was, gently questioning hairy-eyed phone phreaks over the deeper ethical implications of their behavior.

Confronted by this genuinely nice lady, most hackers sat up very straight and did their best to keep the anarchy-file stuff down to a faint whiff of brimstone. Nevertheless, the hackers *were* in fact prepared to seriously discuss serious issues with Dorothy Denning. They were willing to speak the unspeakable and defend the indefensible, to blurt out their convictions that information cannot be owned, that the databases of governments and large corporations were a threat to the rights and privacy of individuals.

Denning's articles made it clear to many that "hacking" was not simple vandalism by some evil clique of psychotics. "Hacking" was not an aberrant menace that could be charmed away by ignoring it, or swept out of existence by jailing a few ringleaders. Instead, "hacking" was symptomatic of a growing, primal struggle over knowledge and power in the age of information.

Denning pointed out that the attitude of hackers were at least partially shared by forward-looking management theorists in the business community: people like Peter Drucker and Tom Peters. Peter Drucker, in his book *The New Realities*, had stated that "control of information by the government is no longer possible. Indeed, information is now transnational. Like money, it has no 'fatherland.' "

And management maven Tom Peters had chided large corporations for uptight, proprietary attitudes in his best-seller, *Thriving on Chaos*: "Information hoarding, especially by politically motivated, power-seeking staffs, had been commonplace throughout American industry, service and manufacturing alike. It will be an impossible millstone aroung the neck of tomorrow's organizations."

Dorothy Denning had shattered the social membrane of the digital underground. She attended the Neidorf trial, where she was prepared to testify for the defense as an expert witness. She was a behind-the-scenes organizer of two of the most important national meetings of the computer civil libertarians. Though not a zealot of any description, she brought disparate elements of the electronic community into a surprising and fruitful collusion.

Dorothy Denning is currently the chair of the computer science department at Georgetown University in Washington, D.C.

There were many stellar figures in the civil libertarian community. There's no question, however, that its single most influential figure was Mitchell D. Kapor. Other people might have formal titles or governmental positions, have more experience with crime or with the law, or with the arcanities of computer security or constitutional theory. But by 1991 Kapor had transcended any such narrow role. Kapor had become "Mitch."

Mitch had become the central civil-libertarian ad-hocrat. Mitch had stood up first, he had spoken out loudly, directly, vigorously, and angrily, he had put his own reputation, and his very considerable personal fortune, on the line. By mid-1991 Kapor was the best-known advocate of his cause and was known *personally* by almost every single human being in America with any direct influence on the question of civil liberties in cyberspace. Mitch had built bridges, crossed voids, changed paradigms, forged metaphors, made phone calls, and swapped business cards to such spectacular effect that it had become impossible for *anyone* to take any action in the "hacker question" without wondering what Mitch might think—and say—and tell his friends.

The EFF had simply *networked* the situation into an entirely new status quo. And in fact this had been EFF's deliberate strategy from the beginning. Both Barlow and Kapor loathed bureaucracies and had deliberately chosen to work almost entirely through the electronic spiderweb of "valuable personal contacts."

After a year of EFF, both Barlow and Kapor had every reason to look back with satisfaction. EFF had established its own Internet node, "eff.org," with a well-stocked electronic archive of documents on electronic civil rights, privacy issues, and academic freedom. EFF was also publishing *EFFector*, a quarterly printed journal, as well as *EFFector Online*, an electronic newsletter with over 1,200 subscribers. And EFF was thriving on the Well.

EFF had a national headquarters in Cambridge and a full-time staff. It had become a membership organization and was attracting grass-roots support. It had also attracted the support of some thirty civil rights lawyers, ready and eager to do pro bono work in defense of the Constitution in Cyberspace.

EFF had lobbied successfully in Washington and in Massachusetts to change state and federal legislation on computer networking. Kapor in particular had become a veteran expert witness, and had joined the Computer Science and Telecommunications Board of the National Academy of Science and Engineering.

EFF had sponsored meetings such as "Computers, Freedom and Privacy" and the CPSR Roundtable. It had carried out a press offensive that, in the words of *EFFector*, "has affected the climate of opinion about computer networking and begun to reverse the slide into 'hacker hysteria' that was beginning to grip the nation."

It had helped Craig Neidorf avoid prison.

And, last but certainly not least, the Electronic Frontier Foundation had filed a federal lawsuit in the name of Steve Jackson, Steve Jackson Games Inc., and three users of the Illuminati bulletin board system. The defendants were, and are, the United States Secret Service, William Cook, Tim Foley, Barbara Golden, and Henry Kluepfel.

The case, which is in pretrial procedures in an Austin federal court as of this writing, is a civil action for damages to redress alleged violations of the First and Fourth amendments to the United States Constitution, as well as the Privacy Protection Act of 1980 (42 USC 2000aa et seq.) and the Electronic Communications Privacy Act (18 USC 2510 et seq. and 2701 et seq.).

EFF had established that it had credibility. It had also established that it had teeth.

In September of 1991 I traveled to Massachusetts to speak personally with Mitch Kapor. It was my final interview for this book.

The city of Boston has always been one of the major intellectual centers of the American republic. It is a very old city by American standards, a place of skyscrapers overshadowing seventeenth-century graveyards, where the high-tech start-up companies of Route 128 coexist with the hand-wrought preindustrial grace of "Old Ironsides," the USS *Constitution.*

The Battle of Bunker Hill, one of the first and bitterest armed clashes of the American Revolution, was fought in Boston's environs. Today there is a monumental spire on Bunker Hill, visible throughout much of the city. The willingness of the republican revolutionaries to take up arms and fire on their oppressors has left a cultural legacy that two full centuries have not effaced. Bunker Hill is still a potent center of American political symbolism, and the Spirit of '76 is still a potent image for those who seek to mold public opinion.

Of course, not everyone who wraps himself in the flag is necessarily a patriot. When I visited the spire in September 1991, it bore a huge, badly erased, spray-can grafitto around its bottom reading BRITS OUT—IRA PROVOS. Inside this hallowed edifice was a glass-cased diorama of thousands of tiny toy soldiers, rebels and redcoats, fighting and dying over the green hill, the riverside marshes, the rebel trenchworks. Plaques indicated the movement of troops, the shiftings of strategy. The Bunker Hill Monument is occupied at its very center by the toy soldiers of a military war-game simulation.

The Boston metroplex is a place of great universities, prominent among them the Massachusetts Institute of Technology, where the term "computer hacker" was first coined. The Hacker Crackdown of 1990 might be interpreted as a political struggle among American cities: traditional strongholds of longhair intellectual liberalism, such as Boston, San Francisco, and Austin, versus the bare-knuckle industrial pragmatism of Chicago and Phoenix (with Atlanta and New York wrapped in internal struggle).

The headquarters of the Electronic Frontier Foundation is on 155 Second Street in Cambridge, a Bostonian suburb north of the River Charles. Second Street has weedy sidewalks of dented, sagging brick and elderly cracked asphalt; large signs warn NO PARKING DURING DECLARED SNOW EMERGENCY. This is an old area of modest manufacturing industries; the EFF is catercorner from the Greene Rubber Company. EFF's building is two stories of red brick; its large wooden windows feature gracefully arched tops and stone sills.

The glass window beside the Second Street entrance bears three sheets of neatly laser-printed paper, taped against the glass. They read: ON TECHNOLOGY. EFF. KEI.

"ON Technology" is Kapor's software company, which currently specializes in "groupware" for the Apple Macintosh computer. Groupware is intended to promote efficient social interaction among office workers linked by computers. ON Technology's most successful software products to date are "Meeting Maker" and "Instant Update."

"KEI" is Kapor Enterprises Inc., Kapor's personal holding

company, the commercial entity that formally controls his extensive investments in other hardware and software corporations.

"EFF" is a political action group—of a special sort.

Inside, someone's bike has been chained to the handrails of a modest flight of stairs. A wall of modish glass brick separates this anteroom from the offices. Beyond the brick, there's an alarm system mounted on the wall, a sleek, complex little number that resembles a cross between a thermostat and a CD player. Piled against the wall are box after box of the September 1991 special issue of *Scientific American*, "How to Work, Play, and Thrive in Cyberspace," with extensive coverage of electronic networking techniques and political issues, including an article by Kapor himself. These boxes are addressed to Gerard Van der Leun, EFF's director of communications, who will shortly mail those magazines to every member of the EFF.

The joint headquarters of EFF, KEI, and ON Technology, which Kapor currently rents, is a modestly bustling place. It's very much the same physical size as Steve Jackson's gaming company. It's certainly a far cry from the gigantic gray steel-sided railway shipping barn, on the Monsignor O'Brien Highway, that is owned by Lotus Development Corporation.

Lotus is, of course, the software giant that Mitchell Kapor founded in the late 1970s. The software program Kapor co-authored, Lotus 1-2-3, is still that company's most profitable product. Lotus 1-2-3 also bears a singular distinction in the digital underground: it's probably the most pirated piece of application software in world history.

Kapor greets me cordially in his own office, down a hall. Kapor, whose name is pronounced KAY-por, is in his early forties, married and the father of two. He has a round face, high forehead, straight nose, a slightly tousled mop of black hair peppered with gray. His large brown eyes are wide-set, reflective, one might almost say soulful. He disdains ties, and commonly wears Hawaiian shirts and tropical prints, not so much garish as simply cheerful and just that little bit anomalous.

There is just the whiff of hacker brimstone about Mitch Kapor. He may not have the hard-riding, hell-for-leather, guitar-strumming charisma of his Wyoming colleague John Perry Barlow, but there's something about the guy that still stops one short. He has the air of the Eastern city dude in the bowler hat, the dreamy, Longfellow-quoting poker shark who only *happens* to know the exact mathematical odds against drawing to an inside straight. Even among his computer-community colleagues, who are hardly known for mental sluggishness, Kapor strikes one forcefully as a very intelligent man. He speaks rapidly, with vigorous gestures, his Boston accent sometimes slipping to the sharp nasal tang of his youth in Long Island.

Kapor, whose Kapor Family Foundation does much of his philanthropic work, is a strong supporter of Boston's Computer Museum. Kapor's interest in the history of his industry has brought him some

> *It would take exactly 157,184 of these primordial toasters to hold the first part of this book.*

remarkable curios, such as the "byte" just outside his office door. This byte—eight digital bits—has been salvaged from the wreck of an electronic computer of the pre-transistor age. It's a standing gunmetal rack about the size of a small toaster-oven: with eight slots of hand-soldered breadboarding featuring thumb-size vacuum tubes. If it fell off a table it could easily break your foot, but it was state-of-the-art computation in the 1940s. (It would take exactly 157,184 of these primordial toasters to hold the first part of this book.)

There's also a coiling, multicolored, scaly dragon that some inspired techno-punk artist has cobbled up entirely out of transistors, capacitors, and brightly plastic-coated wiring.

Inside the office, Kapor excuses himself briefly to do a little mouse-whizzing housekeeping on his personal Macintosh IIfx. If its giant screen were an open window, an agile person could climb through it without much trouble at all. There's a coffee cup at Kapor's elbow, a memento of his recent trip to Eastern Europe,

which has a black-and-white stenciled photo and the legend CAPI-
TALIST FOOLS TOUR. It's Kapor, Barlow, and two California venture-
capitalist luminaries of their acquaintance, four windblown, grin-
ning Baby Boomer dudes in leather jackets, boots, denim, travel
bags, standing on airport tarmac somewhere behind the formerly
Iron Curtain. They look as if they're having the absolute time of
their lives.

Kapor is in a reminiscent mood. We talk a bit about his youth
—high school days as a "math nerd," Saturdays attending Columbia University's high school science honors program, where
he had his first experience programming computers. IBM 1620s,
in 1965 and 1966. "I was very interested," says Kapor, "and then I
went off to college and got distracted by drugs, sex, and rock and
roll, like anybody with half a brain would have then!" After college he was a progressive-rock DJ in Hartford, Connecticut, for a
couple of years.

I ask him if he ever misses his rock and roll days—if he ever
wished he could go back to radio work.

He shakes his head flatly. "I stopped thinking about going back
to be a DJ the day after Altamont."

Kapor moved to Boston in 1974 and got a job programming
mainframes in COBOL. He hated it. He quit and became a
teacher of transcendental meditation. (It was Kapor's long flirta-
tion with Eastern mysticism that gave the world "Lotus.")

In 1976 Kapor went to Switzerland, where the TM movement
had rented a gigantic Victorian hotel in St.-Moritz. It was an all-
male group—120 of them—determined upon Enlightenment or
Bust. Kapor had given the transcendant his best shot. He was
becoming disenchanted by "the nuttiness in the organization."
"They were teaching people to levitate," he says, staring at the
floor. His voice drops an octave, becomes flat. *"They don't levitate."*

Kapor chose Bust. He went back to the States and acquired a
degree in counseling psychology. He worked awhile in a hospital,
couldn't stand that either. "My rep was," he says "a very bright

kid with a lot of potential who hasn't found himself. Almost thirty. Sort of lost."

Kapor was unemployed when he bought his first personal computer—an Apple II. He sold his stereo to raise cash and drove to New Hampshire to avoid the sales tax.

"The day after I purchased it," Kapor tells me, "I was hanging out in a computer store and I saw another guy, a man in his forties, well-dressed guy, and eavesdropped on his conversation with the salesman. He didn't know *anything* about computers. I'd had a year programming. And I could program in BASIC. I'd taught myself. So I went up to him, and I actually sold myself to him as a consultant." He pauses. "I don't know where I got the nerve to do this. It was uncharacteristic. I just said, 'I think I can help you, I've been listening, this is what you need to do and I think I can do it for you.' And he took me on! He was my first client! I became a computer consultant the first day after I bought the Apple II."

Kapor had found his true vocation. He attracted more clients for his consultant service and started an Apple users' group.

A friend of Kapor's, Eric Rosenfeld, a graduate student at MIT, had a problem. He was doing a thesis on an arcane form of financial statistics but could not wedge himself into the crowded queue for time on MIT's mainframes. (One might note at this point that if Mr. Rosenfeld had dishonestly broken into the MIT mainframes, Kapor himself might have never invented Lotus 1-2-3 and the PC business might have been set back for years!) Eric Rosenfeld did have an Apple II, however, and he thought it might be possible to scale the problem down. Kapor, as a favor, wrote a program for him in BASIC that did the job.

It then occurred to the two of them, out of the blue, that it might be possible to *sell* this program. They marketed it themselves, in plastic baggies, for about a hundred bucks a pop, mail order. "This was a total cottage industry by a marginal consultant," Kapor says proudly. "That's how I got started, honest to God."

Rosenfeld, who later became a very prominent figure on Wall Street, urged Kapor to go to MIT's business school for an MBA. Kapor did seven months there, but never got his MBA. He picked up some useful tools—mainly a firm grasp of the principles of accounting—and, in his own words, "learned to talk MBA." Then he dropped out and went to Silicon Valley.

The inventors of VisiCalc, the Apple computer's premier business program, had shown an interest in Mitch Kapor. Kapor worked diligently for them for six months, got tired of California, went back to Boston where they had better bookstores. The VisiCalc group had made the critical error of bringing in "professional management." "That drove them into the ground," Kapor says.

"Yeah, you don't hear a lot about VisiCalc these days," I muse.

Kapor looks surprised. "Well, Lotus . . . we *bought* it."

"Oh. You *bought* it?"

"Yeah."

"Sort of like the Bell System buying Western Union?"

Kapor grins. "Yep! Yep! Yeah, exactly!"

Mitch Kapor was not in full command of the destiny of himself or his industry. The hottest software commodities of the early 1980s were *computer games*—the Atari seemed destined to enter every teenage home in America. Kapor got into business software simply because he didn't have any particular feeling for computer games. But he was supremely fast on his feet, open to new ideas and inclined to trust his instincts. And his instincts were good. He chose good people to deal with—gifted programmer Jonathan Sachs (the co-author of Lotus 1-2-3), financial wizard Eric Rosenfeld, canny Wall Street analyst, and venture capitalist Ben Rosen. Kapor was the founder and CEO of Lotus, one of the most spectacularly successful business ventures of the later twentieth century.

He is now an extremely wealthy man. I ask him if he actually knows how much money he has.

"Yeah," he says. "Within a percent or two."

How much does he actually have, then?

He shakes his head. "A lot. A lot. Not something I talk about. Issues of money and class are things that cut pretty close to the bone."

I don't pry. It's beside the point. One might presume, impolitely, that Kapor has at least forty million—that's what he got the year he left Lotus. People who ought to know claim Kapor has about 150 million, give or take a market swing in his stock holdings. If Kapor had stuck with Lotus, as his colleague friend and rival Bill Gates has stuck with his own software start-up, Microsoft, then Kapor would likely have much the same fortune Gates has—somewhere in the neighborhood of three billion, give or take a few hundred million. Mitch Kapor has all the money he wants. Money has lost whatever charm it ever held for him— probably not much in the first place. When Lotus became too uptight, too bureaucratic, too far from the true sources of his own satisfaction, Kapor walked. He simply severed all connections with the company and went out the door. It stunned everyone— except those who knew him best.

Kapor has not had to strain his resources to wreak a thorough transformation in cyberspace politics. In its first year, EFF's budget was about a quarter of a million dollars. Kapor is running EFF out of his pocket change.

Kapor takes pains to tell me that he does not consider himself a civil libertarian per se. He has spent quite some time with true-blue civil libertarians lately, and there's a political-correctness to them that bugs him. They seem to him to spend entirely too much time in legal nitpicking and not enough vigorously exercising civil rights in the everyday real world.

Kapor is an entrepreneur. Like all hackers, he prefers his involvements direct, personal, and hands-on. "The fact that EFF has a node on the Internet is a great thing. We're a publisher. We're a distributor of information." Among the items the eff.org Internet node carries is back issues of *Phrack*. They had an internal debate about that in EFF and finally decided to take the plunge. They might carry other digital underground publications —but if they do, he says, "we'll certainly carry Donn Parker, and anything Gail Thackeray wants to put up. We'll turn it into a public library, that has the whole spectrum of use. Evolve in the direction of people making up their own minds." He grins. "We'll try to label all the editorials."

Kapor is determined to tackle the technicalities of the Internet in the service of the public interest. "The problem with being a node on the net today is that you've got to have a captive technical specialist. We have Chris Davis around, for the care and feeding of the balky beast. We couldn't do it ourselves!"

He pauses. "So one direction in which technology has to evolve is much more standardized units, that a nontechnical person can feel comfortable with. It's the same shift as from minicomputers to PCs. I can see a future in which any person can have a node on the net. Any person can be a publisher. It's better than the media we now have. It's possible. We're working actively."

Kapor is in his element now, fluent, thoroughly in command in his material. "You go tell a hardware Internet hacker that everyone should have a node on the net," he says, "and the first thing they're going to say is 'IP doesn't scale!' " ("IP" is the interface protocol for the Internet. As it currently exists, the IP software is simply not capable of indefinite expansion; it will run out of usable addresses, it will saturate.) "The answer," Kapor says, "is: Evolve the protocol! Get the smart people together and figure out what to do. Do we add ID? Do we add new protocol? Don't just say, *we can't do it.*"

Getting smart people together to figure out what to do is a skill at which Kapor clearly excels. I counter that people on the Internet rather enjoy their elite technical status and don't seem particularly anxious to democratize the net.

Kapor agrees, with a show of scorn. "I tell them that this is the snobbery of the people on the *Mayflower* looking down their noses at the people who came over *on the second boat!* Just because they got here a year, or five years, or ten years before everybody else, that doesn't give them ownership of cyberspace! By what right?"

I remark that the telcos are an electronic network too, and they seem to guard their specialized knowledge pretty closely.

Kapor ripostes that the telcos and the Internet are entirely different animals. "The Internet is an open system, everything is published, everything gets argued about, basically by anybody who can get in. Mostly, it's exclusive and elitist just because it's so difficult. Let's make it easier to use."

On the other hand, he allows with a swift change of emphasis, the so-called elitists do have a point as well. "Before people start coming in who are new, who want to make suggestions, and criticize the net as 'all screwed up' . . . they should at least take the time to understand the culture on its own terms. It has its own history—show some respect for it. I'm a conservative, to that extent."

The Internet is Kapor's paradigm for the future of telecommunications. The Internet is decentralized, nonhierarchical, almost anarchic. There are no bosses, no chain of command,

> *The Internet is Kapor's paradigm for the future of telecommunications.*

no secret data. If each node obeys the general interface standards, there's simply no need for any central network authority.

Wouldn't that spell the doom of AT&T as an institution? I ask.

That prospect doesn't faze Kapor for a moment. "Their big advantage, that they have now, is that they have all of the wiring. But two things are happening. Anyone with right-of-way is putting down fiber—Southern Pacific Railroad, people like that—there's enormous 'dark fiber' laid in." ("Dark fiber" is fiber-optic cable, whose enormous capacity so exceeds the demands of current usage that much of the fiber still has no light signals on it—it's still "dark," awaiting future use.)

"The other thing that's happening is the local-loop stuff is going to go wireless. Everyone from Bellcore to the cable TV companies to AT&T wants to put in these things called 'personal communication systems.' So you could have local competition—

you could have multiplicity of people, a bunch of neighborhoods, sticking stuff up on poles. And a bunch of other people laying in dark fiber. So what happens to the telephone companies? There's enormous pressure on them from both sides.

"The more I look at this, the more I believe that in a postindustrial, digital world, the idea of regulated monopolies is bad. People will look back on it and say that in the nineteenth and twentieth centuries the idea of public utilities was an okay compromise. You needed one set of wires in the ground. It was too economically inefficient otherwise. And that meant one entity running it. But now, with pieces being wireless—the connections are going to be via high-level interfaces, not via wires. I mean, *ultimately* there are going to be wires—but the wires are just a commodity. Fiber, wireless. You no longer *need* a utility."

Water utilities? Gas utilities?

Of course we still need those, he agrees. "But when what you're moving is *information,* instead of physical substances, then you can play by a different set of rules. We're evolving those rules now! Hopefully you can have a much more decentralized system, and one in which there's more competition in the marketplace.

"The role of government will be to make sure that nobody cheats. The proverbial 'level playing field.' A policy that prevents monopolization. It should result in better service, lower prices, more choices, and local empowerment." He smiles. "I'm very big on local empowerment."

Kapor is a man with a vision. It's a novel vision that he and his allies are working out in considerable detail and with great energy. Dark, cynical, morbid cyberpunk that I am, I cannot avoid considering some of the darker implications of "decentralized, nonhierarchical, locally empowered" networking.

I remark that some pundits have suggested that electronic networking—faxes, phones, small-scale photocopiers—played a strong role in dissolving the power of centralized communism and causing the collapse of the Warsaw Pact.

Socialism is totally discredited, says Kapor, fresh back from the

Eastern Bloc. The idea that faxes did it, all by themselves, is rather wishful thinking.

Has it occurred to him that electronic networking might corrode America's industrial and political infrastructure to the point where the whole thing becomes untenable, unworkable—and the old order just collapses headlong, as in Eastern Europe?

"No," Kapor says flatly. "I think that's extraordinarily unlikely. In part, because ten or fifteen years ago, I had similar hopes about personal computers—which utterly failed to materialize." He grins wryly, then his eyes narrow. "I'm *very* opposed to techno-utopias. Every time I see one, I either run away or try to kill it."

It dawns on me then that Mitch Kapor is not trying to make the world safe for democracy. He certainly is not trying to make it safe for anarchists or utopians—least of all for computer intruders or electronic rip-off artists. What he really hopes to do is make the world safe for future Mitch Kapors. This world of decentralized, small-scale nodes, with instant global access for the best and brightest, would be a perfect milieu for the shoestring attic capitalism that made Mitch Kapor what he is today.

Kapor is a very bright man. He has a rare combination of visionary intensity with a strong practical streak. The board of the EFF—John Barlow, Jerry Berman, formerly of the ACLU, Stewart Brand, John Gilmore, Steve Wozniak, and Esther Dyson, the doyenne of East-West computer entrepreneurism—share his gift, his vision, and his formidable networking talents. They are people of the 1960s, winnowed out by its turbulence and rewarded with wealth and influence. They are some of the best and the brightest that the electronic community has to offer. But can they do it, in the real world? Or are they only dreaming? They are so few. And there is so much against them.

I leave Kapor and his networking employees struggling cheerfully with the promising intricacies of their newly installed Macintosh System 7 software. The next day is Saturday. EFF is closed. I pay a few visits to points of interest downtown.

One of them is the birthplace of the telephone.

It's marked by a bronze plaque in a plinth of black-and-white speckled granite. It sits in the plaza of the John F. Kennedy Federal Building, the very place where Kapor was once fingerprinted by the FBI.

The plaque has a bas-relief picture of Bell's original telephone. "BIRTHPLACE OF THE TELEPHONE," it reads. "Here, on June 2, 1875, Alexander Graham Bell and Thomas A. Watson first transmitted sound over wires.

"This successful experiment was completed in a fifth floor garret at what was then 109 Court Street and marked the beginning of worldwide telephone service."

109 Court Street is long gone. Within sight of Bell's plaque, across a street, is one of the central offices of NYNEX, the local Bell RBOC, on 6 Bowdoin Square.

I cross the street and circle the telco building, slowly, hands in my jacket pockets. It's a bright, windy, New England autumn day. The central office is a handsome 1940s-era megalith in late Art Deco, eight stories high.

Parked outside the back is a power-generation truck. The generator strikes me as rather anomalous. Don't they already have their own generators in this eight-story monster? Then the suspicion strikes me that NYNEX must have heard of the September 17 AT&T power outage that crashed New York City. Belt-and-suspenders, this generator. Very telco.

Over the glass doors of the front entrance is a handsome bronze bas relief of Art Deco vines, sunflowers, and birds, entwining the Bell logo and the legend NEW ENGLAND TELEPHONE AND TELEGRAPH COMPANY—an entity that no longer officially exists.

The doors are locked securely. I peer through the shadowed glass. Inside is an official poster reading:

> New England Telephone a NYNEX Company
> ATTENTION
> All persons while on New England Telephone Company premises are required to visibly wear their identification cards (C.C.P. Section 2, Page 1).

Visitors, vendors, contractors, and all others are required to visibly wear a daily pass.
Thank you.
Kevin C. Stanton.
Building Security Coordinator.

Outside, around the corner, is a pull-down ribbed metal security door, a locked delivery entrance. Some passing stranger has grafitti-tagged this door, with a single word in red spray-painted cursive:

Fury

My book on the Hacker Crackdown is almost over now. I have deliberately saved the best for last.

In February 1991, I attended the CPSR Public Policy Roundtable, in Washington, D.C. CPSR, Computer Professionals for Social Responsibility, was a sister organization of EFF, or perhaps its aunt, being older and perhaps somewhat wiser in the ways of the world of politics.

Computer Professionals for Social Responsibility began in 1981 in Palo Alto, as an informal discussion group of Californian computer scientists and technicians, united by nothing more than an electronic mailing list. This typical high-tech ad-hocracy received the dignity of its own acronym in 1982 and was formally incorporated in 1983.

CPSR lobbied government and public alike with an educational outreach effort, sternly warning against any foolish and unthinking trust in complex computer systems. CPSR insisted that mere computers should never be considered a magic panacea for humanity's social, ethical, or political problems. Members were especially troubled about the stability, safety, and dependability of military computer systems, and very especially troubled by those systems controlling nuclear arsenals. CPSR was best known for its persistent and well-publicized attacks on the scientific credibility of the Strategic Defense Initiative ("Star Wars").

In 1990, CPSR was the nation's veteran cyber-political activist group, with more than two thousand members in twenty-one local chapters across the U.S. It was especially active in Boston, Silicon Valley, and Washington, D.C., where its Washington office sponsored the Public Policy Roundtable.

The Roundtable, however, had been funded by EFF, which had passed CPSR an extensive grant for operations. This was the first large-scale, official meeting of what was to become the electronic civil libertarian community.

Sixty people attended, myself included—in this instance, not so much as a journalist as a cyberpunk author. Many of the luminaries of the field took part: Kapor and Godwin as a matter of course. Richard Civille and Marc Rotenberg of CPSR. Jerry Berman of the ACLU. John Quarterman, author of *The Matrix*. Steven Levy, author of *Hackers*. George Perry and Sandy Weiss of Prodigy Services, there to network about the civil liberties troubles their young commercial network was experiencing. Dr. Dorothy Denning. Cliff Figallo, manager of the Well. Steve Jackson was there, having finally found his ideal target audience, and so was Craig Neidorf, Knight Lightning himself. Katie Hafner, science journalist and co-author of *Cyberpunks, Outlaws and Hackers on the Computer Frontier*. Dave Farber, ARPAnet pioneer and fabled Internet guru. Janlori Goldman of the ACLU's Project on Privacy and Technology. John Nagle of Autodesk and the Well. Don Goldberg of the House Judiciary Committee. Tom Guidoboni, the defense attorney in the Internet worm case. Lance Hoffman, computer-science professor at the George Washington University. Eli Noam of Columbia. And a host of others no less distinguished.

Senator Patrick Leahy delivered the keynote address, expressing his determination to keep ahead of the curve on the issue of electronic free speech. The address was well received, and the sense of excitement was palpable. Every panel discussion was interesting—some were entirely compelling. People networked with an almost frantic interest.

I myself had a most interesting and cordial lunch discussion with Noel and Jeanne Gayler; Admiral Gayler is a former director of the National Security Agency. As this was the first known encounter between an actual no-kidding cyberpunk and a chief executive of America's largest and best-financed electronic espionage apparat, there was naturally a bit of eyebrow-raising on both sides.

Unfortunately, our discussion was off the record. In fact, *all* the discussions at the CPSR were officially off the record, the idea being to do some serious networking in an atmosphere of complete frankness rather than to stage a media circus.

In any case, CPSR Roundtable, though interesting and intensely valuable, was as nothing compared to the truly mind-boggling event that transpired a mere month later: March 25 to 28, 1991, in San Francisco.

"Computers, Freedom and Privacy." Four hundred people from every conceivable corner of America's electronic community. As a science-fiction writer, I have been to some weird gigs in my day, but this thing is truly *beyond the pale.* Even "Cyberthon," Point Foundation's "Woodstock of Cyberspace" where Bay Area psychedelia collided headlong with the emergent world of computerized virtual reality, was like a Kiwanis Club gig compared to this astonishing do.

The "electronic community" had reached an apogee. Almost every principal in this book is in attendance. Civil libertarians. Computer cops. The Digital Underground. Even a few discreet telco people. Color-coded dots for lapel tags are distributed. Free expression issues. Law enforcement. Computer security. Privacy. Journalists. Lawyers. Educators. Librarians. Programmers. Stylish punk-black dots for the hackers and phone phreaks. Almost everyone here seems to wear eight or nine dots, to have six or seven professional hats.

It is a community. Something like Lebanon perhaps, but a digital nation. People who had feuded all year in the national press, people who entertained the deepest suspicions of one another's motives and ethics, are now in each others' laps. "Computers, Freedom and Privacy" had every reason in the world to turn ugly, and yet except for small eruptions of puzzling nonsense from the convention's token lunatic, a surprising bonhomie reigned. CFP was like a wedding party in which two lovers, unstable bride and charlatan groom, tie the knot in a clearly disastrous matrimony.

The Hacker Crackdown is ending in marriage.

It is clear to both families—even to neighbors and random guests—that this is not a workable relationship, and yet the young couple's desperate attraction can brook no further delay. They simply cannot help themselves. Crockery will fly, shrieks from their newlywed home will wake the city block, divorce waits in the wings like a vulture over the Kalahari, and yet this is a wedding, and there is going to be a child from it. Tragedies end in death; comedies in marriage. The Hacker Crackdown is ending in marriage. And there will be a child.

From the beginning, anomalies reign. John Perry Barlow, cyberspace ranger, is here. His color photo in *The New York Times Magazine*, Barlow scowling in a grim Wyoming snowscape, with long black coat, dark hat, a Macintosh SE30 propped on a fencepost and an awesome frontier rifle tucked under one arm, will be the single most striking visual image of the Hacker Crackdown. And he is CFP's guest of honor—along with Gail Thackeray of the FCIC! What on earth do they expect these guests to do with each other? Waltz?

Barlow delivers the first address. Uncharacteristically, he is hoarse—the sheer volume of roadwork has worn him down. He speaks briefly, congenially, in a plea for conciliation, and takes his leave to a storm of applause.

Then Gail Thackeray takes the stage. She's visibly nervous. She's been on the Well a lot lately. Reading those Barlow posts. Following Barlow is a challenge to anyone. In honor of the famous lyricist for the Grateful Dead, she announces reedily, she is going to read—*a poem*. A poem she has composed herself.

It's an awful poem, doggerel in the rollicking meter of Robert W. Service's *The Cremation of Sam McGee*, but it is in fact, a poem. It's the *Ballad of the Electronic Frontier!* A poem about the Hacker Crackdown and the sheer unlikelihood of CFP. It's full of in-jokes. The score or so cops in the audience, who are sitting together in a nervous claque, are absolutely cracking up. Gail's poem is the funniest goddamn thing they've ever heard. The hackers and civil libs, who had this woman figured for Ilsa She-Wolf of the SS, are staring with their jaws hanging loose. Never in the wildest reaches of their imagination had they figured Gail Thackeray was capable of such a totally off-the-wall move. You can see them punching their mental CONTROL-RESET buttons. Jesus! This woman's a hacker weirdo! She's *just like us!* God, this changes everything!

Al Bayse, computer technician for the FBI, had been the only cop at the CPSR Roundtable, dragged there with his arm bent by Dorothy Denning. He had been guarded and tight-lipped at the roundtable; a "lion thrown to the Christians."

At CFP, backed by a claque of cops, Bayse suddenly waxes eloquent and even droll, describing the FBI's "NCIC 2000," a gigantic digital catalog of criminal records, as if he has suddenly become some weird hybrid of George Orwell and George Gobel. Tentatively he makes an arcane joke about statistical analysis. At least a third of the crowd laughs aloud.

"They didn't laugh at that at my last speech," Bayse observes. He had been addressing cops—*straight* cops, not computer people. It had been a worthy meeting, useful, one supposes, but nothing like *this*. There has never been *anything* like this. Without any prodding, without any preparation, people in the audience simply begin to ask questions. Longhairs, freaky people, mathematicians. Bayse is answering, politely, frankly, fully, like a man walking on air. The ballroom's atmosphere crackles with surreality. A female lawyer behind me breaks into a sweat and a hot waft of surprisingly potent and musky perfume flows off her pulse points.

People are giddy with laughter. People are interested, fascinated, their eyes so wide and dark that they seem eroticized. Unlikely daisy chains form in the halls, around the bar, on the escalators: cops with hackers, civil rights with FBI, Secret Service with phone phreaks.

Gail Thackeray is at her crispest in a white wool sweater with a tiny Secret Service logo. "I found Phiber Optik at the pay phones, and when he saw my sweater, he turned into a *pillar of salt!*" she chortles.

Phiber discusses his case at much length with his arresting officer, Don Delaney of the New York State Police. After an hour's chat, the two of them look ready to begin singing "Auld Lang Syne." Phiber finally finds the courage to get his worst complaint off his chest. It isn't so much the arrest. It was the *charge.* Pirating service off 900 numbers. I'm a *programmer,* Phiber insists. This lame charge is going to hurt my reputation. It would have been cool to be busted for something happening, like Section 1030 computer intrusion. Maybe some kind of crime that's scarcely been invented yet. Not lousy phone fraud. Phooey.

Delaney seems regretful. He had a mountain of possible criminal charges against Phiber Optik. The kid's gonna plead guilty anyway. He's a first timer, they always plead. Coulda charged the kid with most anything and gotten the same result in the end. Delaney seems genuinely sorry not to have gratified Phiber in this harmless fashion. Too late now. Phiber's pled already. All water under the bridge. Whaddya gonna do?

Delaney's got a good grasp on the hacker mentality. He held a press conference after he busted a bunch of Masters of Deception kids. Some journo had asked him: "Would you describe these people as *geniuses?*" Delaney's deadpan answer, perfect: "No, I would describe these people as *defendants.*" Delaney busts a kid for hacking codes with repeated random dialing. Tells the press that NYNEX can track this stuff in no time flat nowadays, and a kid has to be *stupid* to do something so easy to catch. Dead on again: Hackers don't mind being thought of as Genghis Khan by the straights, but if there's anything that really gets 'em where they live, it's being called *dumb.*

Won't be as much fun for Phiber next time around. As a second offender he's gonna see prison. Hackers break the law. They're not geniuses either. They're gonna be defendants. And yet, Delaney muses over a drink in the hotel bar, he has found it impossible to treat them as common criminals. Delaney knows criminals. These kids, by comparison, are clueless—there is just no crook vibe off of them, they don't smell right, they're just not *bad.*

Delaney has seen a lot of action. He did Vietnam. He's been shot at, he has shot people. He's a homicide cop from New York. He has the appearance of a man who has not only seen the shit hit the fan but has seen it splattered across whole city blocks and left to ferment for years. This guy has been around.

He listens to Steve Jackson tell his story. The dreamy game strategist has been dealt a bad hand. He has played it for all he is worth. Under his nerdish SF-fan exterior is a core of iron. Friends of his say Steve Jackson *The iron jaws of prison clanged shut without him and now Neidorf looks like a larval congressman.* believes in the rules, believes in fair play. He will never compromise his principles, never give up. "Steve," Delaney says to Steve Jackson, "they had some balls, whoever busted you. You're all right!" Jackson, stunned, falls silent and actually blushes with pleasure.

Neidorf has grown up a lot in the past year. The kid is a quick study, you gotta give him that. Dressed by his mom, the fashion manager for a national clothing chain, Missouri college techie-frat Craig Neidorf outdappers everyone at this gig but the toniest East Coast lawyers. The iron jaws of prison clanged shut without him and now law school beckons for Neidorf. He looks like a larval congressman.

Not a "hacker," our Mr. Neidorf. He's not interested in computer science. Why should he be? He's not interested in writing C code the rest of his life, and besides, he's seen where the chips fall. To the world of computer science he and *Phrack* were just a curiosity. But to the world of law. . . . The kid has learned where the bodies are buried. He carries his notebook of press clippings wherever he goes.

Phiber Optik makes fun of Neidorf for a midwestern geek, for believing that "Acid Phreak" does acid and listens to acid rock. Hell no. Acid's never done *acid!* Acid's into *acid house music.* Jesus. The very idea of doing LSD. Our *parents* did LSD, ya clown.

Thackeray suddenly turns upon Craig Neidorf the full light-house glare of her attention and begins a determined half-hour attempt to *win the boy over.* The Joan of Arc of Computer Crime is *giving career advice to Knight Lightning!* "Your experience would be very valuable—a real asset," she tells him with unmis-takable sixty-thousand-watt sincerity. Neidorf is fascinated. He listens with unfeigned attention. He's nodding and saying yes ma'am. Yes, Craig, you too can forget all about money and enter the glamorous and horribly underpaid world of PROSECUTING COMPUTER CRIME! You can put your former friends in prison —ooops. . . .

You cannot go on dueling at modem's length indefinitely. You cannot beat one another senseless with rolled-up press clippings. Sooner or later you have to come directly to grips. And yet the very act of assembling here has changed the entire situation dras-tically. John Quarterman, author of *The Matrix,* explains the In-ternet at his symposium. It is the largest news network in the world, it is growing by leaps and bounds, and yet you cannot measure Internet because you cannot stop it in place. It cannot stop, because there is no one anywhere in the world with the authority to stop Internet. It changes, yes, it grows, it embeds itself across the postindustrial, postmodern world, and it gener-ates community wherever it touches, and it is doing this all by itself.

Phiber is different. A very fin-de-siecle kid, Phiber Optik. Bar-low says he looks like an Edwardian dandy. He does rather. Shaven neck, the sides of his skull cropped hip-hop close, unruly tangle of black hair on top that looks pomaded, he stays up till four A.M. and misses all the sessions, then hangs out in pay phone booths with his acoustic coupler gutsily CRACKING SYSTEMS RIGHT IN THE MIDST OF THE HEAVIEST LAW EN-FORCEMENT DUDES IN THE U.S., or at least *pretending* to. . . . Unlike "Frank Drake." Drake, who wrote to Dorothy Denning out of nowhere, and asked for an interview for his cheapo cyberpunk fanzine, and then started grilling her on her ethics. She was squirmin' too. . . . Drake, scarecrow-tall with his floppy blond mohawk, rotting tennis shoes and black leather jacket lettered ILLUMINATI in red, gives off an unmistakable air of the Bohemian literatus. Drake is the kind of guy who reads British industrial design magazines and appreciates William Gibson because the quality of his prose is so tasty. Drake could never touch a phone or a keyboard again, and he'd still have the nose ring and the blurry photocopied fanzines and the sampled industrial music. He's a radical punk with a desktop-publishing rig and an Internet address. Standing next to Drake, the diminutive Phiber looks like he's been physically coagulated out of phone lines. Born to phreak.

Dorothy Denning approaches Phiber suddenly. The two of them are about the same height and body build. Denning's blue eyes flash behind the round window-frames of her glasses. "Why did you say I was 'quaint'?" she asks Phiber, quaintly.

It's a perfect description but Phiber is nonplussed. "Well, I uh, you know. . . ."

"I also think you're quaint, Dorothy," I say, novelist to the rescue, the journo gift of gab. . . . She is neat and dapper and yet there's an arcane quality to her, something like a Pilgrim Maiden behind leaded glass; if she were six inches high Dorothy Denning would look great inside a china cabinet. The Cryptographeress . . . Cryptographrix . . . whatever . . . Weirdly, Peter Denning looks just like his wife, you could pick this gentleman out of a thousand guys as the soulmate of Dorothy Denning. Wearing tailored slacks, a spotless fuzzy varsity sweater, and a neatly knotted academician's tie. . . . This fine-boned, exquisitely polite, utterly civilized, and hyperintelligent couple seem to have emerged from some cleaner and finer parallel universe, where humanity exists to do the Brain Teasers column in *Scientific American*. Why does this Nice Lady hang out with these unsavory characters?

Because the time has come for it, that's why. Because she's the best there is at what she does.

Donn Parker is here, the Great Bald Eagle of Computer Crime. . . . With his bald dome, great height, and enormous Lincoln-like hands, the great visionary pioneer of the field plows through the lesser mortals like an icebreaker. His eyes are fixed on the future with the rigidity of a bronze statue. Eventually, he tells his audience, all business crime will be computer crime, because businesses will do everything through computers. "Computer crime" as a category will vanish.

In the meantime, passing fads will flourish and fail and evaporate. . . . Parker's commanding, resonant voice is sphinxlike, everything is viewed from some eldritch valley of deep historical abstraction. Yes, they've come and they've gone, these passing flaps in the world of digital computation. . . . The radio-frequency emanation scandal . . . KGB and MI5 and CIA do it every day, it's easy, but nobody else ever has. The salami-slice fraud, mostly mythical. . . . "Crimoids," he calls them. Computer viruses are the current crimoid champ, a lot less dangerous than most people let on, but the novelty is fading and there's a crimoid vacuum at the moment, the press is visibly hungering for something more outrageous. The Great Man shares with us a few speculations on the coming crimoids. Desktop forgery! Wow. . . . Computers stolen just for the sake of the information within them—data-napping! Happened in Britain awhile ago, could be the coming thing. . . . Phantom nodes in the Internet!

Parker handles his overhead projector sheets with an ecclesiastical air. He wears a gray double-breasted suit, a light-blue shirt, and a very quiet tie of understated maroon-and-blue paisley. Aphorisms emerge from him with slow, leaden emphasis. There is no such thing as an adequately secure computer when one faces a

sufficiently powerful adversary. . . . Deterrence is the most socially useful aspect of security. . . . People are the primary weakness in all information systems. . . . The entire baseline of
computer security must be shifted upward. . . . Don't ever vio-
late your security by publicly describing your security measures.

People in the audience are beginning to squirm, and yet there
is something about the elemental purity of this guy's philosophy
that compels uneasy respect. Parker sounds like the only sane guy
left in the lifeboat, sometimes. The guy who can prove rigorously,
from deep moral principles, that Harvey there, the one with the
broken leg and the checkered past, is the one who has to be,
err . . . that is, Mr. Harvey is best placed to make the necessary
sacrifice for the security and indeed the very survival of the rest of
this lifeboat's crew. . . . Computer security, Parker informs us
mournfully, is a nasty topic, and we wish we didn't have to have
it. The security expert, armed with method and logic, must think
—imagine—everything that the adversary might do before the
adversary might actually do it. It is as if the criminal's dark brain
were an extensive subprogram within the shining cranium of
Donn Parker. He is a Holmes whose Moriarty does not quite yet
exist and so must be perfectly simulated.

CFP is a stellar gathering, with the giddiness of a wedding. It is
a happy time, a happy ending. They know their world is changing
forever tonight, and they're proud to have been there to see it
happen, to talk, to think, to help.

And yet as night falls, a certain elegiac quality manifests itself,
as the crowd gathers beneath the chandeliers with their wine-
glasses and dessert plates. Something is ending here, gone forever, and it takes awhile to pinpoint it.

It is the End of the Amateurs.

INDEX

T

Talsorian's Cyberpunk, 146–47
TAP (*Technical Assistance Program*), 47, 63, 225
"Taran King," 88, 119, 128, 130–31, 251
Tarriffville Rail Disaster, 8, 16
"Techno-Revolution, The," 60–61
Telecom Digest, 261
Telefon Hirmondó, 6
Telenet (network), 102
Telephone Engineer & Management (TE&M), 17, 278
Telephony, 17
Tennessee Valley Authority Police, 220
"Terminus" ("Terminal Technician"), 118–24, 127, 134–36, 141, 148, 278, 279, 283
Thackeray, Gail, 44, 110, 176–87, 195–96, 202, 205, 212, 216, 255, 257, 284, 298, 306–8, 310
Thriving on Chaos (Peters), 288
"Tina," 98, 101, 102, 103
"Tom Edison," 47
"Tony the Trashman," 157
Treasury Police Force, 166
Tribunal of Knowledge, 91
TSR Inc., 145
"Tuc," 86, 278
TuSwF (United SoftWareZ Force), 76
Twist, Steve, 179

2600: The Hacker Quarterly, 63–68, 95, 257
Tymnet (network), 102

U

Underground Tunnel (board), 89
UNIX, 115, 117–27, 130, 131, 134–38, 141, 278, 283
"Unknown User," 130
"Urvile" ("Necron 99"), 97, 102, 103, 104, 106, 112–16, 143, 252, 282
USENET (network), 15
U S West, 24, 98, 213
UTU (United Technical Underground), 76
UUCP network, 123–24, 126, 136, 137

V

Vail, Theodore, 10–11, 13, 19, 25
Van der Leun, Gerald, 292
"VaxCat," 130
"Videosmith, The," 91
Vietnam War, 45–47
VisiCalc (program), 296
VNET (network), 124

ABOUT THE AUTHOR

BRUCE STERLING, author and journalist, was born in 1954. He is the author of four science fiction novels: *Involution Ocean* (1977), *The Artificial Kid* (1980), *Schismatrix* (1985), and *Islands in the Net* (1988). His short stories have appeared in the collections *Crystal Express* (1990) and *Globalhead* (1992), and in the Japanese collection *Semi no Jo-o* (1989). He edited the anthology *Mirrorshades*, the definitive document of the cyberpunk movement, and co-authored the novel *The Difference Engine* (1990) with William Gibson. He writes a critical column for *Science Fiction Eye* and a popular-science column for *The Magazine of Fantasy and Science Fiction*.

His journalistic work has also appeared in *The New York Times*, *Newsday*, *Omni*, *Details*, *Whole Earth Review*, *Mondo 2000*, and other equally unlikely venues. He lives in Austin, Texas, with his wife and daughter.